POCKET BIBLE DICTIONARY

All the major words and themes of the Bible defined and explained.

This edition is adapted from the *Dickson New Analytical Study Bible* and is published by special arrangement with and permission of World Bible Publishers.

Some spellings of proper names and place names have been updated. The abbreviations A.V. (*Authorized Version*) and R.V. (*Revised Version*) have been used throughout. Readers should consult Meridian's *Pocket Handbook of the Bible* for discussions of individual books of the Bible.

PRL4 Pocket Reference Library Edition
ISBN: 0-529-07130-4

Cover design by David Versluis Design
Book design by Blue Water Ink

A Meridian Publication
Published with World Bible Publishers

Manufactured in the United States of America

Abbreviations for books of the Bible

Ac	Acts	**Jude**	Jude
Am	Amos	**1 Ki**	1 Kings
1 Ch	1 Chronicles	**2 Ki**	2 Kings
2 Ch	2 Chronicles	**La**	Lamentations
1 Co	1 Corinthians	**Le**	Leviticus
2 Co	2 Corinthians	**Lu**	Luke
Col	Colossians	**Ma**	Matthew
Da	Daniel	**Mal**	Malachi
De	Deuteronomy	**Mi**	Micah
Ec	Ecclesiastes	**Mk**	Mark
Ep	Ephesians	**Na**	Nahum
Es	Esther	**Ne**	Nehemiah
Ex	Exodus	**Nu**	Numbers
Ez	Ezra	**Ob**	Obadiah
Eze	Ezekiel	**1 Pe**	1 Peter
Ga	Galatians	**2 Pe**	2 Peter
Ge	Genesis	**Ph**	Philippians
Hab	Habakkuk	**Phile**	Philemon
Hag	Haggai	**Pr**	Proverbs
He	Hebrews	**Ps**	Psalms
Ho	Hosea	**Re**	Revelation
Is	Isaiah	**Ro**	Romans
Jam	James	**Ru**	Ruth
Je	Jeremiah	**1 Sa**	1 Samuel
Jo	John	**2 Sa**	2 Samuel
1 Jo	1 John	**Son**	Song of Solomon
2 Jo	2 John	**1 Th**	1 Thessalonians
3 Jo	3 John	**2 Th**	2 Thessalonians
Job	Job	**1 Ti**	1 Timothy
Joel	Joel	**2 Ti**	2 Timothy
Jon	Jonah	**Tit**	Titus
Jos	Joshua	**Ze**	Zechariah
Ju	Judges	**Zep**	Zephaniah

A

AARON (enlightened, bright?) **1.** *Tribe and Family.* Aaron was the oldest son of Amram and Jochebed of the tribe of Levi (Ex 6:16–27). He was three years older than his brother, Moses (Ex 7:7), and some years younger than his sister, Miriam. He married Elisheba, a woman of the tribe of Judah, by whom he had four sons—Nadab, Abihu, Eleazar, and Ithamar (Ex 6:23). **2.** *Divine Commission.* The Lord appointed Aaron the spokesman of Moses and instructed him to meet Moses in the wilderness (Ex 4:27). In Israel's first recorded battle with Amalekites, Aaron and Hur supported the hands of Moses. **3.** *At Sinai.* While Moses was on the mount receiving the law, Aaron granted the request of the people that they should have a visible God. The idol was in the form of an Egyptian deity, the Apis-bull. **4.** *Aaron the High Priest.* Aaron's family was selected for the priesthood and the office was made hereditary. Thus Aaron, the first high priest, became head of the priestly order (Ex 28). His two sons, Nadab and Abihu, were destroyed for unholy conduct (Le 10:1–3). See PRIEST. **5.** *The Period of Wandering.* Aaron and Miriam were jealous of Moses' high position as showed by Miriam's criticism of the marriage of Moses and a Cushite woman. For this offence Miriam was smitten temporarily with leprosy (Nu 12). Aaron died on Mount Hor. Here, in the sight of all the congregation, his priestly robes were transferred to his son, Eleazar, who succeeded him. Aaron died at the age of 123 (Nu 20:23–29, 33:39).

AARON'S ROD A staff carried by Aaron. When thrown down in the presence of Pharaoh, it became a snake (Ex 7:9–12, 15). During sedition in the wilderness, it budded as a sign of divine approval of Moses and Aaron (Nu 17:1–10). It was preserved in the ark (He 9:4).

ABADDON (destruction) **1.** The place of the dead—the place of destruction. The region of the dead is hades, sheol (Job 26:6; Ps 88:11). **2.** The angel of the abyss or bottomless pit, called Apollyon in Greek (Re 9:11).

ABBA (father) A term by which God is addressed. In the mixed Aramaean dialects of Palestine it was commonly used by children in addressing their father (Mk 14:36; Ro 8:15; Ga 4:6).

ABEDNEGO (a servant of Nego). The name given to Azariah, one of the three companions of Daniel. He and the other two were cast into the fiery furnace (Da 1:7, 3:12–30).

ABEL (a breath). One of the sons of Adam and a shepherd. He was a righteous man whose blood offering was accepted by God (Ma 23:35; He 11:4; 1 Jo 3:12). He was slain by his brother, Cain, whose thank offering was rejected because it was not a blood offering like Abel's (Ge 4:2–9).

ABIJAH **1.** A descendant of Eleazar whose family was eighth of the 24 courses into which the priests were divided (1 Ch 24:1, 10). **2.** The wife of Hezron of Judah (1 Ch 2:24). **3.** A son of Samuel and an unworthy judge in Beersheba (1 Sa 8:2; 1 Ch 6:28). **4.** A descendant of Benjamin through Becher (1 Ch 7:8). **5.** A son of King Jeroboam. When the child became ill, Jeroboam sent his wife to Ahijah, the prophet, to inquire as to the outcome. Ahijah spoke the judgment of God upon Jeroboam for his idolatry, declaring the child would die (1 Ki 14:1–18). **6.** The son and successor of King Rehoboam and grandson of Solomon (1 Ch 3:10; 2 Ch 12:16, 13:1–14:1), also called Abijam. During his three-year reign he followed the evil ways of his father and fought against King Jeroboam of Israel (1 Ki 15:6–7), a war in which Israel lost half a million men (2 Ch 13:16–20). He had fourteen wives, twenty-two sons, and sixteen daughters

2 Ch 13:21). **7.** The mother of Hezekiah (2 Ki 18:2; 2 Ch 29:1). **8.** A priest who returned to Jerusalem from Babylon with Zerubbabel (Ne 12:4, 7). Later, a priestly family bore this name (Ne 12:17) and to this family belonged Zacharias, father of John the Baptist (Lu 1:5).

ABIMELECH (royal father?) **1.** A Philistine king at whose court Abraham declared Sarah to be his sister. After Abimelech had placed her in his harem, God appeared to him in a dream threatening him with death, whereupon he restored her to Abraham (Ge 20:1–18, 21:22–34). **2.** Another Philistine king, perhaps son of the preceding, with whom Isaac had a very similar experience (Ge 26:1–33). **3.** A son of Gidon. Assisted by relatives of his mother, Abimelech slew seventy sons of Gideon at Ophrah, with Jotham alone escaping. Thereupon Abimelech became king of Shechem, but in less than three years trouble arose among the people. Abimelech was mortally wounded by a woman who dropped a millstone on his head as he was besieging Thebez. Considering it a disgrace to be killed by a woman, Abimelech ordered his armorbearer to slay him (Ju 9:1–57). **4.** A priest, the son of Abiathar, whose name should probably read Ahimelech (1 Ch 18:16, 24:6). **5.** In the title of Ps 34 Abimelech appears for Achish.

ABNER (father of light) The son of Ner and cousin of King Saul. He was commander-in-chief of Saul's army (1 Sa 14:51) and was present when David slew Goliath (1 Sa 17:55–58). After Saul's death, Abner placed Ish-bosheth on the throne (2 Sa 2:8). David's captain, Joab, defeated Abner (2 Sa 2:12–32), and when the latter was retreating from the battle, he killed Asahel, a brother of Joab, in self-defence. Later Abner had a disagreement with his king and switched his allegiance to David who accepted him. Joab slew Abner in revenge for his brother's death, a deed which horrified David who mourned for Abner and left Solomon to deal with the crime (2 Sa 3:6–39; 1 Ki 2:5).

ABOMINATION OF DESOLATION Dan 11:31 and 12:11 describe "abomination that maketh desolate." The Jews saw in the cessation of the daily sacrifice by Antiochus Epiphanes (168 B.C.), and the erection of an idolatrous altar to Jupiter Olympius, a fulfillment of Dan 11:31. A mistake is made in supposing that our Lord's reference to the abomination that maketh desolate (Ma 24:15) is that of Dan 11:31. That is past. The passage to which he referred is 12:11, and is the abomination to be established by Antichrist during the last of the "seventy weeks" of Daniel, at the close of the age. Of this monster, the last tyrant of human history, Antiochus Epiphanes is indeed a type.

ABRAHAM (exalted father). **1.** *Lineage and Nativity* . A descendant of Arphaxad who was a son of Shem (Ge 11:10–32). Abraham, whose father was Terah, was one of the great patriarchs in the Messianic line. The family lived in Ur of the Chaldees in southern Babylonia, and then in Haran. **2.** *The Call and the Covenant.* Abraham was divinely called from Ur to become progenitor of the chosen people. This is the first great call recorded in the Bible. In the covenant with Abraham three things were promised—the land, a posterity, and the great blessing to all peoples of the earth in that the Messiah would be brought forth from the nation of which Abraham was the founder (Ge 12:1–4). Abraham moved his family from Haran when he was 75 years old and departed for Canaan. He is commended for having obeyed a divine command to undertake through faith this arduous journey (He 11:8). **3.** *In Canaan.* Abraham went to Shechem, then to Bethel (Ge 12). Famine drove him into Egypt where, through his wife, Sarah, whom he introduced as his sister (she was his half-sister), he became embroiled with the king and was ordered to leave (Ge 12:10–20). He returned to

Bethel and divided the land with his nephew, Lot, Abraham moving to Hebron (Ge 13). Lot was captured in a war and was rescued by Abraham, who was blessed by Melchizedek as he was returning home (Ge 14:1–24). Because Sarah was childless, Abraham had a son, Ishmael, by her handmaid, Hagar. Then when Abraham was one hundred years old and Sarah ninety, Isaac was born to Sarah (Ge 21:1–4). Thereupon Abraham exiled Hagar and Ishmael (Ge 21:1–21). Abraham witnessed the destruction of the cities of the plain (Ge 18:20–19:29). The great test of Abraham's faith came when he was divinely commanded to sacrifice Isaac but he followed God's orders completely and was rewarded when the boy was saved (Ge 22:1–19; He 11:17–19). Sarah died when Abraham was 137 years old (Ge 23). Three years later Abraham sent to Mesopotamia and secured Rebekah as a wife for Isaac (Ge 24:67). Another wife of Abraham, Keturah, gave him other sons: Zimran, Jokshan, Medan, Midian, Ishbak, and Shua. Abraham died at the age of 175 years and was buried beside Sarah in the cave of Machpelah (Ge 25:1–9). From this point the Old Testament records the history of this nation which was to bring forth the Savior of mankind.

ABRAHAM'S BOSOM   The blissful state after death. The Jews believed they would have fellowship with Abraham in Paradise. It was to this belief that Jesus referred when he described the state of Lazarus (Lu 16:22–23).

ABRAM   See ABRAHAM.

ABSALOM   (father of peace). David's third son, born in Hebron to Maacah, the daughter of King Talmai of Geshur (2 Sa 3:3). He was physically attractive with beautiful long hair. A half-brother, Amnon, ravished Absalom's full-sister, Tamar, for which misdeed Absalom slew him. His father considered the slaying a crime and exiled Absalom for three years. On his return Absalom was kept from the court for two additional years. Absalom conspired to seize the throne which was intended for Solomon (2 Sa 13:1–19:8). Absalom's tomb, so-called, is in the Kidron Valley.

ABYSS (bottomless) The place of the dead—Hades—also called the bottomless pit; especially the place of evil spirits under Apollyon—Satan (Re 9:11, 17:8, 20:1–3).

ACHAIA Originally the northern part of the Peloponnesus but the name was applied by the Romans (146 B.C.) to all of Greece and Macedonia. Augustus divided the whole into two provinces—Macedonia in the north which extended westward to the Adriatic, and Achaia in the south with Corinth as its capital. The latter division is the province referred to by the New Testament (Ac 18:12, 27; Ro 15:26; 2 Co 1:1).

ACHAN (trouble) A son of Carmi of the tribe of Judah who, after the fall of Jericho, stole a wedge of gold and a Babylonian mantle contrary to the instructions of God. This act caused the defeat of Joshua at Ai. Achan confessed his sin and was stoned to death (Jos 7:1–26).

ADAM (man—human being). The last work in the creation of the world, man was formed in God's own image (Ge 1:26–27). Adam, the first man, was made of dust and was brough to life by God's breathing into his nostrils the breath of life (Ge 2:7, 6:17; Job 10:8–12). He was given dominion over all the animals of the earth (Ge 1:26–28) and lived in the Garden of Eden (Ge 2:8, 15). Through Eve, Adam tasted the forbidden fruit of the tree of knowledge, and because God foresaw that Adam would eat of the tree of life also and live forever, he expelled the couple from the Garden of Eden (Ge 3:1–24). Adam had three children mentioned by name—Cain, Abel, and Seth—and he died at the age of 930. Paul mentions Adam as the first man, a living soul in whom all die, and calls Christ the last Adam, a life-giving spirit in whom all are made alive (Ro 5:12–21; 1 Co 15:22, 45).

ADONIJAH (Jehovah my lord). **1.** The fourth son of David, by Haggith (2 Sa 3:2–4). When David was old, Adonijah attempted to seize the throne although he undoubtedly knew that Solomon was intended to succeed David (1 Ki 1:13; 1 Ch 23:1). When Solomon was proclaimed king, Adonijah fled to the altar for protection and his life was spared, but later, when he gave Solomon reason to suspect him, he was put to death (1 Ki 2:13–25). **2.** A Levite appointed by Jehoshaphat to instruct the people (2 Ch 17:8). **3.** A leader who sealed the covenant with Nehemiah (Ne 10:16).

ADOPTION Moses was adopted by the daughter of Pharaoh and was as her own son (Ex 2:10). Paul speaks of the adoption of Israel by the Lord (Ro 9:4). In the spiritual sense the word denotes the act of God's grace whereby we are made sons of God.

ADULLAM (resting place) A town of Judah which was inhabited by Canaanites in the time of Jacob (Ge 38:1–2). It was conquered by Joshua (Jos 12:15) and was fortified by Rehoboam (2 Ch 11:7). After the Exile, it was occupied by Jews (Ne 11:30). Near the city was a cave in which David hid for a long time and where he was joined by many of his adherents (1 Sa 22; 2 Sa 23:13).

ADULTERY Unlawful sexual intercourse of a married person with one who is not a spouse. It is forbidden by the seventh commandment (Ex 20:14) and was punishable by death (Le 20:10). Christ interpreted adultery to be not only the overt act, but also adulterous thoughts and emotions

(Ma 5:27–28). He gave it as the only legitimate ground for divorce (Ma 5:32). The prophets used the term to signify disloyalty to the Lord through the worship of false gods (Eze 23:37, 43; Ho 2:2–13).

ADVOCATE One who acts in behalf of another. Jesus applied the word to the Holy Spirit, translated *Comforter* (Jo 14:26, 15:26, 16:7). Christ also is called Advocate (1 Jo 2:1).

AGABUS A prophet of Jerusalem in the time of Paul. A famine predicted by him occured in the reign of Claudius (Ac 11:28). He warned Paul about what would happen to him in Jerusalem (Ac 21:10–11).

AGATE A variety of quartz, beautifully colored. The word is translated *ruby* by the Revised Version. Agate was one of the precious stones on the breastplate of the high priest (Ex 28:19, 39:12).

AGE The word is used in two senses: of a particular, limited period and of a period of unlimited duration. Thus age was reckoned by years or months, as in the case of Joshua whose age at his death was 110 years (Jos 24:29). Human life is ordinarily reckoned at seventy years. Lifetimes were orignally reckoned as very long but were shorter after the time of Abraham, who died at the age of 175 years. David died an old man at seventy (Ge 25:7; 2 Sa 5:4; Ep 3:21).

AGRICULTURE In the Scriptures the meaning of this word is rendered *husbandry* and *husbandman*. Adam was placed in the Garden of Eden to care for it (Ge 2:15). The soil was cultivated by Cain (Ge 4:2). Noah planted a vineyard and Isaac sowed (Ge 9:20, 26:12). When the Israelites entered Egypt, they found the people engaged in raising and exporting cereals (Ge 41:49, 57, 43:2). In Palestine such agricultural products as corn, wine, olives, barley, wheat, vines, figs and pomegranates are mentioned (Ge 27:37; Ex 9:31–32; De 6:11). Ezekiel mentions lentils, beans and millet (Eze 4:9) Implements included plows drawn by oxen, pruninghooks and sickles (De 16:9; 1 Ki 19:19; Is 2:4, 18:5; Joel 3:10; Mi 4:3). The Hebrews were devoted to their soil and flocks and, prior to the time of Solomon, did not engage in commercial activities. The law required that the land be permitted to lay fallow every seventh year (Ex 23:10–11; Le 25:3–4).

AGRIPPA See HEROD.

AHAB (a father's brother) **1.** A king of Israel, the son of Omri. His reign began during the closing years of King Asa of Judah (1 Ki 16:29). Idolatry was already established when Ahab came to the throne but it became more widespread, largely because of his wife, Jezebel (1 Ki 16:30–33). Elijah condemned Ahab and Baalism, predicting drought (1 Ki 17:1; Jam 5:17), and at Mt. Carmel called on the Lord to bring down miraculous fire on his sacrifice (1 Ki 18:36). Shalmaneser king of Assyria invaded Israel, defeating Ahab and his ally, Ben-hadad of Damascus. Ahab was slain in his attempt to recover Ramoth-gilead (1 Ki 16:29–22:40). **2.** A prophet, the son of Kolaiah (Je 29:21–23).

AHASUERUS (mighty man, king) **1.** Father of Darius the Mede (Da 9:1). **2.** A Persian king who deposed his queen and replaced her with Esther, a beautiful Jewess (Es 1:19, 2:17). The events of the Book of Esther are represented as occuring between the first and second expeditions from Babylon, 536–458 B.C. Ahasuerus is almost certainly the Persian king known to the Greeks as Xerxes. He was a grandson of Cyrus and ascended the throne in 486 B.C.

AHAZ 1. The son of Jotham, Ahaz was the twelfth ruler on the throne of Judah. His idolatry was most degrading. He sacrificed his son and established false worship in the high places (2 Ki 16:3–4). When King Rezin of Syria and King Pekah of Israel conspired against him, Isaiah admonished him to place his trust in the Lord and then uttered his great Messianic prophecy of the virgin birth of our Lord (Is 7:1–16). Ahaz then secured the aid of King Tiglath-pileser of Assyria for which he gave him the treasures of the Temple and palace. Rezin and Pekah were slain, Damascus taken, and when Ahaz visited this city he saw a pagan altar which he later duplicated at Jerusalem. During his reign Isaiah and Micah prophesied in Judah and Hosea in Israel. His death found the kingdom in a sad state of spiritual decline but Hezekiah, his son, made many corrrections. 2. A Benjamite, descendant of Jonathan, son of Saul (1 Ch 8:35–36, 9:42).

AHAZIAH (the Lord has seized) 1. King of Israel, son and successor of Ahab (1 Ki 22:51–53; 2 Ki 1:2–4). 2. King of Judah, grandson of Ahab and Jezebel. He is best known for his violent death at the hands of Jehu who later became king (2 Ki 9:27–28).

AI (heap of ruins) 1. A town in the territory of Benjamin, east of Bethel (Jos 7:2, 8:11). Following the destruction of Jericho, Joshua attacked Ai and was defeated. This caused great consternation until the Lord told Joshua that there was sin in the camp—the sin of Achan. Achan was punished and a second attack was successful (Jos 7–8). At Jericho the Israelites learned the lesson of faith and at Ai the lesson of obedience. Abraham encamped near this city (Ge 12:8, 13:3). 2. A city of the Ammonites (Je 49:3).

AKELDAMA (field of blood) A small field near Jerusalem purchased with the thirty pieces of silver thrown away by Judas. It is called the potter's field and the field of blood because it was here that Judas died. Traditionally it is located on the southern side of the Valley of Hinnom (Ma 27:7–8; Ac 1:18–19).

ALABASTER A name possibly derived from a place in Egypt called Alabastrum or Alabastron where small vessels for perfumes were made. Modern alabaster is a form of gypsum or sulphate of lime but Oriental alabaster was carbonate of lime. This white stone was much used in antiquity in the ornamentation of buildings and was the expensive material out of which vases and bottles for the holding of precious ointments were made. The box that contained the perfume used in the anointing of Jesus at Bethany was of alabaster (Ma 26:7; Mk 14:3).

ALPHA The first letter of the Greek alphabet. It is derived from the Phoenician and corresponds to Aleph, the first lettter of the Hebrew alphabet. The lsat letter is Omega, hence the statement "I am Alpha and Omega," signifies that Christ is the beginning adn the end of all things (Re 1:8, 11, 21:6, 22:13).

ALPHAEUS (successor?) **1.** Husband of the Mary that stood by the cross of Jesus, and father of James the Less and Joses (Ma 10:3; Mk 15:40). Through the comparison of Ma 27:56, Mk 3:18, and Lu 6:15 it has been ascertained that Mary, the wife of Cleophas and sister of the mother of Jesus, and Mary, the mother of James the Less, were the same, for it is improbable that two sisters should have the same name. Hence it is assumed that Alphaeus was also called Cleophas. **2.** Father of Levi (later called Matthew), one of the apostles (Ma 9:9; Mk 2:14).

ALTAR A structure for the offering of sacrifices or the burning of incense. The first altars were probably built of earth. When Noah left the ark, he built an altar (Ge 8:20) and in the time of the patriarchs altars were made wherever the tents were pitched (Ge 12:7, 35:1, 7). Everything pertaining to the altar in connection with the tabernacle was divinely specified when Moses was given the law at Sinai. He was directed to make two altars. **1.** *The altar of burnt offering.* Ordinarily called simply *the altar*, it was square, small, and portable—five cubits long, five cubits wide, and three cubits high. Its acacia wood frame was overlaid with brass and a horn projected from each corner (Ex 27:1–8). This altar stood in the outer court directly in front of the tabernacle. **2.** *The altar of incense.* This stood within the tabernacle in the holy place before the veil which separated the holy place from the Holy of Holies. It was a cubit square and two cubits high, was made of acacia wood and overlaid with gold (Ex 30:1–10, 34–37; Le 16:18–19). These were the permanent altars on which sacrifices and incense could be offered according to the divine will (De 12:2–7). But in other places where God manifested himself altars could be raised and sacrifices offered, as in the case of Gideon and Manoah (Ju 6:20–25, 13:15–23).

AMALEKITES Descendants of Esau, a nomadic people, inhabiting the peninsula of Sinai and the wilderness between the southern portion of Palestine and Egypt (Ge 36:12; Nu 13:29; 1 Sa 15:7). About the time of the Exodus they occupied the region near Kadesh-barnea. Israel's first battle was fought with these people at Rephidim on their way to Sinai. The Amalekites were defeated but in the next encounter, when the Israelites were at Kadesh, the Amalekites were victorious (Ex 17:8; Nu 14:45). In the time of the judges they were the ally of the Midianites when the latter invaded and oppressed Israel (Ju 3:13, 6:3, 33). They suffered a crushing defeat by Saul (1 Sa 15), and were completely suppressed by David (1 Sa 27:8, 30:1–20).

AMAZIAH (Jehovah is strong) **1.** King of Judah, son of Joash, who took the reins of government when his father was unable to rule on account of sickness (2 Ki 14:1). After defeating the Edomites in the Valley of Salt, he brought back the idols of Edom and worshipped them. He was defeated by King Jehoash of Israel. A conspiracy was formed against him which caused him to flee, and his life was ended by assassins (2 Ki 14:1–20; 2 Ch 25:1–27). **2.** A Levite of the family of Merari (1 Ch 6:45). **3.** A priest of Bethel who brought charges against Amos (Am 7:10–17). **4.** A Simeonite (1 Ch 4:34).

AMETHYST A glassy, clear quartz, violet-blue, nearly purple in color, a precious stone having a place in the high priest's breastplate (Ex 28:19). In the New Jerusalem of Re 21:20 the twelfth foundation is adorned by this stone.

AMMONITES A Semitic people located east of the Jordan between the land of Moab and the River Jabbok, represented as descendants of Ben-ammi, a son of Lot (Ge 19:38). It appears that they had not been long in this land when Israel captured Jericho. Through the following centuries they had many clashes with the Hebrews, notably in the time of Jephthah (Ju 11:4–33) and David (2 Sa 10:6–14, 12:26–31). After the Exile they became an object of hatred for their alleged participation in the destruction of the kingdom (Eze 25:1–7). They obstructed the rebuilding of the walls of Jerusalem (Ne 4:3, 7).

AMNON (faithful) **1.** Son of David and Ahinoam, born at the beginning of David's reign over Judah. He was murdered by Absalom because of his disgraceful treatment of Tamar, his half-sister (2 Sa 13). **2.** Son of Shimon of the family of Caleb (1 Ch 4:20).

AMORITES (mountaineers) A powerful Semitic people who inhabited Canaan prior to the conquest of Joshua (Ge 15:21; Ex 3:8). In the time of Abraham they held a strong position in the hill country and the name was applied to the inhabitants of that region (Ge 15:16), but later it was applied to all the inhabitants of Canaan (Jos 7:7; Ju 6:10). Prior to the Exodus they conquered districts east of the Jordan (Nu 21:26–30). They seized the land from the Arnon to Hermon in the north (Jos 2:10, 9:10; Ju 11:22) and were settled between Jerusalem and Hebron and westward to the Shephelah and to the territory of Ephraim in the north (Jos 10:5–6, 11:3; Ju 1:35). They were not completely expelled by Joshua (Ju 1:35, 3:5) and became a test of the loyalty of Israel to the Lord.

AMOS (burden-bearer). **1.** One of the twelve minor prophets. Although a native of Tekoa, six miles south of Bethlehem in Judah, he prophesied for Israel, the northern kingdom. A herdsman and a dresser of sycomore trees (Am 1:1, 7:14–15), he was not trained in any of the schools of the prophets and was not a prophet by profession. However, in answer to the impudent Amaziah, Amos declared his divine call to prophesy. In the reign of Jeroboam II he appeared at Bethel where Jeroboam I had set up the golden calves. His zeal in denouncing the sins of Israel led Amaziah, the priest at Bethel, to declare to the king that Amos was guilty of conspiracy and a menace to the kingdom. Amos' prophecy is third in the order of the minor prophets. **2.** An ancestor of Jesus (Lu 3:25).

ANAKIM A race of giants, the descendants of Arba (Jos 15:13, 21:11). They are called the sons of Anak (Nu 13:22). The Israelites were terrified by them (Nu 13:28; De 9:2) but, under the leadership of Joshua, drove them out (Jos 10:36, 39) and they settled in the country of the

Philistines (Jos 11:21–22). Caleb expelled three families of them from Hebron (Jos 15:14).

ANANIAS (Jehovah is gracious) **1.** The husband of Sapphira. He and his wife, Christian Jews of Jerusalem, held back from the common fund part of the price they received from the sale of property. Peter denounced the fraud and they were divinely smitten with death (Ac 5:1–11). **2.** A high priest, appointed to office by Herod about A.D. 48. A few years later he was sent to Rome charged with mistreatment of the Samaritans but was cleared and returned to Jerusalem. Paul was tried before him and he was one of the Apostle's accusers before Felix (Ac 23:2, 24:1). Ananias was deposed and assassinated in A.D. 67. **3.** A Jewish disciple at Damascus who aided in the conversion of Paul (Ac 9:10–18).

ANATHEMA The Greek equivalent of the Hebrew word signifying a person or thing devoted to destruction. The word in Paul's writings is usually translated *accursed*, which is explained as excommunication (Ro 9:3; 1 Co 12:3; Ga 1:8–9). *Anathema Maranatha* apparently signified one accursed until the coming of the Lord (1 Co 16:22).

ANDREW (manliness) One of the twelve apostles (Ma 4:18; Jo 1:40) and brother of Simon Peter. Both he and Peter were fishermen and lived at Bethsaida beside the Sea of Galilee (Mk 1:16–18). He brought Peter to Jesus (Jo 1:35–42) and was made an apostle (Ma 10:2; Mk 3:18). According to tradition he preached the Gospel in Greece and died a martyr in Achaia.

ANGEL An order of beings, superior to man, employed in the service of God (Ps 8:5; He 1:14, 2:7). There are different orders of angels as indicated by the expressions archangel and chief angel (Da 8:16, 9:21, 10:13, 21, 12:1; Lu 1:19, 26). In He 1:14 angels are called ministering angels

after the resurrection (Lu 20:36). There were fallen angels who had left their first estate (Ma 25:41; Re 12:7, 9). There are many passages that speak of the angel of God or the Lord (Ge 18:2–4, 13–14, 22:11–12, 15, 32:24, 30; Ex 3:2, 4; Jos 5:13–15).

ANNA (grace) A prophetess in Jerusalem. She was of the tribe of Asher, a widow, and the daughter of Phanuel. When the child Jesus was brought to the Temple to be presented before the Lord, she declared him to be the Messiah (Lu 2:36–38).

ANNAS (grace of Jehovah) The father-in-law of Caiaphas. In Ac 4:6 Annas is called the high priest. In Lu 3:2 both are called high priests. Jesus appeared before Annas as one accused (Jo 18:13). Annas was made high priest in A.D. 7 by Quirinius and held great influence (Lu 3:2). Some believe that Caiaphas was the actual high priest and that Annas was president of the Sanhedrin.

ANOINTING The pouring or rubbing of oil or ointment on the head, hair, beard, or other part of the body, a common Hebrew practice. Aaron and the priests were ordained by anointing (Ex 28:41, 30:30). Saul, David, and Solomon were anointed kings (1 Sa 9:16, 16:1, 12–13; 2 Sa 2:7; 1 Ki 1:34). The altar and tabernacle were anointed (Ex 29:36, 30:26). In the time of Christ it was an act of courtesy to anoint a guest's head with oil (Lu 7:46). The words *Messiah* and *Christ* signify Anointed One. Paul stated that Christians are spiritually anointed by the Holy Ghost (2 Co 1:21).

ANTICHRIST The word means *against Christ,* an *enemy of Christ, in the place of Christ* (1 Jo 2:18, 22, 4:3; 2 Jo 7). The coming of Antichrist, according to John's statement, will mark "the last days" before the second coming of Christ.

Antichrist is apparently a specific person and John empha-
sizes the spirit of Antichrist as it manifests itself in the denial
of Jesus' incarnation and messiahship. While the term is
used by John alone, he is not the only one who teaches this
doctrine. Christ uttered a warning regarding "false Christs"
(Ma 24:23–24; Mk 13:21–22). Paul clearly describes Antichrist and his satanic claims and operations (2 Th 2:3–12),
stating that the lawless one, the masterpiece of Satan, will
appear before the second coming of Christ. John describes
the same person as the "beast" (Re 13) and both Paul and
John declare that he will be destroyed by Christ at his
second coming. According to these teachings Christ will
return to the world when apostasy and iniquity come to full
expression in Antichrist.

ANTIOCH 1. The Syrian Antioch, the capital of Syria in
the time of the Greek dynasty. It was founded by Seleucus
Nicator about 300 B.C., who named it after his father Antiochus. Situated at a bend of the river Orontes on its southern side, it had a mixed population of Gentiles and Jews,
but more of the former. When persecution of Christians at
Jerusalem arose upon the martyrdom of Stephen, many fled
to Antioch. Here they preached the Gospel to the Jews.
Barnabas came from Jerusalem to engage in this work and
was the means of bringing Paul to the city. These labors
continued for a year. It was here that the disciples were first
called Christians (Ac 11:19–26). With the exception of
Jerusalem no other city was so directly related to the history
of the early Church. Antioch flourished under the Seleucid
kings and contained magnificent buildings. It was made a
free city by Pompey. 2. Pisidian Antoich. In Asia Minor
Seleucus Nicator founded another town which he also
named in honor of his father, Antiochus. It was in Phrygia
near the borders of Pisidia, and was called the Pisidian
Antioch to distinguish it from the Syrian Antioch. It was a
military center and was called Caesarea by the Romans. It

had a Jewish synagogue (Ac 13:14) and was visited by Paul and Barnabas on their first missionary journey (Ac 13:14–52, 14:19–21).

ANTIOCHUS (endurer) **1.** *Antiochus the Great.* He came to the throne of Syria in 223 B.C. and was the sixth ruler of the Seleucidan dynasty. After the death of Ptolemy IV he seized Palestine in 198 B.C. He invaded Europe but was defeated in the battle of Magnesia (190 B.C.) and forced to pay Rome an excessive tribute. While plundering a temple in 187 B.C., he was murdered by a mob. **2.** *Antiochus Epiphanes.* The youngest son of Antiochus the Great. A hostage at Rome for fifteen years, he was released shortly after his father's death and came to the throne in 175 B.C., obtaining his kingdom by flatteries (Da 11:21). He enraged the Jews by looting the Temple, setting up in it a statue of Jupiter, sacrificing swine on the altar, adn destroying the walls of Jerusalem. These insults he followed with a frightful massacre of the Jews, and this action precipitated the revolt of the Maccabees.

ANTIPAS 1. A Christian martyr of Pergamos (Re 2:12–13). According to tradition he was the bishop of that place. **2.** Son of Herod the Great. See HEROD.

APOLLOS A learned and eloquent Jew of Alexandrian birth, a disciple of John the Baptist (Ac 18:24–25). His preaching that Jesus was the Christ was attended with great success in Corinth and throughout Achaia (Ac 18:24–28). He was involved in the division of the church at Corinth (1 Co 1:12, 3:4–6, 4:6) and was a friend of Paul (1 Co 16:12; Tit 3:13). Some believe that he was the author of the Epistle to the Hebrews.

APOLLYON (destroyer) The Greek form of the Hebrew word *Abaddon*, the angel of the bottomless pit (Re 9:11).

APOSTLE (one who is sent, a messenger) The name applied to the Twelve selected by Jesus to be with him, receive his training, be witnesses of the events of his life, and preach the Gospel (Ma 4:18–22, 10:2–4; Lu 6:13–16). The original Twelve were plain men of humble occupations and without specialized training apart from that given by Jesus (Ac 1:21–22). Paul was the apostle to the Gentiles.

APOSTOLICAL COUNCIL The council held at Jerusalem about A.D. 50. It was an assembly of apostles and elders of the church (Ac 15).

AQUILA (eagle) A Christian Jew and tent-maker who, with his wife, Priscilla, entertained Paul in Corinth. He was born in Pontus, had come to Italy, but was driven from Rome by an edict of Claudius (Ac 18:1–3). Aquila and Priscilla accompanied Paul to Ephesus where they helped in the Christian training of Apollos (Ac 18:18–19, 26).

ARAMAIC LANGUAGE A group of Semitic languages and dialects including Biblical and Palestinian Aramaic. Documents in Aramaic have been discovered dating from about the tenth century B.C. It spread throughout the Euphrates Valley and Palestine, becoming the common language of most Semitic peoples. During and after the Exile it supplanted the Hebrew language among the Jews. Considerable portions of the books of Ezra and Daniel are Aramaic. The language of Jesus was Aramaic.

ARARAT A district of Armenia, a lofty plateau overlooking the plain of the river Araxes on the north and Mesopotamia on the south. Opinions differ as to the peak on which the ark of Noah rested (Ge 8:4). It is probably to be identified with the lofty snowclad summit of Massis, called by the Persians *Kuh-i-Nuh* (mountain of Noah). It is nearly 17,000 feet above sea level. About seven miles distant is a lesser peak—little Ararat—some 13,000 feet in height.

ARK 1. *Noah's Ark.* Constructed by divine order and specification, it was made to preserve Noah and his family during the flood. Assuming that the cubit was the ordinary cubit of eighteen inches, the length of the ark was 450 feet, the breadth 75 feet, and the height 45 feet. Within its three stories the animals were placed. Although it has been questioned whether two of each species of animals could be accommodated within the dimensions given, computations have shown that there was not only sufficient room, but room to spare (Ge 6:14–8:19; Ma 24:38; He 11:7). **2.** *Ark of the Covenant.* An oblong chest two and a half cubits long and one and a half in breadth and depth. It was made of shittim, or acacia wood, overlaid inside and outside with pure gold. It was covered by a lid of solid gold. By means of staves that passed through two golden rings on each side, it was carried by the Kohathites (Nu 7:9, 10:21). On the cover were two cherubim of gold, one at each end with their wings extended. The cover was called the mercy seat. The cherubim were symbolic of Jehovah's presence dwelling between the cherubim (Ex 25:10–22; Nu 7:89). It contained the two tables of stone having inscribed on them the covenant (Ex 25:21; De 10:3, 5), a pot of manna, Aaron's rod that blossomed, and the book of the law (Ex 16:34; De 31:26; He 9:4). The Kohathites, a family of the Levites to which Moses and Aaron belonged, had charge of the ark (Nu 3:29–31, 4:4–15). The ark, borne by the priests, preceded the Israelites in their desert wanderings and in the crossing of the Jordan (Nu 10:33; Jos 4:9–11). It was carried around Jericho (Jos 6:1–20) and was placed in Shiloh (1 Sa 3:3). In the time of Eli the Israelites took the ark into the battlefield, thinking its presence would give them the victory, but it was captured by the Philistines (1 Sa 4:1–22). The Philistines then returned the ark (1 Sa 1–6:11) and it was next brought by David to Jerusalem and placed in a tent (2 Sa 6:17). Finally, Solomon had it placed within the Holy of Holies of the Temple (1 Ki 8:1–9). Nothing has been known of it since the destruction of Jerusalem by Nebuchadnezzar, 586 B.C. **3.** A box or basket made of bulrushes, slime, and pitch, in which the infant Moses was hidden in the Nile (Ex 2:3–6).

ARMAGEDDON (mountain of Megiddo). A gathering place or battleground (Re 16:16). It was apparently the great plain of Megiddo lying between the Galilaean hills and the mountains of Israel, a notable battleground in Old Testament history. Here Barak defeated the Canaanites, and Gideon the Midianites (Ju 5:19, 7:9). Two national tragedies were enacted at or near the place: the slaying of Saul (1 Sa 31:8); and the slaying of Josiah (2 Ki 23:29).

ARMOR 1. *For defense.* (a) The helmet, made of leather and later of iron and brass, was used by various nations (1 Sa 17:5, 38; Je 46:4; Eze 27:10). (b) The shield was used by all nations. The large shield covered the whole person while a smaller one, the buckler, was used by archers (1 Ch 5:18). They were oblong, round, or oval and were made of layers of leather or of leather-covered wood (Eze 39:9); also of brass (1 Ki 14:27); and even of gold (1 Ki 10:17). (c) The breastplate (cuirass), also called harness, was a coat of mail which protected the breast, shoulders, and back, and was made of leather, iron, or brass (1 Sa 17:5; Re 9:9). (d) Greaves which protected the legs below the knees were made of thin plates of metal (1 Sa 17:6). **2.** *For offense.* Offensive armor consisted of the sword, spear, dart, mace, javelin, sling, bow, and arrow. Paul set forth, in his Epistle to the Ephesians, a detailed description of the Christian's spiritual armor (Ep 6:13–17).

ARTAXERXES (exalted king?) Any one of several Persian kings, as Artaxerxes I, the third son of Xerxes (Ahasuerus). He reigned 464–424 B.C. and was called Artaxerxes Longimanus which, according to some, denoted the long length of his hands, but others regard it as a figurative expression indicating the extent of his kingdom. It was probably he who listened to the enemies of the Jews and stopped the work on the second temple (Ez 4:7) but when the edict of Cyrus was found, the building operations were renewed (Ez 6:1–4). In his twentieth year (445 B.C.), he commissioned Nehemiah to go to Jerusalem and build the walls (Ne 2:1). After an absence of twelve years Nehemiah returned to Persia but in a short time was permitted to return to Jerusalem. During his entire stay in Jerusalem Nehemiah acted in the capacity of governor (Ne 13:6). Longimanus did more for the Jews than any other Persian king except Cyrus.

ASA (physician) **1.** Third king of Judah, the son of Abijam and grandson of Rehoboam. He had a peaceful reign for its first ten years (2 Ch 14:1). He punished his mother for idolatry (1 Ki 15:9–13). He defeated Zerah, the Ethiopian, when the latter invaded Judah (2 Ch 14:9–15) and, aided by Azariah, reformed the people (2 Ch 15:1–15). He made an alliance with Damascus for which he was reproved by Hanani (1 Ki 15:16–22; 2 Ch 16:1–10). In his old age Asa was diseased in his feet and was less loyal to the Lord than he had been earlier (1 Ki 15:23; 2 Ch 16:12). **2.** A Levite, son of Elkanah (1 Ch 9:16).

ASCENSION **1.** The ascension of Enoch in the antediluvian age at the age of 365 years (Ge 5:18–23; He 11:5). **2.** Elijah ascended in a chariot of fire at Jericho (2 Ki 2:9–13). Centuries afterwards he appeared with Moses in the scene of Christ's transfiguration (Ma 17:1–9). **3.** Ascension of Jesus from the Mount of Olives (Ps 68:18; Lu 24:51; Ac 1:9–11;

Ep 4:8–10). **4.** Translation of the Church. Paul writes that this will occur at the time of the resurrection of the dead in Christ at the first stage of Christ's second coming (1 Co 15:51–52; 1 Th 4:13–18).

ASHDOD (fortress) One of five Philistines cities, some twenty miles form Gaza (Jos 13:3; 1 Sa 5:1). It was held by the Anakim and was never taken by the Israelites (Jos 15:46–47). When the ark was captured by the Philistines, it was placed here in the temple of Dagon (1 Sa 5:1–8). Psammeticus, king of Egypt, besieged Ashdod for 29 years. In New Testament times it was called Azotus and from this point to Caesarea Philip the Evangelist labored (Ac 8:40).

ASHER (happy) The eighth son of Jacob and second by Zilpah, the handmaid of Leah (Ge 30:13). The tribe of Asher was assigned the district that ran north from Carmel along the sea shore. To the east of it lay the tribes of Zebulun and Naphtali (Jos 19:24–31).

ASHERAH Name of a Canaanite goddess, frequently associated with Baal. It appears that she was symbolized by sacred poles or trees and that frequently the word does not signify the goddess, but only these symbols. In the Authorized Version Asherahs are called *groves*.

ASHES A priest was required each morning to remove the ashes from the altar of burnt offering and put them in a clean place (Le 6:10–11). The ashes of the red heifer were invested with a purifying power (He 9:13). Sitting in ashes or sprinkling them upon one's person was a symbol of grief (Job 2:8, 42:6; Je 6:26; Ma 11:21). Eating ashes was an expression of humiliation and misery (Ps 102:9; Is 44:20). "Dust and ashes" was a proverbial expression for human fraility (Ge 18:27).

ASHTORETH (a wife) The principal female divinity of the Phoenicians, called Astarte by the Greeks and Romans and Ishtar by the Assyrians. The worship of this goddess was established at Sidon (1 Ki 11:3, 5; 2 Ki 23:13) and was practiced by the Hebrews in the time of the judges (Ju 2:13, 10:6). Solomon gave it his support (1 Ki 11:5; 2 Ki 23:13).

ASIA The word in modern usage denotes the largest of the continents but as used Biblically it refers only to the western portion of Asia Minor. It was the richest, and except for Africa, the most important of the Roman provinces. Its capital was the large and ancient city of Ephesus. To the east lay Bithynia, Galatia, Pisidia, and Lycia. Across the strait, now known as the Dardanelles, lay Macedonia. Asia, especially the section around Ephesus, was the scene of many of Paul's activities (Ac 19:10, 22, 26, 20:4, 6, 18; 1 Co 16:19; 2 Ti 1:15). In this rich province were located the seven churches of Asia (Re 1–3).

ASSYRIA The land lying on the Tigris between Padanaram, Babylon, Armenia, and Media. The name is derived from Asshur, the son of Shem (Ge 10:22) who was later worshipped by the Assyrians as a deity. While Moses appears to have known about Assyria (Ge 2:14, 25:18; Nu 24:22), it did not become important to Jewish history until the reign of Menahem. The Assyrians were a Semitic people who originated in Babylon (Ge 10:11). They conquered Babylonia about 1300 B.C. and under Tiglath-pileser I became the strongest power in the East. They are mentioned in the Bible chiefly for their warlike aggressions.

ATONEMENT In the scriptural sense atonement is the expiation of sin by the sacrificial work of Jesus Christ. It is the means by which reconciliation between God and the sinner is effected. A true study of Scriptures leads to the rejection of the view that the essential truth of the atonement is expressed by what is signified by *at-one-ment*, that is, reconciliation. The words *atonement* and *reconciliation* in Scripture have an entirely different application. The death of Christ looks toward God rather than toward man. In other words, Christ's death affects people spiritually rather than morally. The scriptural significance of atonement is expressed by the following: **1.** Redemption, restored by ransom (Ma 20:28). **2.** The purchase price (1 Co 6:20). **3.** Covering. The Hebrew *cover* as used in sacrificial and propitiatory relations (Ro 4:7) **4.** Responsibility assumed (He 7:22). **5.** Bearing of penalty (Le 24:15; Is 53:4–6; He 9:28). **6.** Propitiation by sacrifice required by God, that is, the securing of the pardon of an offended God (Ro 5:10; 1 Jo 2:2–3). **7.** Escaping the death sentence of the law through one upon whom the sentence fell (Ga 3:13).

ATONEMENT, DAY OF The tenth day of the seventh month was divinely appointed for the expiation of the sins of the nation. On this day the high priest offered sacrifices for the priests, the people and also the sanctuary (Le 16, 23:26–32; Nu 29:7–11). This was the only fast required by the law. Clothed in white linen, the high priest offered a sacrifice for himself and the priests, by which was indicated the imperfection of the Levitical priests, contrasted with which is the perfection of Christ our high priest. The priest then took the blood of the offering into the Holy of Holies and sprinkled it on the mercy seat. This was the only day of the year when he entered this inner sanctuary. He then took the two goats which the nation provided. One was slain as a sin offering for the people and the blood was sprinkled within the Holy of Holies, making atonement for the inner sanctuary and then for the holy place and altar of burnt offering. On the head of the other goat he placed his hands and confessed the sins of the people and then sent it into the wilderness. The goat thus symbolized the sin-bearer, Christ (He 9).

AUGUSTUS The title of Octavius who succeeded Julius Caesar, his great-uncle. Follwoing the death of Caesar he, Antony and Lepidus formed a triumvirate. Augustus afterwards shared the empire with Antony but by his victory in the battle of Actium (31 B.C.), he was made sole emperor by the Senate and had conferred on him the title Augustus (27 B.C.). It was in the reign of Augustus that Jesus was born (Lu 2:1). It was he who issued the decree for the enrollment that brought Joseph and Mary to Bethlehem (Mi 5:2).

AVENGER OF BLOOD When one was slain, either by accident or intent, the nearest relative of the one slain was allowed to avenge his death, hence the expression, *avenger of blood* or *revenger of blood*. One who had slain another might flee to one of the six cities of refuge. Here he was given a trial, and if it was established that the act was accidental and not intentional, he was not put to death (Nu 35:19, 21, 27; 2 Sa 14:11). See CITY OF REFUGE.

B

BAAL (lord, master) **1.** The principal male deity of the Canaanites and Phoenicians. He was adopted by other nations and, as early as the time of Moses, was worshipped by the Moabites (Nu 22:41). In the time of the judges altars were built to him by the Israelites (Ju 2:13, 6:28–32). Jezebel, the wife of King Ahab and a Phoenician by birth, established Baalism in Israel. Through Athaliah, the daughter of Jezebel who married King Jehoram of Judah, this false worship took root in that kingdom (2 Ch 17:3, 21:6). On Mount Carmel Elijah proposed a great test which completely discredited Baal and vindicated Jehovah (1 Ki 16:31–32, 18:17–40). Jehu and Hezekiah checked Baalism but it was revived (2 Ki 21:3). The prophets denounced it (Je

19:4–5). The worship of Baal was attended by lascivious ceremonies and human sacrifice (1 Ki 14:24; Je 19:5). **2.** A town of Simeon (1 Ch 4:33). **3.** A Benjamite, son of Jehiel and brother of Kish (1 Ch 8:30, 9:35–39). **4.** A Reubenite (1 Ch 5:5).

BAAL-PEOR (lord of Peor) A deity worshipped by the Moabites with impure rites on Mount Peor. Through the counsel of Balaam, the Israelites were led to worship this god. For this they were punished by a plague (Nu 25:1–9; Ho 9:10).

BABEL, TOWER OF The huge brick tower erected in the Plain of Shinar (Ge 11:1–9). The purposes of its builders were to make for themselves a name and to possess a citadel as a safeguard against being scattered abroad throughout the earth. The Lord frustrated their plans by confusing their speech.

BABYLON (Babel, confusion) The capital of Babylonia, built on both sides of the Euphrates. It is first mentioned in the Bible as the beginning of the kingdom of Nimrod (Ge 10:10). It was the site of the Tower of Babel. In secular history the city dates back to about 2230 B.C. It was comparatively unimportant until about 1900 B.C. when it became the capital of a dynasty of kings. From that time till near the beginning of the Christian era, it continued, with but brief interruptions, to be one of the greatest cities of southwestern Asia. After the Persian conquest (538 B.C.) it gradually declined and gave place to the cities on the Tigris, of which Baghdad continues to our day. The greatest periods of Babylon's magnificence were the reigns of Hammurabi (about 1800 B.C.) and Nebuchadnezzar (605–562 B.C.) who conquered Jerusalem and carried the Jews into captivity. According to Herodotus and other ancient writers the city was laid out in the form of a huge square with the Euphrates flowing diagonally through it. The walls were fourteen miles in length on each side and were approximately 85 feet thick. It was said to have possessed one hundred gates of brass and 250 towers. The Babylon of Ma 1:11–12, 17 and Ac 7:43 is unquestionably the city on the Euphrates. The Babylon of 1 Pe 5:13 is almost certainly Rome. The Babylon of the Apocalypse (Re 14:8, 17:5, 18:2, 10, 21) is Rome.

BABYLONIA A region of western Asia called Shinar (Ge 10:10, 11:2) and the land of the Chaldeans (Je 24:5, 25:12; Eze 12:13). On the north was Assyria, on the east were the mountains of Elam, on the south the Persian Gulf, and on the west the Arabian Desert. Its ancient cities were Ur (Ge 11:28, 31, 15:7; Ne 9:7), Erech, Babel, Accad (Ge 10:10), and Nippu. At times these were city-states and at other times were confederated under a single king. It was Hammurabi who brought the entire area together under his dominion. From about 1270–747 B.C. Babylonia was, for the most part, under Assyrian rule. In the latter year Nabonassar became king of Babylon, ruling thirteen years. Tiglath-pileser II, after having crushed a revolt, made himself king of Babylon in 729 B.C. Sennacherib burned the city (689 B.C.) but it was rebuilt by Essar-haddon. In 625 B.C. the New Babylonian Empire was founded. For last century of the empire, see BABYLON and NEBUCHADNEZZAR.

BALAAM A soothsayer, the son of Beor of Pethor, a city of Mesopotamia (Nu 22:5, 24:1). King Balak of Moab attempted to have Balaam curse the Israelites who were invading the land but, receiving the word of God, he blessed, rather than cursed, the invaders (Nu 24:1–9). He was slain in battle (Nu 31:8).

BANQUET A means of social enjoyment, the frequent accompaniment of religious festivities. It might be in commemoration of a birthday (Ge 40:20), the weaning of a son

33

(Ge 21:8), a marriage (Ju 14:10; Es 2:18; Ma 22:2–4), or a sheep shearing (1 Sa 25:2, 8, 11; 2 Sa 13:23–29). It usually began in the evening and often extended over a period of days. Invitations were sometimes sent out, the disregarding of which was considered a grave insult.

BAPTISM The subject of baptism is of vital interest to all Christians. However, views and interpretations differ, especially in regard to the *meaning* of baptism, the *modes* of baptism, and the *subjects* of baptism. This article states necessarily briefly and without interpretation, some of the main points of view and doctrines.

1. The Baptism of John. Some regard John's Baptism as Jewish, rather than Christian, because it preceded by some three years the baptism which was instituted by Jesus. Among the Jews, at that time, baptisms or ceremonial purifications were common and there were frequent ceremonial washings, signifying purification and consecration. This was true especially of priestly purifications (Ex 29:4, 40:12; Le 8:6; Mk 7:2–4). John preached "the baptism of repentance for the remission of sins" (Mk 1:4). Those who obeyed John's call to prepare the way of the Lord by repenting and confessing their sins were all baptized by him (Mk 1:3, 5). Lutherans and others hold, on the basis of Mk 1:4, that John's Baptism was a means of grace for the engendering of faith unto the remission of sins.

2. The Baptism of Jesus. Jesus was baptized by John (Mk 1:9), not "unto repentance" nor for "remission of sins" because he had no sins to repent of nor to confess. His baptism, as declared by himself, was "to fulfill all righteousness" (Ma 3:15). The voice, "This is my beloved Son, in whom I am well pleased" (Ma 3:17) set the heavenly seal of approval on his act of righteousness. It was an appropriate and solemn induction into his public ministry.

3. Christian Baptism. Whether Christ personally baptized or delegated this work to his disciples is not definitely known (Jo 3:22; 4:1–2). The difference between the baptisms of John and Jesus is recorded in Ma 3:11; Mk 1:8; Lu 3:16; Jo 1:33; Ac 1:5. Jesus referred to the baptism of John in Mk 11:30 and John referred to the baptism of Jesus in Jo 1:32–33. Some hold that there was no esential difference between the baptism of Christ and that of his way-preparer so far as the object and efficacy are concerned. It was just prior to his ascension that Jesus ordained baptism "in the name of the Father, and of the Son, and of the Holy Spirit" as a permanent institution among "all nations" and "unto the end of the world" (Ma 28:18–20). When Paul found that certain disciples at Ephesus had been baptized with John's baptism, he (Paul) explained it as "the baptism of repentance" and said "they should believe . . . on Christ Jesus. When they heard this, they were baptized in the name of the Lord Jesus" (Ac 19:1–5). Belief in the Lord Jesus Christ, repentance, and baptism in his name for the remission of sins go hand-in-hand in the New Testament. The apostles administered Christian baptism on the day of Pentecost (Ac 2:38, 41).

4. The Meaning of Baptism. The meaning of baptism has been the subject of much controversy. Passages such as, "Repent and be baptized . . . for the remission of sins" (Ac 2:38), "arise and be baptized and wash away your sins" (Ac 22:16), "by the washing of regeneration" (Ti 3:5), "the baptism of repentance for the remission of sins" (Mk 1:4), are taken to support the view that baptism is for the remission of sins, as is held by numerous denominations. Lutherans hold: "The sacred act which constitutes sacramental baptism comprises more than a mere application of water; it is a 'washing of water by the word' (Ep 5:26)—a literal translation. By divine institution, this water is constituted a sacrament, a means whereby men are made disciples of Christ, sanctified and cleansed by him who has redeemed them, giving himself as a ransom for all (Ma 28:19; Ep 5:26). By it we are sanctified, entering into a holy relation to, and union with, that God who has revealed himself as the Triune God, the God of our salvation." Some oppose the view that baptism is essential to salvation. To support this they quote the reply to the jailer's question (Ac 16:30–31) and Paul's statement. "I thank God that I baptized none of you but Crispus and Gaius—for Christ sent me not to baptize, but to preach the gospel" (1 Co 1:14–17). Others point out that baptism is a seal of the work of grace already performed in the soul before baptism is administered, and that the subjects of baptism have already experienced regeneration and because of this are proper subjects for baptism. The Quakers or Friends, for example, who believe in the spiritual character of Christianity, hold that the baptism of the Holy Spirit alone is requisite. The Socinian view regard baptism as merely a mode of professing faith in Christ, a ceremony of initiation into the Christian church. Calvinistic churches hold to the doctrine stated in the Westminster Confession: "Baptism is a sacrament of the New Testament, ordained by Jesus Christ, not only for the solemn admission of the party baptized into the visible church, but also to be unto him a sign and seal of the covenant of grace, of his ingrafting into Christ, of regeneration, or remission of sins, and of his giving up unto God through Jesus Christ to walk in newness of life."

5. Modes of Baptism. (1) *The Immersionist View.* Most immersionists hold to the belief that baptism is one of the ordinances of the church setting forth the central truths of Christianity in sacred symbolism (Ro 6:3–4; Col 2:12). Authority for its practice is based upon the command of Christ as stated in the great commission (Ma 28:19; Mk 16:15–16). The verb used in the New Testament to describe the act of baptizing is *baptizo*. The Greek-English Lexicon by Liddell and Scott gives the meaning of *baptizo* as *dip, dip under*. In agreement with this, Thayer's Lexicon gives the meaning of *baptizo* as being *to dip, to immerse, submerge*. Thayer goes on to say that "it was an immersion in water, performed as a sign of removal of sin." The late Dr. A. T. Robertson, one of the greatest of modern Greek scholars, said "As is well known not only in Greece but all over Russia, wherever the Greek church prevails, immersion is the unbroken and universal practice." (These words were written during the days of religious freedom in Russia.) The Greek word from which the word baptism comes is translated *baptisma*. Of this Liddell and Scott give the meaning as *that which is dipped*. With this Thayer also agrees, saying that *baptisma* is a word peculiar to ecclesiastical writers, meaning *immersion* or *submersion*. The fact that *baptizo* means *to dip*, and that the river of Jordan was the place of baptizing, and that "much water" (Jo 3:23) was needed for baptism, all argue for baptism by immersion. The Greek prepositions used in describing the ceremony also are given as evidence that the baptism, spoken of in the New Testament, was by immersion. In Mk 1:9–10 it is stated that Jesus was baptized of John in (translation into) Jordan and that he came *out of* the water, etc. In Ac 8:38 the same prepositions are found: "They both went down *into* the water, and he baptized him, and when they came up *out of* the water," etc. That baptism should be immersion is also argued from the symbolism used by Paul in Ro 6:3–5. "Don't you know, that so many of us as were baptized into Jesus Christ were baptized into his death? Therefore we are buried with him by baptism into death: that as Christ was raised up from the dead by the glory of the Father, even so we also should walk in newness of life. For if we have been planted together in the likeness of his death, we shall be also in the likeness of his resurrection." The same symbolism is referred to in Col 2:12, where coming out of baptismal waters pictures bodily resurrection. (2) *The Non-immersionist View.* A number of Christian churches hold to the view that what is essential to baptism is not the mode but the application of water "in the name of the Father, of the Son, and of the Holy Spirit." This view admits any mode of baptism—pouring, sprinkling or immersion. According to *The Didache* (The Teaching of the Twelve Apostles, c. A.D. 120), the mode seems to have been pouring. But it is held by historians that immersion wholly in water was the prevailing type of baptism in the first century. Cyprian said in his Epistle concerning the baptism of the sick: "Baptism by sprinkling is pure,—is of the Lord's faithfulness made sufficient." The method of administering the water of separation was sprinkling (Nu 19:17–18; He 9:19). Lutheran doctrine holds: "In apostolic days, there are instances of Christian baptism recorded where immersion was excluded by the circumstances. When the three thousand were baptized in one day, the Day of Pentecost, at Jerusalem, where was the river or pool in the city or its environments in which three thousand men, women, and children might have been immersed? The eunuch (Ac 8:26–39) was on his way through a desert country, where water was and is to this day scarce, the water courses being few and low in their bed. That Philip and the eunuch "went down into the water" and "came up out of the water" is far from establishing an instance of baptism by immersion; it rather describes the simplest way in which the two might get into position to permit Philip to lift water with his hand from a low and shallow brook or pool and pour it upon the eunuch's head." It is thus believed that immersion is not the only mode signified by the Greek word; that it is not sufficient to show that in classical Greek the word always means to immerse, even if true; it must be shown that such is the only use of the word in the New Testament. In Lu 11:38, the word signifies "wash." It does not require that Jesus would be expected to immerse himself before eating. The same is true of Mk 7:4, which refers to the purification of the Jews in coming from public places in case they had become ceremonially unclean. In He 9:10, "which stood only in meats and drinks, and diverse washings," the Greek noun *baptismo*, derived from the verb, is used. It would not be true to fact relative to the Levitical washings to translate this, "and diverse immersions." The argument is that the language used in certain instances does not prove immersion; that "It is contrary to the whole spirit of Christ's teaching to attach great importance to details of ceremony"; also, that baptism, which is a universal rite, may properly and must, of necessity, be varied in mode according to climate and other circumstances.

6. The Subjects of Baptism. (1) *Believers.* Usually most immersionists contend that baptism should be administered only to believers. They reject making infants the subjects of baptism on the ground that the Scriptures require that repentance and faith are essential to baptism (Ac 2:38, 8:36–37, 19:4–5). Since infants are incapable of meeting these requirements, they are not proper subjects of baptism. The following passages support this view: At the conclusion of Peter's great sermon on the day of Pentecost, anxious inquirers asked, "Men and brethren, what shall we do?" In answer Peter said, "*Repent* and be *baptized*" (Ac 2:38) and in the verses that follow it is stated, "Then they that *gladly received his word* were *baptized*" (Ac 2:41). Ac 8:5–8 tells that Philip went into Samaria to preach the gospel, and states further (v. 12) "when they *believed* . . . they were *baptized*, both men and women." The record of Paul's conversion says, "He arose and was *baptized*" (Ac 9:18). Other passages could be quoted but these are sufficient to show that faith in Christ was required by the early gospel preachers of those who were to be baptized. (2) *Infants.* With the exception of the immersionists, most Protestant churches, as also the Roman Catholic Church, practice infant baptism. Baptists and others contend that baptism should be administered only to believers. Many churches, however, from the earliest time have administered it also to children who have sponsors to care for their Christian nurture. The Lutheran doctrine is stated thus: "There is universal sin, universal need of salvation, under the Old

Testament and under the New. Accordingly, when God would make a covenant with his people through Abraham, 'the father of the faithful,' he caused Abraham to receive the seal of that covenant—circumcision. The rule was that people were to be brought into the covenant in infancy, at the age of eight days (Ge 17:12; Le 12:3). If adults and infants in the Old Testament needed to be brought into the covenant, they need the same relationship with God now. In Col 2:11 Paul speaks of a circumcision made without hands and in the next verse we learn that he is speaking of baptism. The law of heredity set forth by Christ states: 'That which is born of flesh is flesh' (Jo 3:6). The offspring of sinners can be nothing but sinners. Being by nature sinners, infants as well as adults need to be baptized. Every child that is baptized is begotten anew of water and of the Spirit, is placed in covenant relation with God, and is made a child of God and an heir of his heavenly kingdom."

7. The Importance of Baptism. The importance of baptism is shown by the fact that the Lord Jesus Christ himself submitted to it "to fulfill all righteousness" (Ma 3:15) and that he included it as a part of his great commission (Ma 28:19; Mk 16:15–16). By observing this sacred ordinance, as instituted by Christ, we honor him and show our love for him.

BARABBAS (son of a father) A prisoner and a robber, who raised an insurrection and commited murder. At the Passover season it was the custom for the procurator to release a prisoner selected by the people. Pilate, anxious to save Jesus, offered the Jews the choice of releasing him or Barabbas. They were induced by the priests to choose Barabbas (Ma 27:16–26).

BARAK (lightning) A man of Kadesh. Israel was oppressed by the Canaanites when Barak, encouraged by Deborah, enlisted 10,000 men of Naphtali and Zebulun.

They completely routed the enemy and broke the yoke of Jabin and his general, Sisera (Ju 4:1–5:12; He 11:32).

BAR-JONA The surname of Peter (Ma 16:17), meaning son of Jona (Jo 1:42, 21:15–17).

BARLEY A grain of Palestine (Le 27:16; De 8:8; Ru 2:17). The Hebrews, especially the poorer class, made it into bread. It was mixed with wheat, millet and other ingredients (Ju 7:13; 2 Ki 4:42; Eze 4:9). It was used as fodder for horses and oxen (1 Ki 4:28). The barley harvest occurred in some regions as early as March and in others as late as May but it preceded the wheat harvest (Ru 1:22; 2 Sa 21:9–10).

BARNABAS (son of exhortation) The surname of Joses, a Levite of the island of Cyprus. He was one of the disciples who sold his holdings and brought the money to the apostles after the day of Pentecost (Ac 4:36–37). It was Barnabas who satisfied the doubting Jewish Christians of the genuineness of Paul's conversion and commended him to the brethren (Ac 9:27). He was sent by the church at Jerusalem to aid in preaching the Gospel at Antioch (Ac 11:19–24). He brought Paul (Saul) from Tarsus (Ac 11:22–26) and later they were sent to Jerusalem to distribute alms (Ac 11:27–30). The church at Antioch then commissioned Paul and Barnabas to preach the Gospel to the Gentiles which resulted in the first missionary journey, Mark accompanying them as far as Pamphylia (Ac 13:1–14, 28). Returning to Antioch, they were sent by that church as commissioners to the council at Jerusalem (Ac 15:1–2, 12). The council commissioned them to report to the churches in Syria and Asia Minor the decree of the council. A second missionary journey was proposed by Paul, but when Barnabas insisted upon taking Mark who had left them on the first journey, Paul objected and chose Silas as his companion (Ac 15).

BARSABAS (son of Saba) **1.** Joseph Barsabas was one of two disciples nominated to fill the place of Judas Iscariot but Matthias was chosen (Ac 1:23). **2.** Judas Barsabas who, with Paul, Barnabas and Silas, was sent with letters to Antioch (Ac 15:22).

BARTHOLOMEW (son of Tolmai) One of the twelve apostles (Ma 10:3; Mk 3:18; Lu 6:14; Ac 1:13). It is probably the surname of Nathanael (Jo 1:45–46).

BARTIMAEUS (son of Timaeus) At Jericho this blind beggar, hearing that Jesus was passing, appealed to him to have mercy upon him and was healed (Mk 10:46).

BATHING In hot countries of the East bathing was fre-quent, as in the case of Pharaoh's daughter (Ex 2:5). In entering a house persons washed the dust from their feet (Ge 18:4, 43:24; Jo 13:10). It was a part of the Jewish system of ceremonial purification (Le 14:8, 17:5; Nu 19:7–8). Before entering the temple, or offering a sacrifice on the altar, the priests washed their hands and feet (Ex 30:19–21). On coming from the market, in case they had touched some-thing that rendered them ceremonially unclean, they washed themselves. In the time of Christ the Jews scrupu-lously washed their hands before eating (Mk 7:3–4).

BATHSHEBA (daughter of an oath) The wife of Uriah the Hittite. The black page of David's history was his adul-terous relations with this woman. Uriah, who had been placed on the most dangerous position of the battlefront by the king's command, was slain, and David married Bathsheba. She became the mother of Solomon (2 Sa 11:3–4, 12:24; 1 Ki 1:11).

BATTERING-RAM An ancient weapon of offensive warfare (Eze 4:2, 21:22, 26:9). Its suspended, heavy horizontal beam resembled a ram's head, hence the name. It was a formidable weapon in siegecraft. Walls were demolished by the impact of its oscillating, metal-headed beam.

BDELLIUM A precious substance listed with gold and onyx as products of the land of Havilah (Ge 2:12). Manna resembled it in appearance (Nu 11:7). It was probably a resinous gum.

BEARD The Jews gave much attention to the beard as expresing the dignity of manhood and regarded the neglect of it as indicative of weakness or infirmity (1 Sa 21:13; 2 Sa 19:24). In times of mourning it was customary to cut it off (Ez 9:3; Is 15:2). The Egyptians shaved the face and the head but allowed the hair to grow as a mark of mourning. Before appearing before Pharaoh, Joseph shaved his beard (Ge 41:14).

BEAST A large four-footed animal (Ge 1:29–30). In the Bible the word includes both wild and domesticated beasts (Le 26:22; Je 50:39; Mk 1:13) and also denotes the lower orders of animals that fly and creep (Ps 147:9; Ac 28:5). Beast is frequently used in the Scriptures in a symbolic sense to designate that which is brutal, sensual, and ferocious (Ps 73:22). Men are represented as wild beasts (1 Co 15:32). In Daniel's prophecy the four beasts are representative of the four great kingdoms (Da 7:3, 17, 23). In Revelation Antichrist and the false prophet are represented as beasts (Re 13:1, 15:2, 17:8).

BEELZEBUB The title of a heathen deity. A slight change in spelling is Baalzebub, the god of Ekron. To the Jews Beelzebub was the prince of evil spirits (Ma 10:25, 12:24; Mk 3:22; Lu 11:15–19). Jesus identifies him with Satan (Ma 12:26; Mk 3:23; Lu 11:18).

43

BEERSHEBA (well of seven or well of the oath). A well dug by Abraham near the Philistine border (Ge 21:22–32). Abraham lived here for several years before moving to Hebron. The wells were filled up but were later opened by Isaac who made a covenant with the king of Gerar here (Ge 26:1–33). On his way to Egypt Jacob sacrificed at this well (Ge 46:1–5) and near it a town arose (Jos 15:28) which was assigned to Simeon (Jos 19:1–2). It was at the southern limit of Palestine, hence the famous expression "from Dan to Beersheba." Samuel's sons were judges here (1 Sa 8:2).

BELIAL (wickedness) Usually wickedness or ungodliness (De 15:9; Ps 41:8; Pr 19:28). Paul applied the term to Satan (2 Co 6:15).

BELSHAZZAR (Bel protect the king) The leader in command of the Babylonian forces at the time Babylon was captured by the Persians (Da 5:28, 30). He was the son of Nabonidus (last king of the New Babylonian Empire) and coregent with the king in the latter years of the reign. His relationship to Nebuchadnezzar was possibly that of grandson—son of the king's daughter (Da 5:11).

BELTESHAZZAR When Daniel was taken to Babylon, this was the name given him by the prince of the eunuchs (Da 1:7).

BEN-HADAD (son of Hadad) The name of three kings who ruled at Damascus. **1.** The grandson of Hezion. He made an alliance with King Asa of Judah against King Baasha of Israel when the latter was building Ramah. Ben-hadad invaded Israel and captured much territory (1 Ki 15:18–21; 2 Ch 16:1–6). **2.** Son of the preceding who, in the time of Ahab, besieged Samaria but was defeated. The following year the war was renewed but he was again defeated and peace was made (1 Ki 20:1–34). He was later joined by Ahab and ten other allies in his conflict with the Assyrians whom they met at Karkar on the Orontes in 854 B.C. Though the Assyrian king claimed a great victory, in reality he suffered a severe reverse. At a later time Ben-hadad besieged Samaria but a panic in the Syrian camp brought the siege to an end (2 Ki 6:8–7:20). He was murdered and was succeeded by Hazael (2 Ki 8:15). **3.** Son of Hazael under whom Damascus lost her conquests in Palestine (2 Ki 13:24).

BENJAMIN (son of the right hand). **1.** The youngest son of Jacob. His mother died at his birth (Ge 35:16–20). The strong paternal affection of Jacob for Benjamin is seen in his hesitancy in allowing him to go to Egypt with his other sons (Ge 43:1–17). Benjamin was also greatly loved by Joseph (Ge 43:29–34). Benjamin had five sons (Ge 46:21; Nu 26:38–41). **2.** The tribe of Benjamin. When the land was divided, the section allotted to Benjamin was between Judah and Ephraim, the eastern limit of which was the Jordan (Jos 18:11–20). Its chief towns were Jerusalem, Jericho, Bethel, Gibeon, Bibeath, and Mizpeh (Jos 18:21–28). It was one of the smaller tribes, numbering at the time of the Exodus only 35,400. For protecting the guilty inhabitants of Gibeah (Ju 19–21), the tribe was nearly annihilated, only 600 escaping. Saul was a Benjamite. When the ten tribes revolted under Jeroboam, a large part of this tribe remained with Judah. Paul, the great apostle to the Gentiles, was a descendant of this tribe (Ph 3:5). **3.** A warrior, son of Bilhan (1 Ch 7:10). **4.** One who took a foreign wife (Ez 10:32), probably the same as in Ne 3:23, 12:34.

BERYL This is the rendering of the Hebrew *tarshish*, a word derived probably from the place of that name. It was the first stone of the fourth row on the breastplate of the high priest (Ex 28:20, 39:13; Eze 1:16; Da 10:6). In Re 21:20 the eighth foundation of the wall of the New Jerusalem is called beryl (Greek *berullos*). It may have been a golden-yellow stone.

BETHANY (house of dates?) **1.** A small town on the eastern slope of the Mount of Olives (Mk 11:1; Lu 19:29) near the road from Jericho to Jerusalem. It was the town of Lazarus and his sisters, Mary and Martha (Jo 11:1, 12:1). More than any other place, it is associated with the closing scenes of Jesus' life. In the house of Simon the leper Jesus was anointed (Ma 26:6–13; Mk 14:3). Here Jesus found retirement and rest and from near it he ascended to heaven. At the present time it is a small wretched hamlet. **2.** A place east of the Jordan where John was baptizing at the beginning of Christ's public ministry (Jo 1:28).

BETHEL (house of God) **1.** An ancient town west of Ai and southwest of Shiloh (Ge 12:8; Ju 21:19). When he arrived in Palestine, Abraham pitched his tent here (Ge 13:3). The Canaanites called it Luz but Jacob named it Bethel because here he had his vision (Ge 28:19, 31:13) and it was the site of an altar he erected (Ge 35:1–15). Bethel was assigned to Benjamin and was on the border between that tribe and Ephraim (Jos 16:2). It became a center of idolatry under Jeroboam (1 Ki 12:29–33, 13:1–32). Because of this, it was denounced by the prophets (Je 48:13; Hos 10:15; Am 3:14, 4:4). Hosea gave it the contemptuous name Beth-aven, meaning house of idols (Hos 4:15). Amos preached here (Am 7:10–13), and Josiah destroyed its pagan altars (2 Ki 23:4, 15–20). **2.** A town of Simeon (Jos 19:4; 1 Sa 30:27).

BETHESDA (house of mercy) A pool or reservoir with five porches at Jerusalem (Jo 5:2, 4). A stone ledge at the pool was large enough to accommodate many sick people. It was supposed to contain healing power.

BETHLEHEM (house of bread) **1.** A town of Judah, one of the oldest of Palestine, formerly called Ephrath and located five miles south of Jerusalem (Ge 35:16, 19, 48:7; Mi 5:2). Rachel died and was buried near this town (Ge 35:16, 19). It was the residence of Naomi, Boaz, Ruth, Obed, Jesse, and David (Ru 1:19, 4:9–11, 21–22; 1 Sa 16:1, 4). It was the city of David (Lu 2:11) and the birthplace of Jesus (Mi 5:2; Ma 2:5). The town's church, called the Church of the Nativity, was built by Helena, the mother of Constantine, on the site of the stable in which Jesus was born. **2.** A town in the territory of Zebulun (Jos 19:15).

BETHSAIDA (house of fish or fishing). A town on the lake of Gennesaret near the Jordan, the native place of Peter, Andrew, and Philip (Jo 1:44, 12:21). Jesus retired to this town after the death of John the Baptist (Mk 6:31; Lu 9:10). Jesus healed a blind man there (Mk 8:22–23) and once denounced the town (Ma 11:21).

BIBLE Chrysostom, patriarch of Constantinople (A.D. 398–404) is believed to have been the first to apply the Greek word Biblia to the Scriptures. **1.** *Language of the Bible.* with the exception of a few sections written in Aramaic, the Old Testament was written in Hebrew and the New Testament in Greek. **2.** *Division into chapters and verses.* The divison into chapters did not occur until the thirteenth century and is generally ascribed to Cardinal Hugo of St. Cher. The New Testament was divided into verses by Robert Stephens in his Greek and Latin New Testament published at Geneva in 1551. It was in the Latin Bible of Sanctus Pagninus in 1528 that division of the entire Bible into chapters and verses first appeared. The first English Bible so divided was the Geneva Bible of 1560.

BILDAD One of Job's three friends with whom he debated the question of suffering and affliction. He is called "the Shuhite," hence was perhaps a desendant of Shuah, Abraham's son by Keturah (Job 2:11, 8:1, 18:1, 25:1).

BIRTHRIGHT The rights of the firstborn son. The father's rank and position as head of the family or tribe passed, at his death, to the oldest son. By right of primogeniture he received a double portion of the father's property (De 21:15–17). The firstborn of the king succeeded to the throne (2 Ch 21:3) unless set aside, by divine appointment, as when Solomon was selected. The firstborn might sell his birthright (Ge 25:29, 34; He 12:16) or by wrongdoing might be deprived of it (1 Ch 5:1).

BISHOP The Greek word *episkospos*, an overseer, occurs first in Paul's injunction to the elders and presbyters of the church at Ephesus (Ac 20:17, 28). In Paul's use of the word it is identical with elders and presbyters (Tit 1:5–7). Thus the words are used interchangeably. In the organization of Christian churches it was necessary to establish a particular order for the superintendence of pastoral work. Hence Peter's exhortation, that the elders tend the flock of God, "taking the oversight" (1 Pe 5:2). He was the shepherd to care for, direct, support, and encourage (1 Th 5:14; He 13:17). Paul specified his qualifications (1 Ti 3:1–7; Tit 1:7–9). That the words elder, presbyter and bishop are identical is seen in the fact that both titles are applied to the same persons (1 Ti 5:17; 1 Pe 5:1–2).

BITHYNIA A province in northwestern Asia Minor (Ac 16:7; 1 Pe 1:1). When Paul purposed to labor in this region, he was divinely directed not to do so. Its chief town, Nicaea, was the scene of the Council of Nicaea (A.D. 325).

BLASPHEMY Language by which God is defamed (Ps 74:18; Is 52:5; Ro 2:24). The Mosaic law made this a capital offence to be punished by stoning (Le 24:16). Jesus and Stephen, the first Christian martyr, were charged with blasphemy (Ma 9:3, 26:65–66; Jo 10:36; Ac 6:11). Blasphemy against the Holy Spirit has been variously explained. But the strict context and the special occasion which elicited from Christ his teaching concerning this form of blasphemy make it appear to consist of ascribing to satanic power the performance of the mighty works which Christ wrought under the direction of the Holy Spirit (Ma 12:22–32; Mk 3:22–30).

BLESS, BLESSING The bestowal of divine favor and benefits (Ge 1:22, 9:1–7, 39:5). It includes recognition of God's goodness in a thankful and adoring manner (Ps 103:1; Ma 26:26; 1 Co 11:24) and invoking God's favor upon another (Ge 27:4, 12, 27–29; Ps 129:8).

BLOOD The blood represented life—the life is in the blood (Le 17:11, 14; De 12:23), and the life God regarded as sacred. After the flood it was forbidden that the blood of animals be eaten (Ge 9:3–4; Ac 15:20, 29). The law was announced that the shedding of man's blood would be punishable by death (Ge 9:6). The penalty of sin was the loss of life (He 9:22) as denoted by the death of animals used in the offerings for sin under the Mosaic law, and signified atonement (Le 17:10–14; De 12:15–16), hence the expressions "the blood of Jesus Christ," or, "the blood of the Lamb" denote the atoning death of our Lord (1 Co 10:16; He 9:14; 1 Pe 1:2, 19; 1 Jo 1:7; Re 12:11).

BOAZ (fleetness?) **1.** A resident of Bethlehem, a man of wealth, a kinsman to Elimelech, the husband of Naomi. He married Ruth, the daughter-in-law of Naomi, and redeemed the estate of her deceased husband. Their son, Obed, became the grandfather of David, hence Boaz became an ancestor of Christ in the line of David (Ru 2–4; Ma 1:5).

2. The name of a pillar, eighteen cubits high, set in the porch of Solomon's Temple (1 Ki 7:15, 21).

BOIL A sore swelling of the skin or an itching skin ulcer which was part of the sixth Egyptian plague (Ex 9:9–11). Job was afflicted with boils (Job 2:7). Isaiah prescribed a poultice of figs for Hezekiah's boil (Is 38:21).

BOOK At an early time inscriptions were made on clay or cut into stone. Skin and papyrus were also used. Skin as a writing material was rolled up and was called a scroll (Ps 40:7; Je 36:2; Eze 2:9). Among the Hebrews books were not mentioned until after leaving Egypt (Ex 17:14). In that country they saw writings in many forms. The Hebrew writings are not limited to the Scriptures. Many other books were written such as the Book of Jasher (Nu 21:14; Jos 10:13), the History of Nathan the Prophet (1 Ch 29:29) and the Chronicles of David, perhaps the beginning of royal annals (1 Ch 27:24). When the books of Chronicles were written, it is evident from the numerous citations that there were many books (2 Ch 13:22, 20:34, 26:22, 33:18–19, 35:25).

BOOTH A structure made of branches. Jacob made booths for his cattle, so his place of residence was called Succoth, which means "booths" (Ge 33:17). In commemoration of their sojourn in the wilderness the Israelites were required to live in booths made of palm and willow branches during the Feast of Tabernacles (Le 23:39–43; Ne 8:14).

BRANCH A limb or shoot of a tree. It is a symbol of prosperity (Ge 49:11; Pr 11:28; Eze 17:6) and is also used to signify uselessness (Is 14:19). Jeremiah and Zechariah apply the word as a title of Christ, the offspring of David (Je 23:5, 33:15; Ze 3:8, 6:12). The term was similarly used by Isaiah

(Is 11:1). In like manner believers are related to Christ as branches to the vine (Jo 15:5–6).

BRASS The Hebrew word *nehosheth* is inaccurately translated brass. The correct translation is copper but in some instances it possibly means bronze which is a compound of copper and tin, while brass is a compound of copper and zinc. Copper was known at an early time. It was taken from the ground and smelted (De 8:9; Job 28:2). It was found in the peninsula of Sinai, in Cyprus and Lebanon. Such articles as basins, pots, pans, spoons, and shovels were made from copper (Ex 38:3; Le 6:28; Nu 16:39). Pieces of armor, such as helmets, mirrors, musical instruments, and later coins were also formed from copper (2 Sa 8:10, 21:16; 2 Ki 25:7, 13; Ma 10:9), also things pertaining to the Temple (1 Ki 7:41–46; 2 Ch 4:1–17).

BRAZEN SEA See MOLTEN SEA.

BRAZEN SERPENT In the wilderness when the Israelites were bitten by fiery serpents, Moses was commanded to form a serpent of metal and place it upon a pole. Looking upon this with faith in the promise of God, the Israelites were healed (Nu 21:8–9). Later, when the Israelites used the brazen serpent as an object of worship, Hezekiah had it destroyed (2 Ki 18:4). The lifting up of the brazen serpent on a pole in the wilderness was likened by Jesus to his death on the cross (Jo 3:14–15).

BREAD The use of bread as an article of food dates back to an early time (Ge 18:6). Among the Hebrews the best bread was made of wheat. It was ground in a mill and sifted (Ju 6:19; 1 Sa 28:24; 1 Ki 4:22). It was made in the form of round flat cakes about an inch thick and nine inches in diameter, as will be found in Palestine today. In the sacred offerings "fine flour" was used (Ex 29:40; Le 2:1; Eze 46:14).

The bread of poor people was made of barley (Jo 6:9, 13). The oven consisted of a metal jar about three feet high with fire in the inside and the cakes of dough placed against the sides (1 Ki 17:12; Is 44:15).

BREASTPLATE **1.** The breastplate of the Jewish high priest was a piece of embroidered cloth about ten inches square. Attached to it were twelve precious stones, each bearing the name of one of the twelve tribes (Ex 28:15–30). **2.** A piece of armor to protect the breast of the warrior. It is used figuratively as the breastplate of righteousness (Is 59:17; Ep 6:14; 1 Th 5:8).

BRIDE, BRIDEGROOM In addition to their usual meaning of persons newly married or about to be married, these words are used figuratively in the New Testament. Christ is represented as the Bridegroom and the church as his bride (Jo 3:29; Re 21:9).

BRIMSTONE The substance known as roll sulphur. It was plentiful in the region of the Dead Sea. Sodom and other cities of the plain were destroyed by brimstone and fire (Ge 19:24; De 29:23; Re 9:17–18, 14:10).

BROTHER The Hebrew word is used in various senses. **1.** A male person having the same parents as another or others; also a half-brother (Ge 27:6, 28:2; Ju 8:19). **2.** A near relation, such as a nephew (Ge 14:16). **3.** A countryman of a kindred nation (De 23:7; Ne 5:7). **4.** A political ally (Am 1:9) or coreligionist (Ac 9:17; Ro 1:13; 2 Co 2:13). **5.** One affectionately or familiarly addressed (2 Sa 1:26; 1 Ki 20:32). **6.** A member of the human race (Ma 5:22, 18:35).

BROTHERS OF THE LORD The four brothers of Jesus as given by the Gospels are James, Joses, Simon, and

Judas (Ma 13:55; Mk 6:3). These are mentioned in connection with Mary (Ma 12:47–50; Mk 3:31–35; Lu 8:19–21). They appeared at Capernaum shortly after Jesus began his ministry (Jo 2:12). None of them were apostles as they did not believe in Jesus' messiahship until after the Resurrection (Jo 7:5) when they joined the company of believers (Ac 1:14). James became the acknowledged leader of the church at Jerusalem (Ac 21:18; Ga 1:19).

BULL The male of any large quadruped, especially of domestic cattle. Bashan was famous for its bulls (Ps 22:12). In De 14:5 and Is 51:20 the Hebrew word is rendered wild ox and wild bull in the Authorized Version but antelope by the Revised Version. A bullock was a young bull (Je 31:18). It was one of the animals offered in sacrifice (Ex 29:1; 1 Ch 29:21).

BULRUSH The Hebrew word *agmon* is variously rendered *reed, rope, rush*, and *bulrush*. It was a plant that grew in swamps and which could be twisted into ropes (Job 41:2; Is 9:14, 58:5). Another Hebrew word *gome* is rendered *rush* in Is 35:7. This was used for making the ark in which the baby Moses was preserved (Ex 2:3). It was also used in the construction of larger boats and in the manfacture of writing material. *Gome* was the famous papyrus plant.

BURIAL When a person died, friends came to the home and lamented the death of the deceased (Mk 5:38). This act was performed even by hired mourners (Je 9:17). After the body was washed and bound with cloth (Ma 27:59; Jo 11:44), those who could afford it anointed the body with perfumes and spices (Jo 12:7, 19:39). The usual type of sepulchre was a cave (Ge 25:9–10; Ma 27:60). See SEPULCHER.

BURNT OFFERING See OFFERINGS.

53

BUSH, BURNING BUSH It is believed to have been a kind of acacia, a thorny tree, that grows in the peninsula of Sinai and in Palestine near the Dead Sea. From it is secured gum arabic (Ex 3:2–3; Mk 12:26).

C

CAESAR The surname borne by the Julian family. After the death of the illustrious Gaius Julius Caesar, Augustus adopted the name as an official title as did practically every other Roman emperor thereafter for some two hundred years. While eleven Caesars (emperors) fall within the scope of New Testament times, only four are mentioned. Caesar Augustus (31 B.C.—A.D. 14) issued the decree that the world should be taxed (Lu 2:1). It was in the fifteenth year of Tiberius Caesar (A.D. 14–37) that John the Baptist began his ministry (Lu 3:1). In the days of Claudius Caesar (A.D. 41–54) the famine predicted by Agabus came to pass. Claudius also commanded all Jews, including Aquila and Priscilla, to leave Rome (Ac 11:28, 18:2). Nero Caesar (A.D. 54–68) is called merely Caesar in Ph 4:22. It was to Nero that Paul made his famous appeal (Ac 25:10–12).

CAESAREA A seaport on the coast of Palestine on the road from Tyre to Egypt, about fifty miles from Jerusalem. It was built by Herod the Great and named in honor of Caesar Augustus. It was the Roman capital of Palestine. In this city Philip the Evangelist preached (Ac 8:40, 21:8) and it was here that the Roman centurion, Cornelius, lived, the first Gentile to come into the church (Ac 10:1, 24, 11:11). Herod Agrippa died here (Ac 12:19, 23). In escaping from Jerusalem, Paul came to Caesarea (Ac 23:23, 33) and remained a prisoner here for two years (Ac 25:1–13). It attained ecclesiastical importance by becoming the seat of a bishop in the second century.

CAESAREA PHILIPPI A city in the extreme northern part of Palestine at the foot of Mount Hermon, the scene of Christ's famous charge to Peter and the Transfiguration (Ma 16:13–20, 17:1–13).

CAIAPHAS (depression?) A Sadducee, the son-in-law of Annas (Jo 18:13) and high priest between A.D. 18 and 36. He demanded the death of Jesus (Ma 26:3–5; Jo 11:49–53, 18:14). Caiaphas participated in the trial of Peter and John (Ac 4:5–7).

CAIN (lance) **1.** Eldest son of Adam and Eve, brother of Abel, whom he slew. An agriculturist, he made a thank offering while that of Abel was a blood offering. For this reason, his offering was rejected. Envious of his brother, he slew him, denied it and expressed no repentance. After God exiled him, Cain went to Nod, built a city which he named after his son Enoch, and became the progenitor of a race distinctive along mechanical lines (Ge 4:1–25; 1 Jo 3:12; Jude 11).

CALEB (dog? bold?) **1.** Son of Jephunneh, called the Kenezite (Nu 32:12; Jos 14:6, 14). He was one of the twelve spies sent from Kadesh to Canaan and strongly advised that the Israelites go forward and take the land. For this demonstration of faith in the Lord, he and Joshua alone of all the people who were over twenty years of age at the time were permitted to enter the Promised Land (Nu 13:2, 6, 30, 14:6, 24, 38; Jos 14:6, 14). He represented the tribe of Judah in the division of the land (Nu 34:19). He received the city of Hebron as an inheritance (Jos 14). His daughter, Achsah, became the wife of his brother, Othniel. **2.** Son of Hezron and father of Hur (1 Sa 25:3; 1 Ch 2:18–20).

CALF A young cow or bullock, used for food (Ge 18:7) and for sacrificial purposes (He 9:12, 19). It was one of the animals worshipped by the Egyptians, which, no doubt, suggested to the Israelites at Sinai the making of a golden calf (Ex 32:4; Ps 106:19–20). When Jeroboam founded the northern kingdom, he set up two golden calves, one at Bethel and one at Dan (1 Ki 12:29). He probably had seen Apis, the sacred bull worshipped in Egypt, where he had fled from Solomon (1 Ki 11:40).

CALVARY (skull) The name is derived from the Latin *calvaria*, a skull (Lu 23:33). It corresponds to the Aramaic word *Golgotha* (Ma 27:33; Mk 15:22; Jo 19:17). Jerome offered as a possible explanation of the name applied to the little hill by Jerusalem the fact that unburied skulls may have been there. Others suggest that it was so called because it was a place of execution. Still others suppose that the skull-like shape of the hill gave rise to the name. It was outside the city wall, and the crucifixion of Christ occurred there (Ma 27:33; Jo 19:17, 20; He 13:11–13). It was perhaps close to a highway (Ma 27:39). There are different opinions about the exact location of Calvary. One is that the site is marked by the Church of the Holy Sepulchre which is within the walls of the present city. To establish this claim it would be necessary to prove that this site was outside the walls of Jerusalem in the time of Christ—a task which appears to be impossible. The site that better meets the conditions is the little hill on the north side of the city about 250 yards outside of the wall.

CANA (place of reeds). A village of upper Galilee, about midway from the Mediterranean to the Sea of Galilee. It was the scene of the first miracle performed by Jesus as well as of his later miracle of healing the nobleman's son (Jo 2:1–11, 4:46–54). It was the native village of the apostle, Nathanael (Jo 21:2).

CANAAN (low) **1.** The son of Ham and grandson of Noah (Ge 10:6; 1 Ch 1:8). His oldest son, Zidon, founded the city of his name (Sidon) in Phoenicia and thus he became the progenitor of that nation. Canaan's other sons were fathers of tribes in Syria and Palestine (Ge 10:15–19; 1 Ch 1:13–16). **2.** By this name the country itself is sometimes understood. It was probably at first employed to denote the coastline of Palestine (Nu 13:29; Jos 11:3). It was then applied to the Jordan district and later to the whole county. It is called the Promised Land because it was promised to Abraham; the Holy Land because it was holy unto the Lord; Palestine, or Philistia, because it was at least in part the land of the Philistines.

CANAANITE Specifically the word denotes a descendent of Canaan, son of Ham. The word is used Scripturally in two senses. In the narrower sense, the Canaanites were those people who inhabited the lowlands of the Mediterranean coast and the Jordan Valley (Ge 10:18–20; Nu 13:29; Jos 11:3). In the broader sense, the word denotes all non-Israelite inhabitants of Palestine (Ge 12:6; Nu 21:3). In De 20:17 they are listed among the inhabitants to be driven out of the land. The expulsion was not complete and those who remained paid tribute (Ju 1:27–36). Solomon made them bond servants (1 Ki 9:20–21).

CANDLESTICK The candlestick of the tabernacle had a base and shaft supporting six branches. It was one of the articles of the holy place (Ex 25:31–40; Le 24:2–4). Pure olive oil was used and the light burned from evening until morning (Ex 27:20–21; 1 Sa 3:3).

CANON OF SCRIPTURE The word *canon* signifies a straight rod or a rule, such as a carpenter's rule. Hence a canon is whatever is qualified to determine or regulate other things. The Scriptures are considered as a rule of faith and practice. If a book has a right to a place in the Bible, it is called canonical; if not, it is declared to be uncanonical. When, for example, the apocryphal books are said to be uncanonical, it means that for certain reasons they are not to be considered as divinely inspired and are not entitled to a place in the Scriptures, and are not a rule of faith or of Biblical doctrine. The Old Testament was formed during an extended period. First came the Pentateuch, the books of Moses (De 31:24–26). This was added to by Joshua (Jos 24:26), and Samuel (1 Sa 10:25). The book of the Law was found in the time of Josiah (2 Ki 22:8–20). The prophets wrote the books bearing their names, and quoted the writings of each other (Is 2:2–4; Mi 4:1–3). The New Testament refers to the Scriptures of the Old Testament as the Word of God (Ma 21:42; 26:56; Mk 14:49; Jo 10:35; Ro 3:2; 2 Ti 3:15; He 5:12; 1 Pe 4:11). In no instance does the New Testament recognize the Apocryphal Books, and the fact that they are excluded from the Hebrew collection is sufficient to establish their non-canonicity. From the time of Ezra the Old Testament appears as a whole. The Canon of the New Testament as we have it was ratified in the fourth century A.D. by the Council of Jamnia.

CAPERNAUM (villages of Nahum) A town on the northwestern coast of the Sea of Galilee (Ma 4:13–16; Lu 4:31; Jo 6:17–24). It was a city of importance, had its own synagogue, and was probably a military post (Ma 8:5–13; Lu 7:1–10). When Jesus was rejected at Nazareth, he made this his headquarters (Ma 9:1; Mk 2:1). It was the scene of many of his miracles and teachings. The centurion's servant, Peter's mother-in-law, a man sick of the palsy, a nobleman's son, and others were healed here (Ma 8:5–13; Mk 1:29–31, 2:1–13; Lu 7:1–10; Jo 4:46–54). Jesus taught in the synagogue and in other places in the city (Mk 9:33–50; Jo 6:24–71). A custom station was located here, and here Matthew, the tax-gatherer, was called as one of the apostles

(Ma 9:9–13; Mk 2:14–17). Jesus predicted the destruction of this unrepentant city (Ma 11:23–24).

CAPTIVITY Using the term in the sense of being held in bondage in a foreign land, the Egyptian bondage is the first of the captivities of the chosen people. But the two instances to which the word usually applies are the captivity of Israel and the captivity of Judah. In the case of the former, Assyria overthrew the kingdom in 722 B.C. After the besieging of Samaria by Shalmaneser, Sargon, in his first year, took it and carried away a great number of the people to Mesopotamia and Media (2 Ki 17:5–6). The captivity of Judah was in three stages, the first in the reign of Jehoiakim in 606 B.C. (2 Ch 36:2–7; Da 1:1–3) by Nebuchadnezzar who carried off Daniel and others. The second stage or deportation was nine years later (597 B.C.) in the reign of Jehoiachin when the king and about 11,000 of the people were taken to Babylon (2 Ki 24:14–16). The third stage was the fall of Jerusalem in 586 B.C. when Nebuchadnezzar destroyed the city and carried away the people, leaving a remnant (2 Ki 25:2–21). The captivity of Judah was predicted 150 years before it happened. The date should be reckoned from the first deportation, 606. It was declared that the captivity would last seventy years, and true to the promise of God the Jews were released by Cyrus in 536 B.C.

CARBUNCLE The Hebrew word in Is 54:12 denotes a bright or shining gem of any kind, such as a garnet. Another word thus rendered—but probably an emerald—appears among the gems of the breastplate of the high priest (Ex 28:17; Eze 28:13).

CARMEL (park) **1.** A high promontory which juts into the Mediterranean some 25 miles west of the Sea of Galilee; also, the short mountain range which begins with the promontory. Running southeastwardly, it joins the central ranges near Samaria. It was the scene of the great test to which Elijah put Baal (1 Ki 18:17–40). It was here the cloud as big as a man's hand was seen that was to terminate the drought. It was visited by Elisha (2 Ki 2:25, 4:25). **2.** A town in the hill country of Judah (Jos 15:55). It was here that Nabal had his posessions (1 Sa 25:2–40).

CARPENTER Carpentry as a distinct occupation is first mentioned in the Scriptures when carpenters of Tyre came to Jerusalem to build David's house (2 Sa 5:11). Various tools are mentioned, such as the hammer, nail, saw, and ax (Je 10:4; Is 10:15), and plane, compass, line (Is 44:13). Carpentry was Christ's occupation in Nazareth (Mk 6:3).

CENSUS The Hebrews had a system of registering by tribe, family and house (Nu 1:18). There was also the numbering of classes, as of the firstborn (Nu 3:43). There were three specific numberings of Israel, the first at Sinai after leaving Egypt (Nu 1). The number of males over twenty years of age was 603,550. The tribe of Levi, counted separately, numbered 22,000 (Nu 3:39). The second census was taken at the close of the wandering and was almost the same as the first—601,730 (Nu 26:1–51), while the Levites numbered 23,000 (Nu 26:62). The third census was taken by David and showed 1,300,000 fighting men (2 Sa 24:1–9; 1 Ch 21:1–6). Shortly before the birth of Christ, Augustus ordered an enrollment of the people which brought Joseph and Mary to Bethlehem, the city of David (Lu 2:1).

CENTURION This word is derived from the Latim *centum* , one hundred. It was the title of a Roman army officer who had command of one hundred soldiers (Ac 21:32, 22:26). Cornelius of Caesarea was a centurion. He was brought into the church by Peter (Ac 10). Julius, who had charge of Paul and other prisoners, was a centurion (Ac 27:1, 3, 43). Two others, whose names are not given, one at

Capernaum (Ma 8:5–13), the other at the cross (Ma 27:54), were also centurions.

CEPHAS (stone) Simon, that is, Peter, thus named by Jesus. Cephas is the Greek for stone (Jo 1:42; 1 Co 1:12, 3:22, 15:5; Ga 2:9).

CHAFF By a winnowing process the straw was separated from the grain. By means of a fork the trodden grain and chaff were tossed together in the wind, which blew away the chaff (Job 21:18; Ps 1:4; Is 17:13, 41:15; Zep 2:2). The Hebrew word rendered *chaff* in Je 23:28 is in Ex 5:7, 10 rendered *straw*. This useless portion of the grain stalk is used figuratively to denote false doctrine or wicked people. (Ps 1:4; Is 33:11; Ma 3:12).

CHALCEDONY This is one of the precious stones in the foundation of the New Jerusalem (Re 21:19). It is a species of quartz found in the mines of Chalcedon near Constantinople. It was probably a greenish stone, silicate of copper.

CHALDEA Originally the southern portion of Babylonia, but the name came to be applied to the entire alluvial plain from the north to above Babylon. The term is used for the Hebrew *Kasdim*. In the south were the cities of Ur and Erech and in the north Babylon, Cutha, and Slippara.

CHALDEAN A native of Chaldea. At first the Chaldeans settled on the shores of the Persian Gulf. They conquered Babylonia but their leader, Merodach-baladan, was defeated by Sennacherib, king of Assyria. Nabo-polassar, a Chaldean, founded the New Babylonian Empire in 625 B.C. and in 605 B.C. was followed on the throne by his illustrious son, Nebuchadnezzar. The magicians, astrologers, and priests, the learned class, were called Chaldeans. It was from Ur of the Chaldees that God called Abraham, the head of the Messianic nation (Ge 11:31, 12:1).

CHARIOT A two-wheeled vehicle used for both hostile and peaceful purposes. The body of the chariot rested on the axle and was open behind. The first mention of the chariot in the Bible is in connection with Joseph who was honored by being placed in chariot of Pharaoh (Ge 41:43) and later rode in his own chariot (Ge 46:29). When used for military purposes, the strength of a nation was considered in terms of the number of its chariots. Pharaoh pursued the Israelites with with 600, Jabin had 900 (Ju 4:3), the Philistines had 30,000 (1 Sa 13:5). They were poorly adapted to the hills of Palestine, hence were not much used by Hebrews. The chariot-borne warrior had a driver and sometimes a shieldbearer (2 Ki 9:24).

CHEDORLAOMER A king of Elam with wide dominion in western Asia. In the time of Abraham, he invaded the region around the Dead Sea with three other kings and subjugated it. Chedorlaomer carried off Lot from Sodom and Abraham rescued him (Ge 14:1–16). He apparently ruled in or about the time of Hammurabi, Babylonian king and lawgiver.

CHEMOSH (fire?) The god worshipped by the Moabites (Nu 21:29; Je 48:46). According to Ju 11:24 he seems also to have been the national god of the Ammonites. But Milcom may be here intended, since the latter was the special deity of the Ammonites. Human sacrifices were sometimes offered to Chemosh (2 Ki 3:27). In the days of his apostasy Solomon built for this god a high place, which Josiah destroyed (1 Ki 11:7; 2 Ki 23:13).

CHERUB, CHERUBIM 1. After the fall and expulsion from Eden, they guarded the tree of life (Ge 3:24). In the

Holy of Holies, on the mercy seat of the ark, golden cherubim with overarching wings faced each other kneeling. They symbolized the presence of Jehovah in the midst of his people (Ex 25:18–20, 37:7–9; Nu 7:89; Ps 80:1). For the Solomonic temple they were much larger, being fifteen feet high, and were overlaid with gold (1 Ki 6:22–28; He 9:5). In the vision of Ezekiel each had four faces—those of a man, an ox, a lion and an eagle; each also had four wings (Eze 10:1–22). Note the living creatures of John's vision and their faces (Re 4:6–9). **2.** A place in Babylonia. From it came persons whose descent as Israelites could not be established (Ez 2:59; Ne 7:61).

CHRIST (anointed) The Greek translation of the Hebrew word 'Messiah' which means 'Anointed One.' With the word "the" prefixed, i.e., the Christ, it signifies the Messiah of Old Testament prophecy (Ma 16:16, 20; Mk 8:29; Jo 1:41). Jesus, the personal name of Christ, given at his birth, is often used with Christ—Jesus Christ—so that the word Christ becomes practically a part of the proper name (Jo 1:17; Ac 11:17; Ro 5:1).

CHRISTIAN A follower of Christ. The name was first applied to the disciples at Antioch in Syria in about A.D. 43 (Ac 11:26). The disciples were also called *brothers* (1 Co 7:12), *disciples* (Ac 9:26; 11:29), and *believers* (Ac 5:14). We are simply told that the disciples were called Christians first in Antioch. Some authorities are of the opinion that it was applied by foes rather than friends. Others reject this view but admit that Agrippa probably used it in derision as seen by the proper rendering of the passage (Ac 26:28). The name came into use very slowly, and was not given until about thirteen years after the founding of Christianity. The word is used three times in the New Testament (Ac 11:26, 26:28; 1 Pe 4:16).

CHRYSOLITE (gold stone) Some golden-colored stone, as yellow as quartz or jacinth, one of the stones of the foundation of the New Jerusalem (Re 21:20).

CHRYSOPRASE, CHRYSOPRASUS (golden-green stone) A chalcedony of golden-tinted, leek-green color, a color produced by the oxide of nickel. This gem was a variety of semi-opaque silica. The tenth foundation of the New Jerusalem is garnished with this stone (Re 21:20).

CHURCH Opinons differ as to the derivation of the word. It is the rendering in the New Testament of the Greek word *Ekklesia*, originally meaning an assembly of citizens convened by a civil authority. The Greek word is employed by the New Testament to denote the body of Christian people, a Christian community, the followers of Christ, and the place of assembly for purposes of worship. This use of the word occurs in the New Testament (Ma 16:18, 18:17). In different cities believers formed themselves into churches, and thus churches signified the various communities of this nature (Ac 9:31, 15:41; Ro 16:4; 1 Co 7:17). Those truly united to Christ by saving faith in him are of the invisible Church and may come into fellowship with an external body (1 Co 1:2, 12:12; Col 1:24; 1 Pe 2:9–10). The officers of local churches were elders or bishops, and deacons (Ac 6:3, 14:23; 1 Ti 3:1, 8; Tit 1:5–9), and had the direction and government of the church (Ac 15:2, 4, 22; 1 Ti 4:14, 5:17; 1 Pe 5:1). The apostles sustained a special relation in matters of authority (Ac 5:2, 6:6; 1 Co 12:28; 2 Pe 3:2).

CIRCUMCISION This was not an exclusively Jewish rite. It was practiced by the Egyptians as early as 3000 B.C. The rite is observed by Muslims, but for the Hebrews it had special significance in that it was divinely instituted—being the seal of God's covenant with Abraham and his desendants (Ge 17:1–14, 21). It was perforrmed on the male child when he was eight days old (Le 12:3). It had been neglected during the period of wandering but was again observed when they were about to take the land of Canan (Jos 5:2–9). In being admitted to Jewish commonwealth all male foreigners were required to receive this rite (Ge 34:14–17, 22; Ex 12:48). The term "uncircumcised," as applied to other nations, was a term of reproach (Ju 14:3; 1 Sa 17:26, 36; 2 Sa 1:20). The expression "the circumcision," as used in the New Testament, denotes the Jewish church and people (Ga 2:8; Col 4:11). In its spiritual significance it means the putting away of the sins of the flesh (Col 2:11).

CITIES OF THE PLAIN Five cities were so called: Sodom, Gomorrah, Admah, Zeboiim, and Bela or Zoar (Ge 13:12, 19:29). Whether they were located at the north or south end of the Dead Sea is a much-disputed point.

CITY OF DAVID See DAVID, CITY OF.

CITY OF REFUGE Six Levitical cities were appointed as cities of refuge for the protection of those who had unintentionally caused the death of another. See AVENGER OF BLOOD. Three of these cities were west and three east of the Jordan. On the east were Bezer in the tribe of Reuben, Ramoth-gilead in the tribe of Gad and Golan in Manasseh. On the west of the Jordan were Kedesh in Naphtali, Shechem in Ephrim and Hebron in Judah. It would not be a difficult thing for anyone to reach the city nearest to him. Here he received a fair trial. If guilty of willful murder, he paid the death penalty. If innocent, he was protected, but if he left the city while the high priest lived, he did so at his own risk (Nu 35; De 19; Jos 20).

COLOSSE A city of Phrygia in Asia Minor. It lost much of its influence as the neighboring cities Laodicea and

Hieropolis became important and wealthy. Under the Romans it remained a free city and was celebrated for its manufacture of wool. The establishment of a church there was probably due to the labors of Epaphras, a disciple of Paul, and to the work of Archippus (Col 1:2, 7, 4:17; Phile 2). Philemon and Onesimus were members of this church (Col 4:9).

COMFORTER, THE See HOLY SPIRIT.

COMMANDMENTS, TEN See DECALOGUE.

CONCUBINE A concubine was a wife of lower rank and was ordinarily selected from slaves or captives. They were not wedded in the usual manner. There were such instances as Hagar (Ge 16:2–3, 21:10) and Bilhah (Ge 29:29). They could be discarded (Ge 21:10–14) and yet they had rights according to Mosaic law (Ex 21:7–11; De 21:10–14). Solomon had three hundred concubines (1 Ki 11:3).

CONSCIENCE Conscience is the moral sense that comes from our decision about what is right or wrong. The Scriptures speak of a *good* conscience (Ac 23:1; 1 Ti 1:5, 19), a *pure* conscience (1 Ti 3:9; 2 Ti 1:3), and a conscience *defiled* or *seared* (1 Co 8:7; 1 Ti 4:2).

CONVERSION The word signifies *turning toward*, and means turning from sin to God; it is used to denote the instrument in bringing about this change (Lu 1:16; Ac 26:18; Jas 5:19–20), and the act of turning on the part of the one thus led to abandon sin. Conversion properly defined in terms of the sinner's action is not be confused with regeneration and justification. The latter have to do with the divine action in which we have no part. It is God who justifies on the ground of the faith exercised by the one who comes by divine action to the state of justification (Ro 5:1).

CONVOCATION An occasion when the Hebrews were required to come together and refrain from all forms of work. Such times were the Sabbath (Le 23:1–3), Pentecost (Le 23:15–21), and the Day of Atonement (Le 23:24–28).

CORNELIUS A Roman centurion stationed at Caesarea and a devout Gentile. Cornelius and those of his household are generally regarded as the first Gentile converts to Christ (Ac 10:1–48).

CORNERSTONE The stone that binds together the sides of a building (Ps 118:22; Is 28:16; Ze 4:7). It was a term often applied to Christ (Ro 9:33; Ep 2:20; 1 Pe 2:6) who was also called the head of the corner (Ma 21:42; 1 Pe 2:7).

COUNCIL This word usually denotes the Sanhedrin, the highest legislative body of the Jews. It was composed of 71 members including the high priest who was its president. It had the power of life and death (Ma 26:3, 57; Ac 4:5–6, 15, 6:12, 15) but could not execute the sentence of death, which was the prerogative of Rome. Jesus was tried before this body (Ma 26:59; Mk 14:55; Jo 11:47), as were the apostles (Ac 4:5–6, 15, 5:21, 27), Stephen (Ac 6:12), and Paul (Ac 22:30, 23:15, 24:20).

COVENANT An agreement or compact (Ge 21:27, 32; 1 Sa 18:3, 23:18; 1 Ki 20:34). God made a covenant with Adam and Eve, promising divine favor in return for obedience (Ge 2:16–17). God covenanted with Noah that he would survive the deluge (Ge 6:18) and that there would never again be such a flood (Ge 9:12–16). Other divine covenants were with Abraham (Ge 13:17, 17:4, 7, 11, 13–14; 2 Ki 13:23; Ac 7:8; Ro 4:13, 17); with the Israelites

(Ex 31:16); with the Levites (Mal 2:4, 8); with Phinehas (Nu 25:12–13); and with David (2 Sa 7:15, 16; 2 Ch 21:7; Ps 89:20–28, 34). There was also given a new covenant of a more spiritual nature (Je 31:31–34; He 8:8–11), designed for all peoples (Ma 28:19–20; Ac 10:44–47) with Christ as the Mediator (He 8:6–13, 9:1, 10:15–17, 12:24), to be administered by the Holy Spirit (Jo 7:39; Ac 2:32–33; 2 Co 3:6–9).

CREATION The Bible opens with the doctrine that God is the author of creation, that he caused to be that which did not previously exist. The things he created are the heavens and the earth, all forms of life, the heavenly bodies, the elements (Ge 1; Ps 51:10, 148:5; Is 40:26; Am 4:13). The general account is given in Ge 1:1–2:3. The second chapter of Genesis gives a more detailed account of the creation of Adam and Eve. The doctrine that all things were created by the mighty power of God is clearly taught in the Old Testament (Ps 33:6–9, 90:2, 104:1–14, 30; Is 40:26–28, 42:5, 44:24, 45:7–13, 18; Je 51:15; Am 4:13). The New Testament further unfolds this teaching by revealing the creative work of Christ, the Word (Jo 1:1–3; Col 1:15–18; He 1:1–3, 10).

CROSS Crucifixion was common among some nations of antiquity. The cross consisted of two pieces of wood, fastened together at right angles, upon which the victim was placed. To the upper part of the cross, above the head of the victim, a sign bearing his name or crime was placed (Ma 27:37; Mk 15:26; Jo 19:19). Crucifixion was regarded with the same feeling of horror that is associated with the electric chair today (Jo 19:31; 1 Co 1:23; Ga 3:13; He 12:2). Paul gloried in the cross of Christ because it signified the atoning work of the Savior (Ga 6:14; Ep 2:16; Col 1:20). See CRUCIFIXION.

CROWN A headdress for ornamentation or denoting high position worn by high priests (Ex 29:6, 39:30;

Eze 21:26). On it was inscribed, "Holiness to the Lord." It was a gold plate attached with blue lace. The royal crown was of gold (Ps 21:3) and was often studded with gems (2 Sa 12:30; Ze 9:16). At his crucifixion a crown of thorns was placed on Jesus' head in derision of his alleged claims of kingship (Ma 27:29). Paul wrote to Timothy of the crown of righteousness (2 Ti 4:8) and Christ is described as being crowned with glory and honor (He 2:9).

CRUCIFIXION A method of capital punishment in which the victim was nailed alive to a cross. It was a common practice of ancient nations. Alexander the Great crucified one thousand Tyrians, and Antiochus Epiphanes used crucifixion as punishment for Jews who refused to renounce their religion. The Jews used stoning as their mode of capital punishment but insisted that the Romans crucify Jesus. The Savior was first scourged (Ma 27:26; Mk 15:15) and then was compelled to carry the cross to the place of execution (Jo 19:17). Often a potion was given the victims to deaden the pain but this was refused by Jesus after he tasted it (Ma 27:34). Two criminals were crucified with him, and the soldiers hastened their death by breaking their legs. But since Jesus had already died, they pierced his side instead (Jo 19:31–36; Ps 34:20). See CROSS.

CUBIT This word is derived from the Latin *cubitum*, an elbow, signifying the length of the arm to the elbow. The royal cubit of Egypt was a little more than twenty and a half inches and the Babylonian a little longer. The common Hebrew cubit was about eighteen inches (De 3:11; 2 Ch 3:3), while another cubit measure was a hand-breadth longer (Eze 40:5, 43:13).

CUP The drinking cup of the Bible was made of earthenware, metal, or horn (2 Sa 12:3; Je 51:7; Mk 9:41). The expression *contents of the cup* was used figuratively for what befalls one (Is 51:17; Je 16:7; Ma 26:39).

CYRENE A city of Libya in northern Africa, in the district now known as Tripoli. Simon, who was forced to carry the cross of Jesus, was a native of Cyrene (Ma 27:32; Mk 15:21; Lu 23:26). Cyrenians had a synagogue in Jerusalem (Ac 6:9). Lucius, a prominent member of the church at Antioch, was a Cyrenian (Ac 13:1).

CYRUS The founder of the Persian empire. Isaiah names him as the divine instrument for the release of the Jews from the Babylonian Exile (Is 44:28, 45:1–14). In 536 B.C., a few years after the fall of Babylon, Cyrus issued a proclamation which permitted the Jews to return to their own land. He restored the sacred vessels of the Temple which had been carried to Babylon by Nebuchadnezzar (Ez 1:1–11, 5:13–14, 6:3).

D

DAGON The national god of the Philistines. Its head, arms and body had the appearance of a human form, while the lower portion was like the tail of a fish (1 Sa 5:3–4).

DAMASCUS This ancient city was the most important of Syria. It lay in a fertile plain, about thirty miles in diameter, which was watered by the Pharpar and Abana Rivers (2 Ki 5:12). Eliezer, servant of Abraham, was a native of Damascus (Ge 14:15, 15:2). Rezin, a subject of King Hadadezer of Zobah, captured Damascus and founded the kingdom of Syria. From this time onward the state was often in conflict with Israel. Ahab held Damascus for a time, but after his death Israel was overrun by the Syrians (1 Ki 20,

22; 2 Ki 6:24, 7:6–7). In the reign of King Ahaz of Judah, Rezin of Damascus and his ally, Pekah of Israel, captured Jerusalem. Ahaz, in league with King Tiglath-pileser of Assyria, captured Damascus and carried off its people (2 Ki 16:5–9; Is 7:1–8:6, 10:9). In 63 B.C. the city became a Roman province. There were Jewish synagogues in Damascus and near this city Paul was converted (Ac 9:2–3, 10, 22:6, 10–11).

DAN (a judge) **1.** Fifth son of Jacob by Bilhah, Rachel's maid (Ge 30:5–6). Jacob foretold the future of the tribe which would descend from him (Ge 49:16–17). **2.** The tribe which descended from the above. In the wilderness census the number of Danites was 62, 700, second in size to the tribe of Judah. Its teritory was in Palestine betweeen Ephraim on the north and east and Judah on the south. Among its towns were Zorah, Ajalon, and Ekron (Jos 19:40–43, 21:5, 23). Samson was a Danite (Ju 13:2, 24). **3.** A town in the northern part of Palestine, hence the expression "from Dan to Beersheba," denoting the extent of the land (Ju 20:1). It was orignally Laish.

DANCE Among the Hebrews dancing was often an expression of rejoicing (Ju 11:34; 1 Sa 18:6–7, 29:5). It was practiced by both men and women (Ps 30:11; Ec 3:4; La 5:15; Lu 15:25) and was accompanied by tambourines. Dancing sometimes formed a part of a religious ceremony or act of worship (Ex 15:20; Ju 21:21, 23; 2 Sa 6:14–23).

DANIEL (God is my judge). **1.** Second son of David, by Abigail (1 Ch 3:1), called Chileab in 2 Sa 3:3. **2.** A priest who signed the covenant with Nehemiah (Ez 8:2; Ne 10:6). **3.** The prophet of the captivity. He belonged to a prominent family of Judah (Da 1:3–7).

DARIUS The name of several kings of Media and Persia. **1.** *Darius the Mede*, son of Ahasuerus (Da 5:31, 6:1, 9:1, 11:1). When Babylon was taken by the army of Cyrus in 538 B.C., he is said to have been made king over Chaldea. **2.** *Darius Hystapsis*, called *the Great*. When the rebuilding of the Temple at Jerusalem was interrupted by foes of the Jews, Darius had a search instituted for an edict previously issued by Cyrus which permitted the work (Ez 6:1–12). He extended his kingdom from India to the Grecian archipelago. He was defeated at Marathon in 490 B.C. and died in 484 B.C. **3.** *Darius the Persian* (Ne 12:22), probably Darius Codomannus, king of Persia (336–330 B.C.).

DAVID (beloved) The son of Jesse and one of the greatest men of the Bible. His life can be roughly divided into five periods: **1.** *His youth in Bethlehem.* He was the youngest of eight brothers (1 Sa 16:10–11, 17:12–14) and is described as ruddy and beautiful in appearance (1 Sa 16:12). He was a shepherd over his father's sheep (1 Sa 16:11, 17:34–36) and was a talented harpist. **2.** *His relations with Saul.* David became Saul's armourbearer and musician. He was also a valiant warrior, as shown by his single-handed defeat of the giant Goliath (1 Sa 16:14–18, 21, 17:32–58). David and Jonathan, a son of Saul, became devoted friends and David married a daughter of Saul. David's deeds in war won him such great renown that Saul became jealous and an enemy of David (1 Sa 15:17–29, 19:4–9). **3.** *His life as fugitive and outlaw.* Fleeing from Saul, David was given food by the high priest at Nob (1 Sa 21:1–9). He took refuge in the cave of Adullam (1 Sa 22:1) and, gathering a band of six hundred men, he defeated the Philistines at Keilah (1 Sa 23:1–5). Twice he refused opportunities to take Saul's life (1 Sa 24, 26). King Achish permitted him to occupy Ziklag, for which kindness he protected the Philistines against the raids of desert tribes (1 Sa 27). Saul was finally slain in battle at Gilboa (1 Sa 31). **4.** *On the throne of Judah.* The tribe of Judah elected David king and he set up his court at Hebron (2 Sa 2:1–10). David had reigned over Judah for about seven years when Ishbosheth, who reigned over the other tribes, died (2 Sa 2:12–4:12). **5.** *King of all Israel.* Israel proposed that both kingdoms be reunited under David (2 Sa 5:1–5). This was done and Jerusalem was taken from the Jebusites and made the capital. The nation was thus centralized (2 Sa 5:6–10). David subjugated the Philistines and captured Gath. The ark was brought to Jerusalem (2 Sa 6:1–23). Worship of the Lord was organized (1 Ch 15–16). David sinned greatly in making Bathsheba his wife but repented deeply (2 Sa 11:1–12, 24; Ps 51). David died after having reigned forty years, and the kingdom was turned over to his son Solomon (1 Ki 2:10–11). He was remembered as the greatest king of Israel.

DAVID, CITY OF 1. The stronghold of Zion which David took from the Jebusites (2 Sa 5:6–9; 1 Ch 11:5, 7). It was on a ridge south of Mount Moriah. David and Solomon were buried here (1 Ki 2:10, 11:43) as were many later kings of Judah (1 Ki 14:31, 15:8, 24; 2 Ki 8:24). **2.** Bethlehem, the birthplace of David (Lu 2:4, 11).

DAY The Hebrews reckoned it form evening to evening (Ex 12:18; Le 23:32). The days of the week, excepting the Sabbath, were numbered rather than named.

DAY-STAR See LUCIFER.

DEACON A member of the early church and later a church official who was charged with a special kind of ministry. The Twelve Apostles appointed seven deacons to administer the charitable funds of the church (Ac 6:1–6). Eventually the deacon came to be regarded as a church official alongside the bishop (Ph 1:1). His qualifications are explicitly stated (1 Ti 3:8–13).

DEAD SEA The modern name of the Biblical Salt Sea and the Sea of the Plain (Ge 14:3; De 3:17; Jos 3:16). It is nearly fifty miles long and nine to ten miles wide and has a level of about 1,300 feet below the Mediterranean. Since it has no outlet, its saltiness is about four times that of the ocean.

DEBORAH (a bee) **1.** The nurse of Rebekah (Ge 24:59, 35:8). **2.** A prophetess, the wife of Lappidoth. She lived in Mount Ephraim where she served as a judge. Aided by Barak, she defeated Sisera (Ju 4:4–14), a victory celebrated in her triumphant song (Ju 5:1–31).

DECALOGUE This word was adopted by the Greeks to designate the Ten Commandments, the laws delivered to Moses in Mount Sinai (Ex 20:1–17; De 5:6–21).

DECAPOLIS (ten cities) A district, containing ten cities, located southeast of Galilee (Ma 4:25; Mk 5:20, 7:31). These were built by the followers of Alexander the Great and consisted of Scythopolis, Damascus, Hippos, Philadelphia, Gadara, Pella, Dion, Gerasa, Kanatha, Raphana.

DECISION, VALLEY OF See JEHOSHAPHAT, VALLEY OF.

DEDICATION, FEAST OF This festival was instituted in 165 B.C. by Judas Maccabaeus to commemorate the purification of the temple and the restoration of worship after the desecration of the temple by Antiochus Epiphanes. It was somewhat of the nature of the feast of tabernacles and continued for eight days. Jesus was present at one of these feasts and spoke to the people (Jo 10:22).

DELILAH (languishing? lustful?) The Philistine woman who lived in the valley of Sorek (Ju 16:4–18). She was paid a large sum of money by Philistine chiefs to induce Samson to disclose to her the secret of his strength.

DEMAS A fellow-laborer of Paul (Col 4:14; Phile 24). Unwilling to endure privation, he deserted Paul and went to Thessalonica (2 Ti 4:10).

DEMETRIUS **1.** A silversmith at Ephesus whose business of making silver shrines of the goddess Diana was threatened by Paul's teachings. Demetrius stirred up a riot, whereupon Paul left Ephesus (Ac 19:24–41). **2.** A Christian whom John commends (3 Jo 12).

DEMON One of the lower order of spiritual beings who left their "first estate," called *devil* in the Authorized Version (Ma 25:41). Satan is the prince of demons (Ma 9:34; Lu 11:15). There were many demons but one devil. Persons possessed by demons suffered from diseases and were tortured (Lu 4:33, 8:30; Jo 7:20). They are represented as speaking (Mk 1:23–24, 5:7), and as being distinct from those whom they possessed (Ma 8:31). They exhibited unusual knowledge (Mk 1:24). The Jews believed that deomons were the spirits of the sinful dead. See DEVIL.

DENARIUS A Roman silver coin in the time of Christ. A typical denarius of Christ's day bore the image of Emperor Tiberius. It was a popular coin among the Jews and is called "a penny." It was the ordinary pay for a day's labor. (Ma 20:2; Mk 12:15; Re 6:6).

DEVIL The translation in the Authorized Version of *daimon.* It is also the rendering in Authorized Version of *diabolos* (slanderer, accuser). The word is used frequently to refer to Satan, the chief of the fallen spirits (Lu 10:18; 2 Pe 2:4; Re 12:7–9). It is generally believed that the sin by which he fell from his former state was pride (1 Ti 3:6). He is the enemy of God and of the divine order (Ma 13:38–39; Re 12:17). He was the tempter of Adam and Eve (Ge 3:1–15; 2 Co 11:3), Jesus (Ma 4:1–11), and man (Jo 13:2; Ac 13:9–10). He is a murderer and liar (Jo 8:44; Re 20:10). Peter represents him as a devouring lion (1 Pe 5:8). He is subtle but can be resisted and put to flight (Ep 4:27, 6:11–16; Jam 4:7). Jesus came to destroy his works (Ge 3:15; 1 Jo 3:8). At Christ's coming he will be bound for 1,000 years (Re 20:2–3).

DIAMOND An unusually hard, transparent mineral. Diamond os the rendering of a Hebrew word for a precious stone (Eze 28:13). It is listed as one of the stones in the breastplate of the high priest (Ex 28:18). The precious stone intended was probably an onyx.

DIANA The Roman goddess of the moon. According to ancient authorities the image of Diana of the Ephesians was of wood (Ac 19:35). Silver models of it were made by Demtetrius and others (Ac 19:24).

DISCIPLE A pupil or learner. The word is used once in the Old Testament in this sense (Is 8:16) and occurs frequently in the New Testament. Meaning followers of a teacher, such as the disciples of Paul or of Christ (Ma 10:24; Lu 14:26–27; Jo 4:1, 6:66), the term is used of the apostles (Ma 5:1, 10:1, 12:1).

DIVINATION The art that claims that things of the future may be ascertained by certain signs or be communicated by a form of inspiration. Such signs were seen in the entrails of animals (Eze 21:21) and in the flight of birds. The stars were declared to exercise an influence in the destiny of persons (Is 47:13) and it was believed that the future could be disclosed by summoning the spirits of the dead (1 Sa 28:8). Diviners were found in great numbers among heathen nations (De 18:9–12; 1 Sa 6:2; Eze 21:21; Da 2:2; Ac 16:16). The Israelites were forbidden to consult such soothsayers (Le 20:6, 27; De 18:10; Is 2:6; Ze 10:2). Diviners were paid (Nu 22:7, 17–18; Ac 16:16).

DIVORCE Divorce was permitted under Mosaic law when the wife was guilty of some unseemly thing. She was permitted to remarry, but if divorced by the second husband, might not again marry the first (De 24:1–4; Je 3:8). In the New Testament divorce appears to be completely forbidden (Mk 10:11–12; Lu 16:18; 1 Co 7:10, 39). In only two passages (Ma 5:32, 19:9) is an allowable exception mentioned. Jesus taught that under God's law a man and his wife were joined together by a permanent compact and that fornication was the only ground for divorce. Furthermore, if a man abandoned his wife on other grounds and married another, he was guilty of adultery, and the same was true if a man married a divorced woman (Ma 5:31–32, 19:3–9; Lu 16:18).

DORCAS (gazelle) A charitable Christian woman of Joppa, also called Tabitha, who gave much of her time making garments for the needy. Through the prayer of Peter, she was raised form the dead, a fact which caused many to accept Christianity (Ac 9:36–43).

DOTHAN (wells?) An ancient town ten miles north of Samaria on the highway which led through Palestine from Babylonia (Ge 37:17; 2 Ki 6:13). It was here that Joseph was cast into a pit (Ge 37:17–28).

DOVE, PIGEON A bird frequently mentioned in the Scriptures, many varieties of which (including the turtledove) were native to Palestine. Turtledoves and pigeons might be offered in sacrifice (Le 1:14; Lu 2:24). Rocks and valleys served them as nesting places (Je 48:28). The plumage of doves was strikingly beautiful (Ps 68:13). Their eyes were like those of lovers (Son 1:15, 4:1). Other characteristics include their swift flight, their mournful cooing, their gentleness, harmlessness, and innocence. The dove is a symbol of the Holy Spirit (Lu 3:22).

DOWRY It was the custom among the Hebrews for the bridegroom or his father to pay a sum of money as a dowry to the father of the bride (Ge 29:15–20; Ex 22:17; 1 Sa 18:25). The average amount of dowry was apparently fifty shekels (De 22:29). The bride's father might also give the bride a gift (Jos 15:19; 1 Ki 9:16).

DRAGON Rendering in Authorized Version of different Greek and Hebrew words for various land and water animals. It frequently refers to a howling desert animal such as the wolf and is translated *jackal* in the Revised Version (Job 30:29; Ps 44:19; Is 13:22, 34:13, 35:7; Je 10:22, 49:33). In the sense of crocodile it is applied to Pharaoh (Eze 29:3) and as a crocodile or sea serpent to Nebuchadnezzar (Je 51:34). In the New Testament the Greek *drakon* is applied to Satan (Re 12:3–4, 7, 9, 13, 16–17; 20:2).

DREAM A series of images, thoughts, or emotions occuring during sleep. Throughout the Bible significance is attached to dreams (Ge 37:6, 9; Ju 7:13; Da 2:28, 7:1; Ma 1:20, 2:12–13, 19). They were not infrequently regarded as genuine communications from God (Job 33:14–17; Je 23:28). There are warnings against deception by false dreamers and their lying dreams (Je 23:25, 32; Ze 10:2). The interpretation of dreams belongs to God (Ge 40:8).

DRINK The chief drink of the Hebrews was water. Milk was commonly served with meals (Ge 18:8; De 32:14; Ju 4:19, 5:25). Light beverages were probably made from barley and water and fig cakes and water. Diluted vinegar and sour wine was much used by the poorer classes. Wine and other intoxicants were well known.

DRINK OFFERING An oblation (Le 23:13). See OFFER-ING.

DROUGHT A lack of moisture, especially of the kind needed for growing crops and watering cattle. Between May and October there is practically no rain in Palestine, hence the great value of the excessively heavy dews. Mention is made of the drought by day and of summer (Ge 31:40; Ps 32:4). It makes the heavens like brass and the earth like iron (De 28:23).

DRUNKENNESS The state characterized by being drunken or intoxicated. Its earliest Biblical mention is in connection with Noah (Ge 9:21). Warnings against strong drink are frequent in the Bible (Le 10:9; Pr 23:29–32). Drunkenness is a reproach (Ro 13:13; Ga 5:21; Ep 5:18; 1 Th 5:7). It is represented as a vice to which the wealthy were particularly addicted (Da 5:1–4). Drunkards are to be excluded from Christian fellowship and from the kingdom of heaven (1 Co 5:11, 6:10).

DUST In countries having extended periods of drought, the soil works into the form of dust which is carried by the winds as heavy dust storms. The Israelites were told that if they forsook Jehovah, a storm of dust and ashes should descend upon them (De 28:24). Covering the head with dust was expressive of deep grief (Jos 7:6) and sitting in the dust denoted degradation (Is 47:1). To "lick the dust" expressed humiliating submission (Ps 72:9).

E

EAR At consecration blood was put on the right ear of the priest (Le 8:23) and also on the right ear of a leper who was to be cleansed (Le 14:14). As a mark of perpetual servitude, holes were bored in the ears (Ex 21:6; De 15:17).

EARTH The world in which we live as distinguished from the heavens (Ge 1:1); dry land (Ge 1:10); and the inhabitants of the world (Ge 11:1). Mention is made of the foundations of the earth (Ps 102:25, 104:5–9; Is 48:13). The earth is represented as supported by pillars erected by God (1 Sa 2:8; Job 9:6; Ps 75:3).

EARTHQUAKE A shaking of the earth caused by subterranean forces. A remarkable instance in Palestine occurred in the time of Uzziah (Am 1:1; Ze 14:5) which Josephus interpreted as an expression of divine judgment upon Uzziah (2 Ch 26:16). During severe earthquakes mountains may appear to rock to and fro and their very foundations be shaken (Ps 18:7; Je 4:24). In the seventh year of Herod the Great an earthquake destroyed much cattle and about 10,000 people. At the time of the crucifixion of Jesus there was an earthquake accompanied with darkness (Ma 27:45, 51–54). Another earthquake occurred at the time of the resurrection (Ma 28:2). Philippi was shaken by an earthquake (Ac 16:26).

EDEN 1. The name applied to the Garden of Eden. There has been controversy over its location but it is generally conceded that the Euprates and Tigris are branches of the river that flowed through it (Ge 2:8, 10). It is here that Adam and Eve were tempted, ate of the tree of knowledge, and were expelled from the garden (Ge 3:4–6).

2. A Levite, son of Joah (2 Ch 29:12). **3.** A region that was associated with Damascus (Am 1:5).

EGYPT A country in northeast Africa, called Kemet by the Egyptians because of the black soil. The Canaanites knew it as Misri and the Hebrews used the name Mizraim, meaning two Egypts, the upper and lower.

EHUD (union?) **1.** The deliverer of the Israelites from King Eglon of Moab. He went to the king on the pretext that he had a present for him from the children of Israel. When Ehud was left alone with the king, he stabbed him and fled to the hill country of Ephraim. Ehud was left-handed (Ju 3:12–30). **2.** A Benjamite, son of Bilhan (1 Ch 7:10).

EKRON (eradication) One of the five chief cities of the Philistines (Jos 13:3; 1 Sa 6:16–17). It was assigned to Judah (Jos 15:45–46), later to Dan (Jos 19:43). It was recaptured by the Philistines. When the ark was taken from the Israelites in the time of Eli, it was sent to Ekron and then returned to Israel (1 Sa 5:10).

ELDER An officer who was head of a family or tribe (Ju 8:14, 16; 1 Ki 8:1–3). The name signified that he was a man of mature age. The elder exercised authority over the people (De 27:1; Ez 10:8) and in matters of state, elders represented the people (Ex 3:18; Ju 11:5–11; 1 Sa 8:4). A body of seventy elders aided Moses when he was over-burdened with the responsibility of supplying the people with food (Nu 11:16, 24). The elders of a town had charge of civil and religious affairs. In the early Christian church such designations as elder, presbyter and bishop, if not strictly synonymous, were interchangeable (Ac 20:17; Tit 1:5, 7). Elders were in the church at Jerusalem in A.D. 44 (Ac 11:30). On his first journey Paul appointed elders in every church

(Ac 14:23). They cooperated with the apostles in the government of the church (Ac 15:2, 4, 6, 22, 16:4). They had spiritual care of the congregation (1 Ti 3:5, 5:17; Tit 1:9; 1 Pe 5:1–4).

ELECTION Used in the Scripture in three ways. (1) Of elect nations, such as Israel (Ex 19:5–6; Ps 135:4; Is 41:8; Is 45:4). (2) Of individuals, such as the Apostles, divinely elected to a certain service (Lu 6:13). (3) Of certain individuals elected to salvation in Christ. This last usage has been the cause of many bitter theological controversies, two views resulting. *Calvinistic View* stated well in the Westminster Confession: "God from all eternity did by the most wise and holy counsel of His own will freely and unchangeably ordain whatsoever comes to pass; yet so as thereby neither is God the author of sin, nor is violence offered to the will of the creatures, nor is the liberty or contingency of second causes taken away, but rather established. Although God knows whatsoever may or can come to pass upon all supposed conditions, yet has He not decreed anything because He foresaw its future, or as that which would come to pass upon such conditions. By the decree of God, for the manifestation of His glory some men and angels are predestinated unto everlasting life and others foreordained to everlasting death. These angels and men thus predestinated and foreordained are particularly and unchangeably designed, and their number is so certain and definite that it cannot be either increased or diminished." (Ac 2:23; Ro 8:29–30; Ep 1:4–11; 1 Pe 1:2–20). *Arminian View* states that election is not absolute but conditioned "contingent upon the proper acceptance of such gifts of grace as God by His Spirit and providence puts withing the reach of men." To this view the Scriptures teach that man's eternal destiny is settled by his own choice and that though God desires the salvation of all men, only those will perish who wickedly resist his will (Jo 5:40; Ac 7:51; 1 Ti 2:4, 4:10). Also this view states that certain passages of Scripture by their various exhortations and warnings teach that the number of the elect can be increased or diminished. (Ma 24:4, 13; 2 Pe 1:10–11).

ELI High priest at the temple of Shiloh during the eleventh century B.C. He helped to train Samuel (1 Sa 1:9, 24–28). Although a man of great piety, he was unable to control his sons, Hophni and Phinehas, whose conduct was disgraceful (1 Sa 2:23–25, 3:13). God's denunciation of Eli and his house was spoken through the boy Samuel and through an unnamed prophet (1 Sa 2:27–36, 3:11–18).

ELIJAH 1. One of the greatest of the prophets, a Tishbite who lived in Gilead (1 Ki 17:1). Little else is known of his origin. He appeared suddenly during the reign of Ahab (About 876–854 B.C.) to denounce the king and his wife, Jezebel, for their idolatry and crimes. His purpose was to save Israel from the worship of Baal. On Mount Carmel he succeeded in discrediting the 400 prophets of Baal; God caused a fire from heaven to burn the water-soaked sacrifice (1 Ki 18:19–46). Following the scene on Mount Carmel, Elijah fled from the furious Jezebel to Mount Horeb, where, like Moses, he was divinely taken care of for a period of forty days (Ex 24:18, 34:28; De 9:9, 18; 1 Ki 19:8). The Lord rebuked him for leaving Israel and commanded him to return. When Naboth was murdered at the instigation of Jezebel, Elijah met Ahab and declared the judgments of God upon him (1 Ki 21:1–29). Like Enoch, Elijah was translated to heaven without dying. This was on the east of the Jordan. Elisha was with him when he was carried away by a whirlwind into heaven (2 Ki 2:1–12). Elijah appeared with our Lord in the transfiguration (Ma 17:4; Lu 9:30). He was one of the most rugged and colorful characters of the Scriptures. The last two verses of the Old Testament predict that Elijah will appear on earth before the dreadful day of the Lord (Mal

4:5–6). While the New Testament explains this in terms of John the Baptist, who, in some respects, was like Elijah (Ma 3:4; Mk 1:6; Lu 1:17), it is believed by some that, while John appeared in the spirit and power of Elijah, the prophet is yet to come in person before the second advent of Christ. **2.** A son of Jeroham, a Benjamite, who resided at Jerusalem (1Ch 8:27). **3.** A son of Harim, a priest, who married a Gentile (Ez 10:21). **4.** An Israelite in the time of Ezra who renounced his foreign wife (Ez 10:26).

ELIZABETH (God is an oath) A descendant of Aaron, wife of Zacharias and mother of John the Baptist. An angel revealed to her the fact that she was to be the mother of the forerunner of Christ. She was a kinswoman of Mary, mother of Jesus (Lu 1:5–45).

ELISHA The son of Shaphat who lived in Abel-meholah in the Jordan valley. He was plowing his father's field when Elijah found him and appointed him his successor (1 Ki 19:16, 19). Leaving his home, Elisha joined Elijah and was with him when Elijah was transported to Heaven (2 Ki 2:1–18). His miracles were designed to establish the being and truth of Jehovah at a time when the kingdom of Israel was committed to Baal. Included among his miracles: causing water to spring from barren land (2 Ki 2:19–22); the death of the children who mocked his bald head (2 Ki 2:23–25); the increase in the oil to pay the widow's debts (2 Ki 4:1, 7); the son restored to life (2 Ki 4:8–37); the feeding of the hundred men (2 Ki 4:42–44); the healing of Naaman (2 Ki 5:1–19); the blinding of the Syrian soldiers who pursued him (2 Ki 6:17–23); and the prediction of the death of Ben-hahad (2 Ki 8:7–15). The body of a dead man, who was placed in the same sepulchre as Elisha, touched the prophet's bones and was restored to life (2 Ki 13:20–21).

ELOHIM The plural of ELOAH (mighty), sometimes used in the sense of gods, true or false (Ex 12:12, 35:2, 4). On the use of Elohim and Jehovah in the O.T., Dr. W.H. Green says: "Jehovah represents God in His special relation to the chosen people, as revealing Himself to them, their guardian and object of their worship; Elohim represents God in His relation to the world at large, as Creator, providential ruler in the affairs of men, and controlling the opeations of nature. Elohim is used when Gentiles speak or are spoken to or spoken about, unless there is a specific reference to Jehovah, the God of the chosen people. Elohim is used when God is contrasted with men or things, or when the sense requires a common rather than a proper noun."

EMERALD A type of precious stone imported into Tyre by the Syrians (Eze 27:16). They were used in the second row of the breastplate of the high priest (Ex 28:18, 39:11). The fourth foundation of the wall of the New Jerusalem is garnished with emeralds (Re 21:19).

EMMAUS The real site of this town is a matter of dispute. It was about seven miles from Jerusalem (sixty furlongs). Near this town Christ revealed himself to two of his disciples after the resurrection (Lu 24:13).

ENOCH 1. The eldest son of Cain (Ge 4:17–18). 2. Son of Jared and father of Methuselah; he belonged to the Seth line, "the antediluvian line of the Messiah" (Ge 5:18–24). A prophecy of Enoch is found in the Epistle of Jude (Jude 14–15).

EPAPHRAS A member of the Colossian church and possibly the founder of it. He came to Paul at Rome during his first imprisonment. In Paul's epistle to that church he joined the apostle in sending salutations (Col 1:7–8, 4:12). Paul speaks of him as "my fellowprisoner" (Phile 23).

EPAPHRODITUS A Christian sent with gifts from the church at Philippi to Paul, then a prisoner at Rome. Epaphroditus became ill while there but, upon recovery, he returned to Philippi taking with him Paul's epistle to that church (Ph 2:25–30, 4:18).

EPHOD (a covering) **1.** Father of Hanniel, a leader of the tribe of Manasseh in the wilderness (Nu 34:23). **2.** An official garment of the Jewish high priest which he was required to wear when engaged in religious duties (Ex 28:4). It was suspended from the shoulders and covered both back and front. On the shoulders were two onyx stones on which the names of the tribes were engraved (Ex 28:9, 39:6–7). Attached to the ephod was the breastplate (Ex 28:25–28, 39:19–21).

EPHRAIM (fruitful) **1.** Joseph's younger son. His mother, Asenath, was the daughter of Potipherah, priest of On. He was born after Joseph became prime minister of Egypt (Ge 41:45–52). When Jacob placed his right hand on the head of Ephraim, the younger son, he explained to Joseph that Ephraim would be the greater and would be the ancestor of a multitude of peoples. The descendants of the two sons were to be regarded as two tribes (Ge 48:8–20). **2.** *The tribe of Ephraim* (Jos 16:4, 10; Ju 5:14). A year after the Exodus, when the census was taken, the tribe numbered 40,500. At the close of the wandering, in the second census, they numbered 32, 500 (Nu 26:37). Joshua was an Ephraim-ite (Jos 19:50, 24:30). In the division of the land, on the south of Ephraim was Benjamin, on the north Manasseh, and on the west Dan. Strongest of the northern tribes, Ephraim was resentful of Judean supremacy and was critical of the undertakings of other tribes, such as those led by Gideon and Jephthah (Ju 8:1–33, 12:1–6). **3.** *Mount Ephraim*, part of a mountain ridge in central Palestine within the territories of Ephraim and the western half-tribe of

Manasseh. Samuel's parents were from Mount Ephraim (1 Sa 1:1). **4.** A city of Judea to which Jesus fled after restoring Lazarus (Jo 11:54). **5.** Forest or wood of Ephraim which was the scene of the decisive battle between the armies of David and his rebellious son, Absalom (2 Sa 18:6). **6.** *Gate of Ephraim.* A gate of Jerusalem, probably in the northeast portion of the wall (2 Ki 14:13; 2 Ch 25:23; Ne 8:16, 12:39).

EPHRATAH **1.** The name by which Bethlehem was originally known; the place where Rachel was buried (Ge 35:19, 48:7; Ru 4:11). The city was also called Bethlehem Ephratah (Mi 5:2). **2.** The wife of Caleb and mother of Hur (1 Ch 2:19, 50, 4:4).

EPISTLE A letter, particularly one with a formal style and containing a specific teaching or doctrine. Twenty-one of the 27 books of the New Testament are in the form of formal letters, or epistles. Usually they were addressed to individuals, groups, or churches. With two exceptions they open with a statement as to authorship or destination. About a dozen such letters are attributed to Paul. Four others claim as their authors James, Peter, and Jude. Three are ascribed to John. The author of the Epistle to the Hebrews is not named. These letters were written to meet definite needs, such as correcting the conditions of the churches, teaching Christian doctrine, or refuting heretical ideas.

ESARHADDON Son of Sennacherib, king of Assyria. His being favored by his father so angered two of his brothers that they assassinated their father and fled into Armenia (2 Ki 19:36–37; 2 Ch 32:21; Is 37:37–38). At that time Esarhaddon was conducting a campaign in Armenia. When he heard of this foul deed, he returned with his army to Nineveh but on the way encountered the rebel forces and defeated them. In 680 B.C., he succeeded to the throne.

ESAU (hairy) The oldest son of Isaac and Rebekah; a hunter. He sold his birthright to his brother, Jacob, for a mess of red pottage. For this he was given the name Edom which means red (Ge 25:27–34; He 12:16–17). He married Judith and Adah, both Hittites (Ge 26:34–35, 36:1–2), and a daughter of Ishmael (Ge 28:9, 36:3). Esau was cheated from receiving the blessing of his father by the deception of Jacob and Rebekah. Esau's fury at this caused Jacob to flee to Mesopotamia (Ge 27:1–31:55). However, he treated Jacob kindly when he returned from Mesopotamia (Ge 32:3–33:15). His descendants were called Edomites (De 2:4, 12, 22).

ESDRA-ELON, PLAIN OF See MEGIDDO.

ESTHER (star) The beautiful daughter of Abihail, a Benjamite (Es 2:15). Her Hebrew name was Hadassah (myrtle). After being brought up by her uncle, Mordecai, she became the favorite wife (or concubine) of King Ahasuerus.

EUCHARIST The Lord's Supper. It is based on the Greek word *eucharistesas*, to give thanks. At his last supper Jesus gave thanks for the bread and wine. He told his disciples to eat and drink for the bread would symbolize his body, the wine his blood (Ma 26:26–28; Lu 22:15–20).

EUNUCH (bed-keeper) A chamberlain, one who had charge of beds and bedchambers. Those chosen for the office were rendered impotent (Is 56:3; Ma 19:12). This class frequently rose to high position and considerable authority. Three under Pharaoh were eunuchs (Ge 37:36, 40:2, 7), translated *officer*. They were in Babylon (Da 1:3) and in the service of the Persian king (Es 1:10, 2:21). They served Jezebel (1 Ki 22:9; 2 Ki 8:6, 9:32). Mariamne, the wife of Herod the Great, was served by a eunuch. The treasurer of

Candace, queen of Ethiopia, was a eunuch and was converted to Christianity (Ac 8:27–38).

EUPHRATES One of the great rivers of Asia, the Euphrates rises in northeast Turkey, flows through Syria and Iraq, and empties into the Persian Gulf. It is 1,780 miles long. About 90 miles above its mouth it is joined by the Tigris. In ancient times the greatest city along its banks was Babylon. It was the eastern boundary of the land of Israel (Ge 15:18; 1 Ki 4:21, 24).

EUTYCHUS (good fortune) A young man of Troas who, while sleeping, fell from a window. Paul restored him to life (Ac 20:9–10).

EVANGELIST (messenger of good tidings) In the early church a class of men who went from place to place preaching the Gospel. They were distinct from apostles, pastors, and teachers (Ep 4:11). Philip, who was instrumental in the conversion of the eunuch, was an evangelist (Ac 6:5, 8:5, 26, 21:8) and should not be confused with Philip the apostle. Paul enjoined Timothy to do the work of an evangelist (2 Ti 4:5).

EVE (life) The mother of all living (Ge 3:20), fashioned from a rib taken from the side of Adam (Ge 2:18–22). She and Adam were forbidden to eat the fruit of a particular tree, as a test of their obedience. The serpent induced Eve to violate the command and she induced Adam to do likewise (Ge 3:1–24; 2 Co 11:3; 1 Ti 2:13).

EVIL The Bible alone has given us the origin of evil in the story of the fall in Eden. Our first parents were created innocent, having moral capacity, the power to act morally, but, in the nature of the case, could not be created *holy* in the moral sense of that term. They were placed under law which they had the power to obey or violate. God is not, and could not be, the author of sin, but under the conditions of our moral constitution he permitted it. The fall afforded God the opportunity of manifesting his grace and infinite love in Jesus Christ, the Savior of mankind, the rejection of whom lays upon the sinner the consequences of sin under the law.

EXILE See CAPTIVITY.

EXODUS (a way out) The departure of the Israelites from their life of bondage in Egypt. They were led by Moses. This marks the beginning of the history of the Israelites as a nation. They left Rameses in Goshen and traveled to Succoth (Ex 12:37). The shortest route to Canaan would have been through the land of the Philistines. But, because they might encounter war by this route, they were led instead through the wilderness by the Red Sea (Ex 13:17–18). At Pi-hahiroth they passed through the Red Sea, which had been made dry for them (Ex 14:1–31). They then entered the wilderness of Shur (Ex 15:22; Nu 33:8) and traveled along the coast of the Red Sea toward Mount Sinai. They reached the land of Canaan 40 years after they left Egypt.

EZEKIEL (God strengthens) One of the major prophets, a Zadokite priest and the son of Buzi (Eze 1:3). He was among the captives taken by Nebuchadnezzar to Babylonia in about 597 B.C. (2 Ki 24:10–16). During the captivity he was consulted by the elders on important matters (Eze 8:1, 14:1, 20:1).

EZRA (help) **1.** A famous priest, reformer, scribe, and student of law who lived during the time of the Babylonian captivity. Artaxerxes, the Persian king, permitted Ezra and a group of his followers to return to Jerusalem. When he arrived there, he found religious affairs at a low ebb. He thereupon initiated reforms, among them the decree that foreign wives be divorced (Ez 10:9–17). Ezra disappears from the Biblical narrative here although, as Ezra the scribe, he reappears later to read the law of Moses (Ne 8:1–13). **2.** A priest who accompanied Zerubbabel from Exile in Babylon to Jerusalem (Ne 12:1, 13, 33).

F

FAITH Faith is the belief or trust in things unseen (2 Co 4:18, 5:17; He 11:1). In a religious sense faith is applied particularly to God or to Christ, the author and finisher of our faith (Mk 11:22–24; Jo 3:16, 33–36, 20:31; He 12:2; 1 Jo 5:9–14). Belief generally indicates intellectual assent to the evidence establishing the claims of the Scriptures (1 Co 15:12–17; 1 Ti 6:20–21; 2 Ti 2:18). Faith implies a confidence or trust which comes after the belief has been established (Ma 13:3–17; Lu 8:10; Jo 8:30–32; 1 Co 2:9–16). Many Old Testament heroes of faith are listed in He 11. Some believe that saving faith is the only condition of salvation (Ac 16:31) and one of the fruits of the spirit (Ga 5:22). Others believe that saving faith includes repentance, confession of sins, and obedience to Christ (Ac 2:37–38; Ro 10:8–17; Ga 3:11, 23–29).

FAMINE Crop failure was the chief cause of famines in Biblical times, although they also occurred in cities under siege. Notable famines in the Scriptures took place in the time of Abraham (Ge 12:10), Isaac (Ge 26:1), Joseph in Egypt (Ge 41:27–57), Jacob (Ge 42:1–3, 47:1–13), the judges (Ru 1:1), David (2 Sa 21:1), Elijah (1 Ki 17:1–18:46), Elisha (2 Ki 4:38, 8:1), in the reign of Claudius, A.D. 41—54

91

(Ac 11:28), at the siege of Samaria (2 Ki 6:24–7:20), and at the siege of Jerusalem (2 Ki 25:1–3).

FAST The words *to fast* and *fasting* are not found in the Pentateuch and injunctions to fast do not appear in the Mosaic law. The first instance of voluntary fasting is that of David when he refused to eat during the sickness of his child (2 Sa 12:22). Many instances of fasting are recorded in the later books (Ez 8:21; Ne 9:1; Es 4:3; Ps 69:10; Da 6:18, 9:3). In times of calamity fasts were sometimes proclaimed to create a serious attitude of mind (Je 36:9; Joel 1:14). It signified a state of humility before God because of sin (1 Sa 7:6; 1 Ki 21:9, 12). In the post-exile period there were fasts in the fourth, fifth, seventh, and tenth months (Ze 8:19). These commemorated the siege and capture of Jerusalem, the destruction of the Temple, and the slaying of Gedaliah, the governor. The Pharisees fasted twice a week (Lu 18:12), a formalism criticised by Jesus (Ma 6:16–17).

FATHER A word with various meanings in the Scriptures, including the begetter of children, a forefather, the founder of a tribe or nation, originator of an art, and a protector or benefactor. The father held unquestioned authority in a family. Some of his iniquities could be visited upon his children. Much importance was attached to receiving his blessing (Ge 27:27–40, 48:15–20, 49). Jesus often referred to God as Father (Jo 17:1).

FEAST Feasts are often mentioned in the Bible. They celebrated important or joyful events. Three annual feasts were required by Mosaic law. The first was Passover, on the fourteenth day of the first month, which was followed the next day by the feast of unleavened bread (Le 23:5–6). The second annual festival was the Feast of Weeks, later called Pentecost, occurring fifty days after Passover (Le 23:15–16; Ac 2:1). The third festival was the Feast of Tabernacles, on the fifteenth day of the seventh month. Lasting for seven days, it commemorated the period in the wilderness (Le 23:34–44). All adult males were required to appear before God on these three occasions (Ex 23:17; De 16:16). Another important religious feast is the Feast of Purim celebrating the deliverance of the Jews at the time of Esther (Es 9:21–28). The Feast of Dedication, instituted by Judas Maccabaeus, is another.

FELIX (happy) He was liberated from slavery by Claudius, by whom he was appointed procurator of Judea. When Paul spoke before Felix and his wife, Drusilla, who was a Jewess, Felix was terrified. However, failing to receive a bribe from Paul and to placate the Jews, he left Paul in prison (Ac 24:24–27).

FESTUS, PORCIUS The successor of Felix as procurator of Judea (Ac 24:10, 27) about A.D. 60. He listened to Paul's defence in the presence of Agrippa II. Festus was satisfied as to Paul's innocence but proposed that he be tried in Jerusalem. This was unwise and Paul asserted his right to appeal to Caesar (Ac 24:27–26:32).

FIG A tree of Palestine and its edible fruit. Some of these trees grow to a height of fifteen feet. Looking like a small green knob, the young fruit appears in the early spring before the leaf buds. This fact is alluded to by Jesus in the parable about the barren fig tree (Mk 11:13–14). Figs were a staple article of food in Palestine and a crop failure caused great distress. Occasionally figs were used medicinally (2 Ki 20:7; Is 38:21).

FIRE Among the Hebrews it symbolized the Lord's presence and was used to consume the sacrifice (Ge 4:4, 8:20). It was also used for cooking and heating (Je 36:22; Mk 14:54; Jo 18:18).

FIRMAMENT The expanse of space surrounding the earth, which includes everything between the earth and the stars. This expanse is compared to a tent spread out above the earth (Ps 104:2; Is 40:22) and also to a mirror (Job 37:18). It was spoken of as having doors and windows (Ge 7:11; 2 Ki 7:2; Ps 78:23).

FIRSTBORN God claimed the firstborn, of both men and animals. In the tenth plague of Egypt the firstborn of the Egyptians were slain and by the sprinkling of blood the firstborn of the Hebrews were preserved, hence they were dedicated to Jehovah (Ex 12:12–13, 23, 29). Every firstborn male was presented to the Lord at the sanctuary (Nu 18:15; Lu 2:22). In place of each firstborn the tribe of Levi was chosen (Nu 3:12, 41, 46, 8:13–19) for the service of the sanctuary. Thus the firstborn were redeemed by this substitution, but a redemption price, not exceeding five shekels, was paid (Nu 18:16).

FIRSTFRUITS The first ripe fruits of the season which many ancient peoples, including the Hebrews, presented as divine offerings. The offering of firstfruits was required by Mosaic law (Ex 23:19).

FLESH In the ordinary sense the word *flesh* denotes the human body as distinct from the human spirit (Job 14:22; Is 10:18; Col 2:5). It is also used to contrast mortal men with God who is the spirit (Ps 56:4; Is 31:3; Joel 2:28–29; Ma 16:17). The term *having mind for the flesh* means having carnal desires (Ro 8:5–8).

FLOOD The deluge at the time of Noah which, according to the Scriptures, was divine judgment for the wickedness of man (Ge 6:5–7:24). Only the righteous Noah, his family, and a large number of animals were permitted to escape by riding out the flood in an ark. The rain began on the

seventeenth day of the second month and on the seventeenth day of the seventh month the ark rested on the mountains of Ararat (Ge 8:1–4). Three months later the tops of the mountains appeared. Noah left the ark on the twenty-seventh day of the second month of the new year. The flood had lasted about a year (Ge 8:14–19).

FOOD The diet of the Hebrews in Palestine was almost entirely vegetarian. Meat was eaten occasionally by the rich. Mosaic law stated that only animals which chewed the cud and had cloven hoofs were edible. Serpents, creeping things, and fish without scales were forbidden (Le 7:26, 11:10, 17:10–14; De 12:16). Bread was the staple of the table. Lentils were also important. Onions, leeks, cucumbers, and garlic were used as relishes. Preferred condiments were cummin, fitches, dill, mint, and mustard. Edible fruits were figs, olives, grapes, pomegranates, almonds, and melons. Foods derived from the animal kingdom were honey, locusts, milk, curds, meat, and fish.

FOREIGNER In the Authorized Version the translation is usually *stranger*, signifying someone not of Israel and having no allegiance to the God of Israel—an Egyptian (Ex 2:22), a Philistine (2 Sa 15:19). A proselyte to Judaism would not be considered a foreigner (Is 56:6–8; Ac 2:10). Intermarriage with foreigners was forbidden (Ex 34:16; De 7:3; Ez 10:2; Ne 13:26–27). Foreigners among the Israelites were required to abstain from idolatrous worship (Le 20:2), to honor the Sabbath (Ex 20:10), not to eat leavened bread during the passover season (Ex 12:19). They were accorded civil rights and enjoyed protection under Israel's laws (Le 25:47). In order to have the full rights of citizenship a foreigner should receive the rite of circumcision (Ex 12:48; Ro 9:4).

G

GABRIEL (man of God). A heavenly messenger high in rank among the angels. He was sent to Daniel to interpret a vision received by the prophet (Da 8:16–27). The same occurred in connection with the prophecy of the Seventy Weeks (Da 9:21–27). Centuries afterwards he appeared to Zacharias to announce the birth of John the Baptist (Lu 1:11–22) and at Nazareth he declared to Mary her great distinction and honor (Lu 1:26–31).

GALATIA A district of central Asia Minor named for the Gallic tribes from Macedonia and Greece who lived there. They were given the territory by Nicomedes, king of Bithynia, in return for military service (Ac 16:6, 18:23; Ga 1:2).

GALILEE (circle, district) In New Testament times Galilee was one of the three provinces of Palestine. It was located in the northern part. In the Old Testament it was considered to be roughly the territories of Asher, Naphtali, Zebulun, and Issachar. Many Canaanites lived in this district (Ju 1:30–33, 4:2). Many Gentiles also lived here as was indicated by the expression "Galilee of the nations" (Is 9:1; Ma 4:15). Jesus was raised in Galilee, and performed several miracles there.

GALILEE, SEA OF This lake was called first the Sea of Chinnereth (Nu 34:11), later the Lake of Gennesaret (Lu 5:1) and the Sea of Galilee or Tiberias (Jo 6:1, 21:1). It is fed by the river Jordan. Its greatest length is about twelve miles and its greatest breadth about seven and a half miles. Its surface is about 680 feet below the Mediterranean. It was the center of a busy, industrious life. A chief industry was fishing.

GALL 1. A Hebrew word meaning bile, the bitter secretion of the liver. The ancients believed that the poison of asps was their bile (Job 20:14). The "gall of bitterness" signified a venomous attitude toward that which is good (Ac 8:23). 2. A bitter, poisonous herb called *rosh* in Hebrew (De 29:18, 32:32; Ps 69:21). Wine mixed with gall was a stupefying drink given to those about to be crucified to deaden the pain. Such a drink was offered to Jesus at the crucifixion (Ma 27:34).

GAMALIEL (reward of God) 1. Son of Pedahzur, head of the tribe of Manasseh in the wilderness (Nu 1:10, 2:20, 7:54, 59). 2. A doctor of the law, a Pharisee, and a member of the Sanhedrin. He was held in high regard by the Jews. Paul received his training in the law under this man (Ac 22:3). Gamaliel opposed the persecution of the apostles (Ac 5:34–39). He died in about A.D. 50.

GARDEN The first garden mentioned in the Scriptures was the garden of Eden occupied by Adam and Eve (Ge 2:8–17, 3:4–6, 23). In Egypt, water stored up from the overflow of the Nile was released by a foot-operated contrivance to water the gardens (De 11:10). There were gardens at Jerusalem (2 Ki 25:4) and in Shushan (Es 1:5). Gardens were usually protected by walls or hedges (Son 4:12; Is 5:2, 5). Some used them for idolatrous purposes (Is 1:29, 65:3, 66:17) and some for burial purposes (Jo 19:41).

GATH (wine press) A city of the Philistines (Jos 13:3; 1 Sa 6:17, 7:14). The Anakim, men of strong build and of great stature, lived here (Jos 11:22). One of these men was Goliath (1 Sa 17:4; 2 Sa 21:15–22). The town was taken by David (1 Ch 18:1), and was later fortified by Rehoboam (2 Ch 11:8). Hazael captured it (2 Ki 12:17).

GAZA One of the five main cities of the Philistines, the scene of many struggles between the Israelites and the Philistines (Jos 13:3; Ju 1:18; 1 Sa 6:17). It is located on the Mediterranean Sea not far from the desert. It was the scene of many exploits in Samson's career, including the destruction of the temple of Dagon (Ju 16:23–31). Dire predictions were made about the city by the prophets (Je 47:1, 5; Am 1:6–7; Zep 2:4; Ze 9:5). It is referred to as Azzah three times in the Authorized Version.

GEHENNA See HELL.

GENEALOGY It was very essential that ancestral records be kept by the Jews to safeguard succession to the throne, the high priesthood, tribal headship, and head of the father's house. From the earliest days of their nation such records were kept (Nu 1:2, 18; 1 Ch 5:7, 17). In the time of Ezra those who could not support their claim by genealogical evidence were expelled from the priesthood (Ez 2:61–62; Ne 7:63–64). It was of first importance that registers be kept to secure the rights provided by the Year of Jubilee when all alienated property was restored to the original owners.

GENERATION Biblical usage of this term varies according to different periods through which the Hebrews lived. In the patriarchal age, a generation was reckoned at a century—the 400 years of the sojourn in Egypt were referred to as four generations (Ge 15:13–16). In other passages the word refers to a period of about thirty-five to forty years (Job 42:16). It also implies the group of ancestors one joins at death (Ps 49:19), or the posterity which comes after one (Le 3:17), or, in the present-day sense, one's children and grandchildren, etc. (Ex 20:5).

GENNESARET The land of Gennesaret is mentioned in connection with the crossing of the Sea of Galilee by Jesus and his disciples (Ma 14:34; Mk 6:53). See GALILEE, SEA OF.

GENTILES The Hebrew word meaning nations, i.e., political and religious groups other than Israel (Ju 4:2, 13, 16). Sometimes the word is translated *nations* (Ge 10:5, 20) or *heathen* (Ne 5:8; Ps 2:1). The word usually had an unfavorable meaning. In the New Testament the term is used for the word *nations* (Ma 24:7; Ac 2:5) and for the word *Greek* (Ro 2:9; 1 Co 12:13).

GERIZIM The mountain of the Gerizites across the valley from Mount Ebal. It was on Mount Gerizim that Abraham was directed to sacrifice Isaac, according to the Samaritans. At the base of the mountain is the well of Jacob (Jo 4:6) and a little to the north is the tomb of Joseph (Jos 24:32). After entering the valley, Moses directed that the law be read from Mount Gerizim and Mount Ebal (De 11:29; Jos 8:33).

GETHSEMANE (an oil press) A garden traditionally located near the foot of Mount Olivet (Lu 22:39). At the time of Christ it contained many olive trees but these were probably cut down in the first Christian century by Titus. This garden was often visited by Jesus and his disciples (Jo 18:2). It was here that, betrayed by Judas, Jesus was taken prisoner by soldiers and priests.

GIANT The Hebrew word *nephilim* is used to describe demigods, or men of great renown, who were the offspring of the sons of God and the daughters of men (Ge 6:4). The word *rephaim* was used to denote true giants as far as stature was concerned. They were found by the Israelites among the Canaanite inhabitants of Palestine. Among them were the Anakims of Philistia and the Emims of Moab (De

2:10–11). The word *giant* is also used for the four mighty Philistines—Ishbi-benob, Saph, Goliath the Gittite, and a giant with 12 fingers and 12 toes (2 Sa 21:15–22).

GIDEON (feller of trees) A Manassite, son of Joash. He lived in Ophrah (Ju 6:11–15). By clever strategy and God's power he managed to defeat the Midianites with only a very small army (Ju 7:19–24). He was probably the greatest of the judges.

GOD The Bible opens with the fact of God—"In the beginning God." The Bible is the record of the revelation of God. It is because man by searching cannot "find out the Almighty unto perfection," cannot know God as he has revealed himself, that such a revelation of God is necessary—the fact grounded in the need. The Bible does not reach a conception of God by a philosophical process. The Greek philosopher worked from the world and its phenomena up to God. The Grecian philosophical procedure was not that of the Hebrew thinker. The latter did not think from the world to God; he began with God as the source, and the world and all things followed.

1. Elohim, Jehovah. These are the two chief names used throughout the Old Testament for the Divine Being. Elohim is usually translated *God*, and Jehovah in the A.V. *Lord*. The former is the plural of Eloah. The short form *El* is often used. It signifies strength, as in El-Shaddai, *God Almighty*, by which name God was known to the patriarchs (Ge 17:1, 28:3; Ex 6:3). For the significance and use of Elohim representing God in his relation to the world as Creator, providential ruler in the affairs of men, and controlling the operations of nature, and the use of Jehovah which represents God in his special relation to the chosen people, see ELOHIM. The word *Lord* as the translation of the Hebrew word for Jehovah is better is a better choice, as in the R.V.

2. Unity of God. There is but one self-existing being. The Bible reveals God to us as one, and the only God. There cannot be more than one God, for eternity, infinity, omnipresence, etc., cannot apply to more than one such being. Two such beings would limit and exclude each other and thus render impossible the being of God. God makes himself known in the Scriptures as Father, Son and Holy Spirit, three separate pe[s]onalities, three persons in one Godhead, but not three Gods. It is trinity, not tri-theism (De 6:4; 1 Ki 8:60; Is 44:6; Mk 12:29; Jo 10:30; 1 Co 8:4; Ep 4:6).

3. God the Creator. Creator of the heavens and the earth (Ge 1:1; Ex 20:11; Ps 8:3, 19:1; Jo 1:3; Ac 14:15; Ro 11:36; He 1:2). Creator of man (Ge 1:26, 5:1; Ex 4:11; Job 10:8–12; Ps 33:15; Ec 12:1; Is 43:1; Ac 17:25–29; 1 Co 15:38).

4. Natural Attributes. Properties or qualities of the Divine Being. The true representations of God as revealed by himself in his Word. They are inseparable from his nature. Being God he must be what he is in these essential attributes or perfections. **1.** *Infinity.* His infinitude expressed in all things. In no matter limited. He is unconditioned (1 Ki 8:27; Ps 139:8; Ac 15:18; He 4:13). **2.** *Eternity.* He is infinite, not finite in the duration of his being. Time has no place in his eternal nature. There can be no progression, advancing from point to point, in his being (Ge 21:23; Ex 3:14–15; Ps 90:2; 2 Pe 3:8). **3.** *Omnipotence.* Unlimited in might and power as expressed by the name Elohim (Ge 1:1, 3; 18:14; De 32:39; Ps 66:3; Is 40:12; Da 4:35; Ma 19:26; Ro 1:20). **4.** *Omniscience.* The all-knowing God is infinite in understanding as in power, and as in the case of his eternity and all other perfections, there can be no advance or progression in knowledge. In this he is unconditioned (Job 37:16; Ps 33:13, 119:168; Je 23:24; Ma 10:29; Ac 1:24; 15:18). **5.** *Omnipresence.* His presence extends over all his works (Job 34:21–22; Ps 139:7–12; Is 66:1; Ac 17:27). **6.** *Immutability.* God is no more subject to change than to any other limitation (Ps 33:11; Is 46:10; Mal 3:6; He 1:12, 6:17–

18; Jam 1:17). **7.** *Wisdom.* (Job 36:5; Ps 104:24; Is 28:29; Ro 16:27; 1 Ti 1:17).

5. Moral Perfections. As the natural attributes appear in the statements relative to his own nature, and in relation to his acts of power, his relations to the universe and to his creatures, so the Scriptures reveal his moral attributes in his dealings with man in his moral constitution and conduct, and his relation to the moral order. In a marvelous manner the Bible sets forth the ethical God. **1.** *Holiness.* God is as essentially and infinitely holy as he is essentially omnipotent, and requires holiness of the beings made in his image (Le 19:2; Jos 24:19; 1 Sa 2:2; Job 36:2–3; Ps 89:35; Is 5:16, 6:3; Ho 11:9; 1 Pe 1:15). **2.** *Justice.* In the Scriptures justice and righteousness are used synonymously. In the beings of God it is a necessary outflow from his holiness, the manifestation of that holiness in the moral government of the world. He is perfectly just as the righteous governor of the world, and his perfect righteousness appears in the penalties pronounced and rewards bestowed (Ge 18:25; De 10:17; Job 8:3, 20; Ps 9:8, 119:142; Je 11:20; Da 9:7; Ro 2:11; Re 15:3). **3.** *Mercy.* The divine goodness and compassion exercised toward the guilty and wretched in harmony with truth and justice, the ministry of love for the relief of those unworthy of it (Ex 34:7; De 4:31; Ps 51:1, 117:2; Is 55:7; Je 3:12; Lu 1:50, 6:36; Ep 2:4; Tit 3:5; He 4:16). **4.** *Faithfulness.* This divine attribute is noted especially in the Psalms. By it we are assured that God will fulfill his promises. As regards temporal necessities (Ps 84:11; Is 33:16; 1 Ti 4:8). Support in temptation and persecution (Is 41:10; 1 Co 10:13; 1 Pe 4:12–13). In afflictions (He 12:4–12). Guidance in trouble (2 Ch 32:22; Ps 32:8). Power to persevere (Je 32:40). Spiritual blessings and final glory (1 Co 1:9; 1 Jo 2:25). **5.** *Love.* Our conceptions of God must be derived from the revelation of himself in his Word, and in that revelation he declares this attribute of love. Not only so, but it is the only attribute by which his being as such is defined—"God is love." In no instance is another attribute so employed, as "God is power," or "God is omniscience." Love is the distinctive characteristic of God in which all others harmoniously blend. In both the Old and New Testaments God's gracious love to men is so strongly and frequently declared that it would take considerable space to set down all the passages (Ex 34:6; Is 63:9; Je 31:3; Jo 3:16; 1 Jo 4:10). The highest expression of divine love is in redemption—God in Christ reconciling the world unto himself (Ro 5:8; 8:32–39; 1 Jo 4:9–10).

6. The Triune God—Father, Son, Holy Spirit.

The Scriptures set forth the Godhead in this distinction of persons with absolute unity of essence. At the beginning of our Lord's ministry the three persons are exhibited at his baptism: the Holy Spirit as a dove resting upon him, the Father speaking and acknowledging the Son. In the formula of baptism the doctrine of the trinity is established by the resurrected Lord (Ma 28:19). **1.** *The Father is God.* (Ma 11:25; Jo 6:27, 8:41; Ro 15:6; 1 Co 8:6; Ep 4:6; Jam 1:27). **2.** *The Son is God.* (Jo 1:1, 18, 20:28; Ro 9:5; Ph 2:6; Col 2:9; He 1:8; 2 Pe 1:1). **3.** *The Spirit is God.* (Ac 5:3–4; 1 Co 2:10–11; Ep 2:22). **4.** *The distinctness of the three from one another.* (Jo 15:26, 16:13–14, 17:1–8, 18–23).

GOG **1.** Son of Shemaiah, a Reubenite (1 Ch 5:4). **2.** The prince of Meshech and Tubal. It was prophesied that he would be defeated in his expedition against Israel (Eze 38–39). **3.** Figuratively, the terms Gog and Magog are used to represent the nations Satan will gather about him to attack the forces of the Messiah (Re 20:8–15).

GOLD It has been used from earliest times (Ge 2:11). At first it was used for ornaments (Ge 24:22) and not until much later was it coined as money. In ancient times it was abundant (1 Ch 22:14; 2 Ch 1:15; Da 3:1). It was found in Arabia, Sheba and Ophir (1 Ki 9:28, 10:1; Job 28:16), also in

Uphaz (Je 10:9; Da 10:5), and Parvaim (2 Ch 3:6). Working with gold is mentioned in Ps 66:10; Pr 17:3, 27:21; and Is 46:6. The sacred articles of the tabernacle and temple were overlaid with gold (Ex 25:18; 1 Ki 6:22, 28).

GOLGOTHA See CALVARY.

GOLIATH (exile) A Philistine giant of the city of Gath. For forty days he defied the army of Israel (1 Sa 17). Estimating a cubit as eighteen inches he was over nine feet tall, and over ten feet if the cubit is reckoned as twenty-one inches. He was challenged by David, and in the valley of Terebinth he was slain by a stone from David's sling.

GOMER 1. The oldest son of Japheth (Ge 10:2–3). He was included by Ezekiel in the army of Gog (Eze 38:3, 6). He represents the people known as Cimmerians whose original home was north of the Black Sea and who later migrated to Asia Minor. 2. The daughter of Diblaim, and wife of Hosea (Ho 1:3).

GOMORRAH One of the five cities of the plain. With the exception of Zoar (formerly Bela) these cities were destroyed by fire from heaven (Ge 19:23–29). It was in Zoar that Lot, a resident of Gomorrah, took refuge and was spared.

GOSPEL (from god and spell, Anglo-Saxon, good message or news) This is applied to the four inspired histories of the life and teaching of Christ. They were not written until the latter half of the first century—Matthew and Mark prior to the destruction of Jerusalem, Luke about A.D. 64, and John towards the close of the century, or not earlier than about A.D. 90. Thus ten of Paul's Epistles were written before any of the Gospels, and John's Gospel about twenty-two years after the death of Paul. "As a matter of literary history," says Dr. William Smith, "nothing can be better established than the genuineness of the Gospels."

GRAVEN IMAGE An image made by a sharp instrument as distinguished from one made in a mould. Stone, wood, and metal were used (Is 30:22, 44:15, 17, 45:20). They were made by the Canaanites before the land was taken by the Israelites (De 7:5, 12:3) and in other countries (Je 50:38, 51:47). The sin of making them was constantly impressed upon the Jews (Ex 20:4; De 5:8, 27:15; Is 44:9; Je 51:17).

H

HAGAR Sarah's Egyptian bondwoman (Ge 16:1). She bore Abraham a son, Ishmael, after the patriarch decided to wait no longer for God's promise of an heir to be fulfilled through his 76-year old wife, Sarah. When Sarah bore Isaac, Ishmael mocked the boy with result that Hagar and Ishmael were expelled from Abraham's house into the wilderness. When Hagar's water supply was exhausted the Lord directed her to a well (Ge 21:19).

HAIR The Hebrews regarded long hair on the chin and head as a mark of manliness. The men wore it quite long but not to an extreme length (Nu 6:5; 2 Sa 14:26). It was also worn long by the Assyrians, while the Egyptians cut theirs short except for times of mourning. It was a pagan custom to cut off the hair about the temples but the Israelites were forbidden to do this (Le 19:27). Hebrew women wore their hair longer than the men. Both sexes used hair oil (Ps 23:5; Ma 6:17).

HAM The youngest son of Noah, born when Noah was five hundred years old (Ge 5:32, 6:10, 9:18). He and his two brothers survived the flood with Noah. After Ham saw his father naked, Noah cursed Ham's son, Canaan, to a life of continued servitude to his brothers (Ge 9:22–27). Ham was founder of one of the three great families that repeopled the earth after the flood (Ge 10:1, 6–20). **2.** A term for Egypt used only in Biblical poetry (Ps 78:51, 105:23, 27, 106:22). **3.** A place east of the Jordan where the Zuzim were defeated by Chedorlaomer (Ge 14:5). **4.** Some of the inhabitants of Gedor were men of Ham (1 Ch 4:40).

HAMAN Son of Hammedatha (Es 3:1). He was called an Agagite (Es 3:1, 9:24), based on his real or alleged descent from Agag whom Samuel cut to pieces (1 Sa 15:33). He was a high official in the court of King Ahasuerus. His intrigue against the Jews was exposed by Esther (Es 7–9).

HANNAH (grace) One of the two wives of Elkanah; the mother of Samuel. She was especially favored by her husband which aroused the hostility of the other wife who subjected her to annoyances. Hannah was childless, but vowed that if she became the mother of a son, she would dedicate him to the Lord's service. Samuel was born and Hannah kept her vow (1 Sa 1:1–28). Her triumphant song (1 Sa 2:1–10) may have been in the mind of Mary (Lu 1:26–55).

HARAN **1.** A city of Mesopotamia in which Abraham settled after leaving Ur. He remained there until after the death of his father, Terah, and then he started for Canaan. The city was a commercial center. Jacob lived in Haran for a time (Ge 28:10, 29:4). It was near this city that Crassus was defeated by the Parthians in 55 B.C. **2.** A son of Terah and brother of Abraham, he died in Ur. Lot was his son and Milcah and Iscah were his daughters (Ge 11:29). **3.** A son of Caleb and Ephah (1 Ch 2:46). **4.** A Gershonite Levite of the family of Shimei (1 Ch 23:9).

HARVEST In the southern portion of Palestine and in the plains the crops ripened about the middle of April but in the northern sections about the first week of May. Barley preceded wheat by about two weeks (Ru 2:23). In the Jordan valley, where the heat was more intense, barley was harvested in April (Jos 3:15; 1 Sa 12:17-18). Great rejoicings attended the harvesting (Is 9:3).

HARVEST, FEAST OF See WEEKS, FEAST OF.

HEART The word in the Scriptures has a wide signification. *First*, the physical heart, the center of bodily life (Ps 40:8, 10, 12), and the things that contribute to its health and strength (Ju 19:5; Ac 14:17). *Second*, the higher rational, spiritual activities. The set purpose to do a thing (Es 7:5; Ro 6:17); holding firmly and steadfastly to a purpose (1 Co 7:37); its rational activities in thought, perception, understanding (De 29:4; Pr 8:5, 14:10; Is 44:18), reflecting (Lu 2:19) and judging (Pr 16:9). The seat of the affections and emotions like joy (Is 65:14); fear (De 28:28; Ps 143:4); hatred (Le 19:17); love (1 Ti 1:5). *Third*, as expressive of moral characteristics and conditions. The hardening of the heart (Is 6:10, 63:17; Je 16:12; 2 Co 3:15); the keeping of the heart because it determines the issues of life (Pr 4:23), as true of thoughts, words and deeds (Ma 12:34; Mk 7:21); the seat of passions (Mk 4:15; Ro 1:24); for the moral government of life God's law is written in the heart (Is 51:7; Je 31:33; Ro 2:15; He 10:22). *Fourth*, the deeper spiritual life. The dwelling place of Christ (Ep 3:17) and of the Holy Spirit (2 Co 1:22); where the love of God is felt (Ro 5:5), and his peace is realized (Col 3:15); where we enjoy the deeper communion with God (Ep 5:19).

HEATHEN Worshipers of false gods, or those who do not worship the God of the Bible. The Greeks *Ethnos*, of which heathen is frequently the rendering, denotes a nation or people. Their hostility to the true religion brought them under divine judgment (Ps 79:1, 6, 10; Je 10:25; Eze 36:6–7, 15). The Jew under strict legal requirements did not eat food that came from the heathen, and did not sit at meat at a Gentile table (Ac 11:3; Gal 2:12).

HEAVEN, THE HEAVENS **1.** The region about the earth—the heavens and the earth (Ge 1:1), comprising the universe (Ge 14:19; Je 23:24). The mass beyond the visible firmament (Ge 1:7; Ps 108:4). To the Jews the highest, or seventh heaven, was God's dwelling place. Paul relates a personal experience in which he was carried into the third heaven, but whether he was bodily transported to it, or it was a vision, he did not know (2 Co 12:1–4). **2.** The place of God's presence from whence Christ came and to which he returned (Ps 80:14; Is 66:1; Ma 5:16, 45, 48; Jo 3:13; Ac 1:11). It is from here that he will come in his return to the earth (Ma 24:30; Ro 8:33–34; 1 Th 4:16; He 6:20). Heaven is the dwelling place of angels (Ma 28:2; Lu 22:43) and the future home of the redeemed (Ep 3:15; 1 Pe 1:4; Re 19:1–4).

HEBREW (pertaining to Eber) **1.** A designation first applied to Abraham, a descendant of Eber (Ge 14:13). It was applied by foreigners to the Israelites (Ge 39:14, 17, 41:12; Ex 1:16; 1 Sa 4:6, 9) and the Israelites used the word in regard to themselves (Ge 40:15; Ex 1:19). In the New Testament it is used to describe those whose speech was Aramaic to distinguish them from Greek-speaking Jews (Ac 6:1). Paul called himself a Hebrew of the Hebrews, indicating that his parents were of Hebrew stock (Ph 3:5). **2.** Hebrew was the language of the Israelites. It is a Semitic language consisting of twenty-two consonants and reads from right to left. The Old Testament, with the exception of a few portions written during the Exile and the Restoration, was written in Hebrew. To the time of the Captivity the language was quite pure, but following the Exile it was mixed with Aramaic until it ceased to be used. By the time of Christ the Aramaic prevailed and was called Hebrew (Jo 19:13, 17, 20; Ac 21:40, 22:2, 26:14).

HEIR Hebrew law relative to inheritance was simple. The property was divided between the sons of legitimate wife. The sons of a concubine did not inherit. Ishmael, the son of Hagar, the bondwoman, could not inherit because of Abraham's other son, Isaac, the son of Sarah, the free woman (Ge 21:10). The birthright falling to the eldest son secured for him a double portion of the property (De 21:15–17). When the children consisted wholly of daughters, they received the property (Nu 27:1–8) but they were required to marry in their tribal family (Nu 36:1–12). If a man died childless the brothers inherited and if he had no brothers, the property went to his father's brothers (Nu 27:9–11). In the case of a childless widow, the law required the nearest of kin on her husband's side to marry her, and if he refused, the next of kin was to marry her (Ru 3:12–13).

HELL A word meaning the place of the dead. It is a frequent translation of the Hebrew word *sheol* and the Greek words *hades* and *gehenna*. The early Hebrews regarded it merely as the place to which the dead go, but later the word comes to mean a place of punishment. **1.** *Sheol* in Hebrew meant the realm of the dead. But the Semitic conception of it was vague. They thought of it as beneath the earth (Eze 31:17; Am 9:2), entered by gates (Is 38:10). In Sheol the sinful and the righteous were respectively punished or rewarded. **2.** *Hades*, a Greek term used in the New Testament. According to a parable told by Jesus it was a place where good and evil people lived close together, but were separated by a chasm (Lu 16:26). Those who had led a good life on earth were comforted; those who had not were punished. **3.** *Gehenna*, the place of eternal punishment, the antithesis of heaven, to which the wicked were cast after the last judgment. It is depicted as a fiery furnace (Ma 13:42), and as a lake of fire (Re 19:20, 20:10, 14–15, 21:8).

HEROD The name of a number of Palestinian rulers. The most famous was Herod the Great, king of Judea (37–4 B.C.). He was jealous of his power and killed many, even his sons, because he feared they would take his throne. When he heard that the King of the Jews had been born, he ordered the death of all infants in the area of Bethlehem so that Jesus might be destroyed (Ma 2:16). He was succeeded by his three sons, Archelaus, Herod Antipas, and Philip. The grandson of Herod the Great was Herod Agrippa, who became king under Gaius, and who persecuted the Christians. Herod Agrippa II, called King Agrippa by Paul, was the last of the Herods. He ruled Chalcis for a time and later was given the tetrarchies of Philip and Lysanias.

HEZEKIAH **1.** King of Judah, son of Ahaz. Unlike his godless father, he was a man of outstanding piety in his service of Jehovah. He reorganized the temple service and celebrated the Passover to which he invited the tribes of Israel (2 Ch 29:1–30:13). He brought about a revival of religion and worked earnestly to drive out idolatry. He was greatly assisted by the prophet, Isaiah. **2.** A son of Neariah of Judah (1 Ch 3:23). **3.** Head of a family which returned from Exile (Ez 2:16; Ne 7:21). **4.** Ancestor of the prophet Zephaniah (Zep 1:1).

HIGH PLACE The Hebrew *bamah*, originally a height or elevation; specifically a place of worship (Nu 22:41). In the course of time the term was extended to include sanctuaries regardless of elevation—some were even in valleys. It was a center of worship often used by Israelites as well as by their heathen neighbors. It usually consisted of a small plot of comparatively level ground containing a rude altar and religious symbols, especially stone pillars and asherahs, or wooden poles. Before the building of Solomon's Temple, Israel often worshipped Jehovah in a high place (1 Sa 9:12–14, 19). But because of the heathenism pervading these centers, worship of Jehovah became increasingly corrupted. They were condemned by law (Nu 33:52; De 33:29) and by the prophets (Is 16:12; Je 7:31; Eze 6:13).

HIGH PRIEST See PRIEST.

HIRAM 1. A king of Tyre who greatly enlarged his city. When David captured Jerusalem, Hiram sent an embassy to him and later furnished the timber and workmen for David's house (2 Sa 5:11). He was also a friend of Solomon and contracted with him to furnish timber and workmen for the building of the Temple (1 Ki 5:1–12; 2 Ch 2:3–16). He assisted Solomon in securing precious metals from Ophir (1 Ki 9:26–28). Solomon offered him twenty towns in Galilee which he did not accept (1 Ki 9:10–12; 2 Ch 8:1–2). **2.** One whose mother was a widow of either the tribe of Naphtali or of Dan. His father was from Tyre (1 Ki 7:13–14). Hiram was a workman on Solomon's Temple (1 Ki 7:13–46; 2 Ch 2:13–14).

HITTITES In Ge 10:15 they are called the sons of Heth. In the time of Abraham they dwelt near Hebron (Ge 23:1–20) and it was from one of them that Abraham bought the cave of Machpelah. Esau married two Hittite women (Ge 26:34–35, 36:2). They were in the land when the spies were sent to Canaan by Moses (Nu 13:29). Ahimelech, a follower of David, was a Hittite (1 Sa 26:6), as was Uriah, whom David so greatly wronged (2 Sa 11:3, 17, 21).

HOLY Separated or set apart; sacred. Things which in themselves were ordinary, such as utensils, became sacred or holy when devoted to the service of the sanctuary. The same was true of those separated from the body of the people for the sacred office of the priesthood. Certain seasons and days were also holy (Ex 20:8, 31:10; Le 21:7; Ne 8:9). Holiness is ascribed to God, since he is apart from and above every being in his infinite perfections and attributes. (1 Sa 2:2; Is 6:3; Re 4:8).

HOLY PLACE, HOLY OF HOLIES
See TABERNACLE.

HOLY SPIRIT Frequently "the Spirit" or "the Spirit of the Lord" or "the Holy Spirit." Designated in O.T. only three times as "Holy Spirit" (Ps 51:11; Is 63:10–11), though his work is frequently mentioned. *Personality*. He is the third person of the Trinity, thus not simply a divine energy or influence proceeding from God. As a person, he possesses intelligence, self-consciousness and self-determination. His personality is explicity described (Ma 3:16–17; 28:19; Jo 14:16–17, 15:26). Personal pronouns used of him (Jo 16:13–14; Ac 13:2). His personal freedom (1 Co 2:10, 12:11). *Divinity*. When the personality of the Holy Spirit is admitted there is little disputation as to his divinity. He is distinctly addressed as God and designations are used that belong only to God (Ac 5:3–4; 2 Co 3:17–18; He 10:15). He has the divine attributes of eternity, knowledge, sovereignty (1 Co 2:11, 12:11; He 9:14). Operations ascribed to him are of a divine nature, as creation (Ge 1:2; Job 26:13) and regeneration (Jo 3:5–6, 8). The unpardonable sin is the sin against the Holy Spirit (Ma 12:31–32), and sin is not committed against an influence or an energy; it is committed against God alone. In his relation to Father and Son he is the same as they in divine substance, in power, and in glory. He proceeds from the Father and Son and in this relation is subordinate (not inferior) to them as they operate through him (Jo 15:26, 16:13; Ph 1:19). *O.T. Teaching*. Described as brooding over chaotic matter (Ge 1:2; Ps 139:7). Giver of life, physical, mental, moral (Ge 6:3; Job 32:8, 33:4, 34:14; Ps 104:30). Inspired the prophets (1 Sa 10:6; Hos 9:7; Mi 3:8; Ze 7:12). Prediction of effusion of the Spirit in Messianic times (Is 44:3; Eze 36:26; Joel 2:28; Ze 12:10). *Beginning of the Christian Age.* Conception of Jesus (Ma 1:18–20). Baptism of Jesus (Ma 3:16; Mk 1:10; Jo 1:32). Effusion of the Spirit at Pentecost (Ac 2:4).

HORN The Israelites had many uses for the horns of animals. They made them into trumpets (Jos 6:13), and they used them as containers for oil (1 Sa 16:1, 13). The horn was also a symbol of power (Ps 132:17; Je 48:25) and of the monarchy (Da 7:8, 11, 21; Ze 1:18–19). The corners of the altar for burnt offerings resembled horns (Ex 29:12; Le 4:7). When one's horn was exalted by God, it signified divine favor (1 Sa 2:10; Ps 89:24). The expression *to lift up one's horn* denoted arrogance and pride (Ps 75:4–5).

HOSEA (salvation) One of the minor prophets; son of Beeri, a native of the northern kingdom. His labors extended over a long period, probably to the overthrow of Israel in 722 B.C.

HOUSE It was not until the Israelites were dwellers in Egypt and in Palestine after taking the country that they lived in houses. The houses of the common people consisted ordinarily of one story and often of a single room. The materials were furnished by the locality. In Egypt mud or sunburnt brick were used. In Palestine brick, lime, and sandstone were used, while only the houses of the rich were made of hewn stone (1 Ki 7:9; Is 9:10). Houses of the more prosperous classes were built around a courtyard having a well (2 Sa 17:18). The second story contained the upper room or chamber (1 Ki 17:19; 2 Ki 4:10; Mk 14:15; Ac 1:13, 9:37). The roof, surrounded by a low wall, was flat for storing things (Jos 2:6), for social intercourse (1 Sa 9:25–26) and for religous purposes (2 Ki 23:12; Ac 10:9). The roof could be reached by an outside stairway (Ma 24:17).

HYACINTH, JACINTH A precious stone. It was one of the twelve stones in the high priest's breastplate (Ex 28:19) and garnishes one of the foundations of the New Jerusalem (Re 21:20).

I

IDOL The likeness of a god in gold, wood, silver, or stone which was an object of worship (Ex 20:4–5; Ju 17:3; Ps 115:4, 135:15; Is 44:13–17; Ro 1:23). When metal was melted and molded, it was called a molten image. An idol was called a graven image if it was carved from wood (Is 40:19–20, 44:9–20; Je 10:8).

IMMANUEL, EMMANUEL (God is with us). The symbolic name of the child whose birth Isaiah promised as a sign of deliverance and safety to King Ahaz (Is 7:14). The name is repeated in Is 8:8. This prophesy was made at a time of national crisis (735 B.C.) when the kingdom of Ahaz was threatened with defeat by the combined armies of Syria and Ephraim. In addition to its immediate significance as a sign to Ahaz, it has always been regarded as a forewarning of the Messiah. This prophecy was fulfilled in the birth of Christ (Ma 1:23).

IMMORTALITY The doctrine of continued existence after the death of the body. The question, "If a man die, shall he live again?" (Jo 14:14) was answered in the affirmative by the Hebrews who regarded man as a body inhabited by a soul (Ge 2:7). At death the body returns to the ground

(Ge 3:19; Ec 12:7), but the soul lives on. In the later books of the Old Testament there is a marked development in the idea of resurrection (Job 19:25–27; Ps 49:15; Da 12:2–3). One distinguishing difference between the Pharisees and Sadducees was that the former believed in a resurrection and immortality while the latter denied both (Lu 20:27–38). The New Testament teaches that the righteous will be rewarded and the wicked punished after death (Ma 13:37–43; Jo 6:47–58, 14:1–2; 1 Co 15:19–58; Ga 6:7–8; 1 Th 4:13–18; Re 14:13, 20:12–15).

INCARNATION (in flesh) This doctrine teaches that Christ, the Son of God, became man, having the body and nature of human beings, and that in one person were united two natures, divine and human. In his first Epistle, John refuted the false teaching that denied that Jesus came in the flesh.

INCENSE A fragrant substance burned in the religous services of the Israelites (Ex 25:6, 35:8, 28). Frankincense and other aromatic substances gave forth perfume when burned. The high priest burned incense each morning (Ex 30:1–9). The burning of incense is symbolic of the rising to heaven of the prayers of the saints (Re 8:3–4).

INN A place to pass the night. The characteristic hospitality of the people of ancient Palestine to travelers made the inn less necessary than it is in modern society (Ju 19:15–21; 2 Ki 4:8; Ac 28:7; He 13:2). The inns of the Old Testament were located near a well or stream. The traveler provided food for himself and his animals. In New Testament times inns in the modern sense were built.

INSPIRATION There are many reference in the Bible to the fact that its words were the inspiration of God, although they were spoken or written down by men (Je 14:1; 2 Ti 3:16; 2 Pe 1:20–21).

ISAAC (laughter) The son and heir of Abraham and Sarah who was born in Beersheba when his father was about one hundred years old and his mother about ninety (Ge 17:17, 21:2–3, 22:1–2). The parents were amazed to learn that Isaac would be born to them (Ge 18:9–15). Isaac had reached young manhood (Ge 22:6) when his father was commanded to offer him as a burnt offering. When the Lord was convinced that Abraham passed this test of faith, he spared Isaac's life (Ge 22:12). Unlike his father, Isaac was gentle and reflective. When forty years old he married Rebekah, sister of Laban (Ge 25:20, 26). They settled in Gerar because of famine (Ge 26:1, 6). Two sons were born to them, Esau and Jacob (Ge 27–28). Later Isaac moved to Hebron where he died at the age of one hundred and eighty years. There he was buried beside his parents and his wife in the cave of Machpelah (Ge 35:28, 49:30–31).

ISCARIOT (man of Kerioth) Judas, who betrayed his Lord, is thus designated (Ma 10:4; Lu 6:16). By this designation he was distinguished from Judas, another apostle (Lu 6:16; Ac 1:13, 16). It probably denotes that he was a native of Kerioth (Jos 15:25).

ISHMAEL (God hears) **1.** The son of Abraham by Hagar, Sarah's Egyptian maid. At Ishmael's birth Abraham was eighty-six years old (Ge 16:3, 15). Ishmael was about fourteen years of age when Isaac, the child of promise and heir to the covenant promises, was born (Ge 21:5). When Ishmael mocked Isaac, Ishmael and his mother were expelled from the home of Abraham, and in their distress in the wilderness were divinely provided for. Ishmael married an Egyptian (Ge 21:3–21) and became the ancestor of princes (Ge 17:20, 25:12–16). His daughter became the wife of Esau (Ge 28:9, 36:10). He died at the age of 137 (Ge 25:17). Paul uses the tension between the two sons and mothers as an allegory (Ga 4:22–31). **2.** Son of Azel, a descendant of Saul (1 Ch 8:38, 9:44). **3.** The father of Zebadiah, a leader of Judah in the time of Jehoshaphat (2 Ch 19:11). **4.** Son of Jehohanan; the captain of a company. He aided Jehoiada in the uprising against Athaliah and placed Joash on the throne of Judah (2 Ch 23:1–24:2). **5.** Son of Pashur who abandoned his foreign wife (Ez 10:22). **6.** Son of Nehaniah who played a leading role in the murder of Gedaliah (2 Ki 25:22–26; Je 40:7–41:15).

ISRAEL (having power with God) **1.** The name of Jacob. His name was changed the night he spent at Peniel on his way to Canaan from Mesopotamia. It marked a turning point in his life (Ge 32:22–30). **2.** The covenant people, descendants of Jacob. Dating from the change of his name, the people were called "the children of Israel" (Ge 32:32). The name was often used during the period in the wilderness (Ex 32:4; De 4:1, 27:9). While the name designated the Hebrew people as a whole, a separation began to exist between Judah and the other tribes prior to the actual disruption of the kingdom (1 Sa 11:8, 17:52, 18:16). **3.** The designation of the northern kingdom after the disruption of the united kingdom. Division took place when the already rebellious northern tribes were confronted with the fact that Rehoboam, Solomon's son and successor, would not reduce the taxes and other burdens imposed by Solomon (1 Ki 12:9–17). The new kingdom was not allowed to use the central sanctuary at Jerusalem. The northern kingdom set up its own religous centers which eventually became centers of idol worhsip, particularly of Baal. Idolatry was especially strong during the reign of Ahab because of the encouragement given it by Ahab's wife, Jezebel (1 Ki 16:30–33). Elijah labored in vain to end the idolatry. The kingdom of Israel fell apart and ended with the fall of

Samaria in 721 B.C.) at which time many of the people were carried away to Assyria (2 Ki 17:3–6).

ISSACHAR (he will bring reward) **1.** The ninth son of Jacob by his first wife, Leah (Ge 30:17–18, 35:23). He and his four sons went to Egypt with Jacob (Ge 46:13; Ex 1:3). **2.** Tribe of Issachar. It consisted of four tribal families, the descendants of the four sons (Nu 26:23–24). When the land was divided, the territory of Issachar was south of Zebulun and Naphtali; south of it lay Manesseh, and its eastern boundary was the Jordan. **3.** A son of Obed-edom, a Korhite Levite (1 Ch 26:5).

J

JABBOK (effusion) One of the principal eastern tributaries of the Jordan. It was the western boundary of the Ammonites (Nu 21:24; De 2:36–37; Jos 12:2–6).

JACINTH See HYACINTH.

JACOB The twin brother of Esau and the son of Isaac and Rebekah. Jacob was the favorite of his mother, Esau of his father. In his youth he tricked Esau into giving up his birthright and his father's blessing. Jacob then fled Esau's wrath to Haran where he lived in the home of Laban. He married Laban's daughters, Leah and Rachel. The latter, his favorite, gave birth to Joseph, his favored son. Later he returned, had a reconciliation with Esau, and settled in Canaan. On the return trip he changed his name to Israel. Joseph, who had been carried captive to Egypt, later brought his family to Egypt to escape a famine. Jacob died there but was buried in Canaan.

JAEL (wild goat) The wife of Heber the Kenite (Ju 4:17). When Sisera, Jabin's captain, was defeated by Barak, he (Sisera) fled to the tent of Heber. While he was asleep she drove a nail (wooden pin) into his head (Ju 4:11–22).

JAMES (a form of the name Jacob or Jacobus) **1.** James the son of Zebedee and brother of John (Ma 4:21, 17:1; Mk 3:17). We know nothing of his birthplace or early life. He and John were partners of Peter and Andrew in the fishing business (Lu 5:10). These men were the first four apostles called by Jesus (Ma 4:21; Mk 1:19). James' mother, Salome, was the sister of Mary, mother of Jesus. James is always mentioned in connection with John, and his name is written first, implying that he was older than John (Ma 10:2; Mk 5:37; Lu 5:10). James, John, and Peter were intimate with Jesus as seen in their association with him on various occasions—the raising of the daughter of Jairus (Mk 5:37; Lu 8:51), the transfiguration (Ma 17:1; Mk 9:2), and in Gethsemane (Mk 14:33). The two brothers had mistaken views of our Lord's kingdom and, desirous of having a high place in it, they joined in the request made by their mother to Jesus that they sit on either side of Jesus in his kingdom (Ma 20:20–23; Mk 10:35). James was the first of the apostles to die for his Lord, under the persecution of Herod (Ac 12:2). **2.** James the son of Alphaeus was one of the apostles (Ma 10:3; Mk 3:18; Lu 6:15; Ac 1:13). He was called James the Less, either on account of his stature or because he was younger than James son of Zebedee (Mk 16:1). Assuming that the James of Ma 27:56; Mk 15:40, 16:1; Lu 24:10 is this James, then his mother was Mary, wife of Cleophas (Jo 19:25). **3.** James, the Lord's brother. That James and his sisters were the children of Joseph and Mary the mother of Jesus is the most natural interpretation of Ma 13:55 and Mk 6:3. This James was not an apostle (Ma 10:2–4) and was not a believer in the Messiahship of Jesus (Jo 7:5) until after the resurrection (Ac 1:13–14). Then he headed the church in Jerusalem. He is believed to have authored the Epistle of James.

JAPHETH (let him enlarge) One of the three sons of Noah, born when Noah was about five hundred years old (Ge 5:32, 6:10, 10:21).

JASPER This precious stone is a variety of quartz of various colors (Ex 28:20; Eze 28:13; Re 4:3).

JEBUS A name for Jerusalem, in use when the city was in possession of the Jebusites (Jos 15:63; Ju 19:10; 1 Ch 11:4).

JEBUSITE A member of the mountain tribe which was encountered by the Israelites on their conquest of Canaan (Nu 13:29). After the Jebusite king was slain by Joshua, their territory was assigned to Benjamin (Jos 10:23–26, 18:28). The tribe was small and, as it was not exterminated by the Hebrews, the Jebusites lived on among their conquerors. King Adoni-zedek and Araunah are the only two Jebusites specifically named (Jos 10:1, 23; 2 Sa 24:21–25).

JEHOAHAZ **1.** Son of Jehu. He followed his father on the throne of Israel and reined seventeen years (2 Ki 10:35, 13:1). **2.** Son of Josiah; he followed his father on the throne of Judah. He reigned three months, was deposed by Pharaoh-necho and taken to Egypt (2 Ki 23:30–34; 2 Ch 36:1–4). He is called Shallum in Je 22:11. **3.** Another name of Ahaziah (2 Ch 21:17).

JEHOIACHIN (Jehovah establishes) The son of Jehoiakim. He followed his father on the throne of Judah and reigned only three months. The forces of Nebuchadnezzar of Babylon took Jerusalem, and Jehoiachin and many of the leading people of Jerusalem, among them Ezekiel, were carried to Babylon. When Evil-merodach came to the throne of Babylon, he soon released Jehoiachin from prison (2 Ki 25:27–30; Je 52:31–34). He is frequently called Jeconiah and Coniah.

JEHOIAKIM A son of Josiah, king of Jerusalem and Judea (2 Ki 23:34, 36). His orignal name was Eliakim. He was placed on the throne by Pharaoh-necho, who deposed his brother Jehoahaz and carried him to Egypt. He required the prophet, Jeremiah, to write his prophecies but after listening to a few of them, cut the roll and threw it in the fire (Je 36). In 606 B.C. Nebuchadnezzar came to Jerusalem, carried to Babylon the first deportation of captives, and made Jehoiakim a subject king (2 Ki 24:1; Je 46:2). He reigned eleven years and was succeeded by his son Jehoiachin (2 Ki 23:36, 24:6).

JEHORAM (exalted by Jehovah) **1.** Son and successor of Jehoshaphat of Judah (2 Ki 8:16). His wife was Athaliah, daughter of Ahab and Jezebel of Israel. **2.** Son of Ahab and king of Israel (2 Ki 3:1). **3.** A priest appointed by Jehoshaphat to teach the people (2 Ch 17:8).

JEHOSHAPHAT **1.** Son and successor of Asa and one of the better kings of Judah. Conjointly with Asa, then alone, he reigned 25 years (1 Ki 22:41–42; 2 Ch 17:1). He honored Jehovah, carried forward the reforms of Asa, and commissioned the Levites to instruct the people in the law (2 Ch 17:7–9). He also brought an end to the conflicts between Israel and Judah. However, he made an alliance with Ahab and fought with him against the Syrians at Ramoth-gilead. Ahab was slain but Jehoshaphat escaped (1 Ki 22:1–38; 2 Ch 18:1–34). After his death he was succeeded by his son, Jehoram (1 Ki 22:50). **2.** Son of Ahihud. He was recorder in the court of David and Solomon (2 Sa 8:16, 20:24; 1 Ki 4:3). **3.** A priest who blew the trumpet when the ark was brought to Jerusalem (1 Ch 15:24).

JEHOSHAPHAT, VALLEY OF The valley between Jerusalem and Mount of Olives, also called the valley of the Kidron and the valley of Decision. Here Jehoshaphat defeated the enemies of Israel (2 Ch 20:26).

JEHOVAH One of the names of God (Ex 17:15). The later Hebrews and translators of the Septuagint substituted the word Lord. What it denotes is essentially different from El-Shaddai and Elohim. The latter signifies God the mighty creator, sustainer, and moral governor of the universe. El-Shaddai signifies the covenant God of the patriarchs, their strength and hope, God almighty. Jehovah signifies the covenant-keeping God of grace who dwells with his people, guiding them, manifesting his grace (1 Ki 8:43; Ps 9:10, 91:14; Is 52:6; Je 16:21). See ELOHIM.

JEHOVAH-NISSI (Jehovah my banner) The name Moses gave the altar which he built at Rephidim (Ex 17:15–16).

JEHOVAH-SHALOM (Jehovah is peace). The name given by Gideon to an altar erected by him in Ophrah (Ju 6:23–24).

JEHU (Jehovah is He) **1.** Son of Hanani, a prophet. He denounced Baasha, king of Israel, for his idolatry (1 Ki 16:1–4, 7). He reproved Jehoshaphat, king of Judah, for his alliance with Ahab (2 Ch 19:2). He was the author of a book which recorded the acts of Jehoshaphat (2 Ch 20:34). **2.** A Benjamite who came to David at Ziklag (1 Ch 12:3). **3.** Son of Obed and father of Azariah of Judah (1 Ch 2:38). **4.** Son of Josibiah, a chief Simeonite in the time of Hezekiah. He was with those who captured the valley of Gedor (1 Ch 4:35–41). **5.** Son of Jehoshaphat and grandson of Nimshi (1 Ki 19:16; 2 Ki 9:2), the founder of the fifth dynasty of the kingdom of Israel. He was in the service of

Ahab (2 Ki 9:25). Elijah was divinely directed to anoint him king of Israel (1 Ki 19:16–17) which was done later by Elisha. He was commanded to destroy the house of Ahab. The king at that time was Jehoram, son of Ahab. He executed his commission with bloody zeal. Jezebel, wife of Ahab, was slain (2 Ki 9:1–37). His acts were needlessly brutal and Hosea, the prophet, condemned the spirit of them (Ho 1:4). He then destroyed the prophets of Baal in the temple of Baal (2 Ki 10:12–28). He reigned 28 years, and in fulfillment of God's promise, this was the longest of the nine dynasties of Israel.

JEPHTHAH   (he opens) A son of Gilead; he was expelled from his home by his brothers because of his illegitimate birth (Ju 11:1–2). He went to Tob where he became a famous hunter. At this time the Ammonites were holding the tribes east of the Jordan in subjection. Those who had driven Jephthah away now urged him to be their chief and deliver them from this oppression. A very religious man, Jephthah made a vow that if he were victorious he would sacrifice to God whatever came from his house first on his return. It was his daughter. Some believed that he did sacrifice her, for in Ju 11:39 it says that he "did with her according to his vow." He judged Israel six years (Ju 10:6–12:7; 1 Sa 12:11). He is one of the heroes of faith (He 11:32).

JEREMIAH   (Jehovah establishes) **1.** The great prophet who worked at the time of the fall of Judah. He was the son of Hilkiah (Je 1:1). It is believed that the family was descended from Abiathar who was expelled to Anathoth by King Solomon (1 Ki 2:26–27). Jeremiah began his work in the thirteenth year of the reign of King Josiah (627 B.C.), and continued through the declining years of the kingdom and for some time after its fall (586 B.C.). The last evidences of his work come from Egypt where he was taken with a group of fugitives. Throughout his life he protested against the evils of idolatry. **2.** A warrior of Benjamin who allied himself with David at Ziklag (1 Ch 12:4). **3.** The father of Hamutal, the wife of Josiah, king of Judah (2 Ki 23:31, 24:18; Je 52:1). He lived in Libnah. **4.** A head of a family of east Manasseh (1 Ch 5:24). **5.** Two Gadites who joined David at Ziklag (1 Ch 12:10, 13). **6.** A priest who signed the covenant with Nehemiah (Ne 10:2). **7.** A priest who came with Zerubbabel from Babylon (Ne 12:1). **8.** Son of Habazaniah (Je 35:3).

JERICHO (fragrant) A city in the valley of the Jordan near the Dead Sea, over 800 feet below the level of the Mediterranean (De 34:1, 3). It was called the city of palm trees (Ju 3:13). It is first mentioned when the Israelites reached Moab (Nu 22:1, 26:3). After the Israelites crossed the Jordan, it was the first place to fall in the conquest of the country. A curse was pronounced against anyone who should fortify the city (Jos 5:13–6:26).

JEROBOAM **1.** Son of Nebat, of the tribe of Ephraim, the founder of the northern kingdom of Israel. His father was an official under Solomon (1 Ki 11:26) and Jeroboam, because of his ability, was made overseer of a part of Solomon's building operations at Jerusalem (1 Ki 11:27–28). Jeroboam represented the ten tribes in demanding that the tax burdens be lightened. Rehoboam's foolish reply brought about the disruption and, with Jeroboam as their leader, ten tribes revolted. To keep the people from going to Jerusalem to worship, Jeroboam set up two centers of worship, at Dan in the north and Bethel in the south with a golden calf at each place, thereby violating the commandment that God must not be worshipped by means of images (1 Ki 12:26–30; 2 Ch 13:8). When the the priests and Levites in this territory returned to Judah (1 Ki 12:31; 2 Ch 11:13–15, 13:9), he instituted his own priestly system. Thus idolatry became firmly rooted in Israel and continued until the fall of the kingdom (1 Ki 15:26, 34, 22:52; 2 Ki 3:3, 13:2,

11). He made Shechem the capital and reigned twenty-two years (1 Ki 14:20). **2.** Jeroboam II, son and successor of Joash of the fifth dynasty of Israel, the dynasty of Jehu. From about the year 790 B.C., he reigned forty-one years, the longest reign of Israel. He was a man of unusual executive and administrative ability. He captured Damascus and Hamath and restored to Israel the territory from Hamath to the Dead Sea, successes that were predicted by Jonah (2 Ki 14:23–28). It was during his reign that the three prophets of Israel arose, Jonah, Amos, and Hosea.

JERUSALEM An ancient city, which was known as Salem in the time of Abraham (Ge 14:18; Ps 76:2), and later called Jebus at the time of its occupation by the Jebusites (Ju 19:10–11). In the time of Joshua the name Jerusalem began to be used and by the time it was captured by David, it was the common name for the city. Jerusalem is situated about fifteen miles from the Jordan River, in the Judean highlands at an elevation of about 2,500 feet. The ancient city captured by David from the Jebusites was built on the southern end of a steep hill overlooking the Kidron Valley to the east. See ZION. Solomon enlarged the city to include the area on the eastern hill lying north of the old city in which were located the Temple and the palaces. Jerusalem has an almost unbroken history of over four thousand years. It was mentioned in records of the conquering Pharaohs. There are still in existence letters written in the fourteenth century B.C. by its Hittite ruler. Its capture by David around 1000 B.C. laid the basis for its subsequent religious and political importance. After Solomon built the Temple, the city became the religious center of Israel. Present day Jerusalem consists of two parts, the old walled city approximately a mile square with its Armenian, Jewish, Moslem and Christian quarters, and the new modern city.

JESUS Jesus is an imitation of the Greek form of Jeshua. It means, Jehovah is salvation. **1.** A military leader of the Israelites (Ac 7:45; He 4:8); he is also called Joshua. **2.** An ancestor of the family of Christ; also called Jose (Lu 3:29). **3.** A Jewish Christian associated with Paul (Col 4:11). He was also called Justus. **4.** The name given the Messiah (Ma 1:21).

JESUS CHRIST

1. Name. The name Jesus, announced by the angel as that divinely selected for Mary's son (Ma 1:21; Lu 1:31–33), signifies *the Lord is salvation.* The word Christ (the anointed one) is essentially an official title borne by Jesus as the Messiah (Jo 1:41) and as the Son of the living God (Ma 16:16).

2. Date. Jesus was born in the year 4 (some say late 5) B.C. The Roman abbot who (prior to A.D. 550) devised the Christian calendar fixed the year 1, the year intended for Christ's birth, too late.

3. Political situation. The political situation in Palestine in the time of Jesus was complicated and seething with discontent. The country, since the Exile, had been successively under Persian, Greek, Egyptian, and Syrian domination. Foreign rule was followed by about a century of independence under the Maccabees which ended near the middle of the first century B.C. when the country was incorporated into the Roman Empire as part of the province of Syria. Jewish reaction to Roman rule ranged from mildly critical to hostile but was usually tempered with the spirit of opportunism.

4. Religious situation. The religious life of Judaism in Jesus' time was at low ebb. Formal religion was dominated by two powerful sects, the Pharisees and the Sadducees. The former were the more influential and they added much religious tradition and theological subtleties to the word of God. The latter, while rejecting the traditions of the Pharisees, were more interested in politics than religion. Sadducees controlled the Sanhedrin and limited the high priests to members of their own families. Both sects were denounced by John the Baptist and Jesus warned against them (Ma 3:7, 16:6; Lu 11:42–52). It was to the common people that the Gospel of Jesus was destined to appeal (Mk 12:37; Lu 19:47–48).

5. Early life. The events and circumstances connected with the birth of Jesus (Ma 1–2; Lu 1:26–35, 2:1–39) are well-known. The genealogy of the family is traced by Matthew to Abraham and by Luke to Adam. The political situation is reflected in episodes such as the flight into Egypt and the return to Nazareth (Ma 2:13–15, 19–23). Only his boyhood experience of visiting the Temple at the age of twelve has been recorded(Lu 2:41–52). Carpentry became his vocation (Mk 6:3).

6. His baptism. John the Baptist, probably in the summer of A.D. 26, began to proclaim the approach of the day of the Lord. John called upon individuals and the nation to repent and be baptized. Among the Galilaeans who came to the region of the lower Jordan to be baptized was Jesus. As an individual Jesus had no need of baptism, but by submitting to it he identified himself with men as their Redeemer. It was at his baptism that he heard the heavenly voice declaring him to be the beloved Son in whom God was well-pleased (Ma 3:1–17; Mk 1:10–11).

7. His temptation. After the baptism, Jesus was led by the Spirit into the wilderness to be tempted (Ma 4:1–11; Lu 4:1–13). The attractions of the world were presented to him in three successive visions or experiences, yet he did not yield (He 4:15, 7:26; 1 Pe 2:21–22).

8. Early Judean ministry. After certain rather informal opening events which included the calling of some disciples and the miracle at Cana (Jo 1:35–47, 2:1–11), Jesus began his work in Judea, making occasional visits to Galilee (Jo 4:3). Among the recorded events of this period were the cleansing of the Temple, the conversations with Nicodemus and with the woman at the well (Jo 2:13–17, 3:1–21, 4:3–26).

9. The early or main Galilaean ministry. Jesus' fame in Judea preceded him into Galilee (Jo 4:43–45). The synagogue at Nazareth rejected him at the outset (Lu 4:16–30) but the people generally gave him a tumultuous welcome. He declared that the Spirit of the Lord was upon him and that he was anointed to preach the gospel to the poor of this earth (Lu 4:18–21). He moved his residence from Nazareth to Capernaum; called additional disciples; and performed many miracles of healing (Ma 4:13, 18–22, 9:2–6, 9; Jo 4:46–54). A new phase of this early work in Galilee began with a visit to Jerusalem where he incurred the opposition of the Pharisees by healing a crippled man on the Sabbath (Jo 5:1–16). This antagonism was intensified by other deeds performed on the Sabbath (Ma 12:1–14). Jesus continually proclaimed himself to be the fulfillment of Old Testament prophecy (Ma 5:17–18; Lu 24:44–48). He chose twelve apostles and sent them forth (Ma 10; Lu 6:13–16). Jesus presented doctrine through his powerful Sermon on the Mount (Ma 5:1–7:29), various discourses, and parables (Ma 13:1–53).

10. The later Galilaean ministry in northern Galilee and beyond. In these northern districts (including the vicinity of Capernaum) and in Decapolis he exercised a ministry of some six months. His purpose was primarily that of preparing his disciples for his approaching death. He elicited from Peter his great confession, foretold his death and resurrection, and was manifested to certain disciples in the transfiguration (Ma 16:13–28, 17:1–13).

11. The Perean ministry. During this period it seems clear that he moved back and forth between Perea and Judea. The seventy disciples had been sent out to announce his coming (Lu 10:1–24). At this time he uttered many of his most famous parables (Lu 10:30–37, 15:1–16:12, 19–31).

He delivered discourses on prayer, on the coming of the kingdom, and against the Pharisees (Lu 11:1–13, 37–54, 17:20–37).

12. Passion Week. Six days before the Passover Jesus went to Bethany where Mary anointed his head with precious ointment (Jo 12:1–8). On the next day (the beginning of Passion Week) he made his triumphal entry into Jerusalem (Ma 21:1–11; Jo 12:12–19), then returned to Bethany, probably to the house of Mary, Martha, and Lazarus. On Monday he entered Jerusalem, cleansed the Temple and cursed a barren fig tree which by the following day had withered away (Mk 11:11–26). On Tuesday he was challenged by the religious leaders (Ma 21:23–27). They asked him three questions, to each of which Christ gave a silencing reply (Ma 22:15–46). He pronounced woes against the scribes and Pharisees but commended the poor widow who cast two mites into the Temple treasury (Ma 23; Mk 12:41–44). He delivered a lengthy discourse on the destruction of the Temple, the end of the world, and the last judgment (Ma 24:1–51, 25:31–46). It was on this day that Judas Iscariot conspired to betray him (Ma 26:3, 14–16). On Wednesday he remained in retirement at Bethany. On Thursday he instituted the Last Supper and delivered farewell discourses (Ma 26:17–30; Jo 13:1–17:26). On Friday he underwent the agony in Gethsemane, was betrayed by Judas, and was arrested (Lu 22:39–54; Jo 18:1–28). He was tried first before the Jewish authorities, then before Pilate. Pilate found no fault in him but, in order to pacify the Jews who clamored for his death, turned him over to them for execution (Jo 18:29–19:22).

13. His death, burial and resurrection. When death came to Jesus on the cross, the crowd had dispersed but a few faithful followers remained. Joseph of Arimathaea, a secret disciple of Jesus and member of the Sanhedrin who had not consented to his death, went boldly to Pilate and asked for the body, a request which was granted. Nicodemus, another secret disciple and a member of the Sanhedrin, also came, bringing myrrh and aloes. The little group bound the body with linen cloths and spices, then placed it in a new, rock-hewn tomb (Ma 27:26–66; Mk 15:16–47; Lu 23:32–56; Jo 19:23–42). Despite the huge stone which had been rolled against the door of the tomb and the watch which had been placed on guard, Jesus rose on the third day and later ascended into heaven (Ma 28; Mk 16; Lu 24; Jo 20). See CRUCIFIXION, RESURRECTION, ASCENSION.

JEZEBEL (chaste) **1.** A Phoenician princess, daughter of Ethbaal, king of Sidon (1 Ki 16:31). She married Ahab, king of Israel, and became the power behind the throne. She was a zealous worshipper of Baal and established that idolatry in Israel (1 Ki 16:32–33). She killed the prophets of Jehovah (1 Ki 18:4–13) and by false judicial action had Naboth slain (1 Ki 21:16–22). The divine judgment that she would be devoured by dogs was fulfilled when Jehu put to death the house of Ahab (2 Ki 9:7–10, 30–37). **2.** The name is applied to the lewd woman of Revelation (Re 2:20, 23).

JEZREEL (God sows) **1.** A town of the mountainous district of Judah (Jos 15:56). Probably from this place David secured his wife, Ahinoam (1 Sa 25:43, 27:3). **2.** A descendant of Hur of Judah (1 Ch 4:3). **3.** A son of Hosea, the prophet, so called because of the slaughter predicted by Ho 1:4–5. **4.** A town in the territory of Issachar near Mount Gilboa (Jos 19:17–18; 1 Ki 21:23). It was the camping place of the forces of the Israelites in Saul's last battle with the Philistines (1 Sa 29:1). It was here that Jezebel, wife of Ahab, was destroyed by the dogs (2 Ki 9:10, 30–35), and here the heads of the seventy sons of Ahab were stacked when the house of Ahab was destroyed (2 Ki 10:1–11). The name *valley of Jezreel* was afterwards extended to the whole plain of Esdraelon (Jos 17:16; Ju 6:33).

JOAB (Jehovah is father) **1.** Son of Zeruiah the half sister of David (2 Sa 8:16; 1 Ch 2:16). He was a companion of David in his exile and commander-in-chief of his troops throughout his reign. Joab was an efficient general who was also independent in his attitude toward King David. Occasionally he disobeyed David's instructions, as in the case of the slaying of Abner and Absalom (2 Sa 3:22–39, 18:10–15). **2.** Son of Seraiah of the line of Kenaz. He was the progenitor of the inhabitants of the valley of Charashim (1 Ch 4:13–14). **3.** The head of a family (Ez 2:6; Ne 7:11).

JOASH **1.** Father of Gideon of the family of Abiezer of the tribe of Manasseh (Ju 6:11, 15). He erected an altar to Baal which Gideon destroyed (Ju 6:11–32). **2.** A descendant of Shelah the son of Judah (1 Ch 4:22). **3.** Son of Shemaah, a Benjamite of Gibeah. He allied himself with David at Ziklag (1 Ch 12:3). **4.** Perhaps a son of Ahab, but the rendering is questionable. He was ordered by that king to imprison the prophet Micaiah because Micaiah had advised against the plan to seize Ramoth-gilead (1 Ki 22:26; 2 Ch 18:25). **5.** A Benjamite of the family of Becher (1 Ch 7:8). **6.** One whom David appointed to have charge of his oil supplies (1 Ch 27:28). **7.** Son of Ahaziah, king of Judah. His grandmother Athaliah usurped the throne and tried to exterminate the royal heirs of Judah. Joash escaped by being hidden in the Temple by his aunt, Jehosheba, the wife of the high priest Jehoiada. The latter headed a revolt with the result that Joash was crowned king, Athaliah was slain, and the house and images of Baal were destroyed (2 Ki 11:1–20; 2 Ch 23:10–21). **8.** Son of Jehoahaz, king of Israel. During the sixteen years of his reign he supported the worship of calves set up at Bethel and Dan. His son Jeroboam II succeeded him and had the most brilliant reign of the kingdom of Israel (2 Ki 14:8–16; 2 Ch 25:17–24).

JOB. **1.** Son of Issachar (Ge 46:13), called Jashub (Nu 26:24; 1 Ch 7:1). **2.** An Old Testament saint who lived in the land of Uz (Job 1:1). He is mentioned by Ezekiel (14:14, 16, 20).

JOEL (Jehovah is God) Son of Pethuel, a minor prophet of whose history nothing is known. Author of the book of Joel.

JOHN THE BAPTIST The son of Zacharias. His mother, Elisabeth, was a descendant of Aaron (Lu 1:5) and a cousin of the Virgin Mary. His parents lived in the hill country of Judea. When the angel informed Zacharias that a son was to be born to them, he instructed him to name him John (Lu 1:8–17). John's early years were spent in seclusion in the wilderness, and there, near the Jordan, he began his preaching as the forerunner of Jesus (Ma 3:1–3). His preaching was designed to prepare the hearts of the people for the acceptance of the Christ about to appear. Repenting of their sins, the people obeyed John's preaching and were baptized (Ma 3:5–6). They were not baptized in any name and this baptism should not be confused with Christian baptism instituted much later by our Lord (Ma 28:19; Ac 19:1–5). When our Lord at baptism began his public ministry, it was John who baptized him (Ma 3:13–17). John denounced Herod Antipas for taking as his wife Herodias, the wife of his half-brother Philip, and Herod imprisoned him. (Lu 3:19–20). Later at the solicitation of Herodias he was beheaded (Ma 14:1–12).

JOHN THE APOSTLE He and James were sons of Zebedee. It is believed their mother was Salome. They were fishermen on the Sea of Galilee in partnership with Peter and Andrew (Lu 5:10). He was called the disciple whom Jesus loved, and he wrote the gospel of John (Jo 21:20, 24). After Pentecost he remained in Jerusalem during the persecutions of the early Christians and was active with Peter in missionary labors (Ac 3:1, 15:6; Ga 2:9).

JONAH **1.** Father of Peter the apostle (Ma 16:17; Jo 1:42, 21:15). **2.** A prophet of Israel and the son of Amittai. He was a resident of Gath-hepher in Galilee. His prediction about the expansion of Israelite territory in 2 Ki 14:25 is all that is known of him outside of the Book of Jonah.

JONATHAN (God given) **1.** A Levite descendant of Gershom, the son of Moses. He and his sons served the tribe of Dan until the Exile (Ju 18:30). His grandfather's name, though rendered Manasseh in Ju 18:30, was Moses. **2.** Saul's eldest son. His father gave him the command of 1000 men at Geba at which point he defeated the Philistine garrison (1 Sa 13:3). This brought on war. Accompanied by his armor-bearer, Jonathan climbed the gorge of Michmash, surprised an outpost of the Philistines, slew twenty of them and created a panic. When Saul arrived with his army he found the Philistines confused and demoralized (1 Sa 14:1–14). The friendship of David and Jonathan began when David slew Goliath and it continued in the face of Saul's persecution of David (1 Sa 18:1–4). Jonathan acted on behalf of David (1 Sa 20:1–42), and they entered into "a covenant before the Lord" (1 Sa 23:15–18). We hear nothing more of Jonathan until Saul's last battle at Gilboa when Jonathan and his two brothers were slain by the Philistines and Saul took his own life (1 Sa 31:1, 11–13; 1 Ch 10:2, 8–12). David deeply lamented their deaths (2 Sa 1:17–27) and took care of Jonathan's crippled son, Mephibosheth (2 Sa 4:4). **3.** Son of Abiathar, the high priest. The latter was loyal to David at the time of Absalom's rebellion (2 Sa 15:27, 36). Jonathan sent David information of what was occurring in Jerusalem during Absalom's rebellion (2 Sa 15:36, 17:15–22). He brought the news to Adonijah that Solomon had been proclaimed king (1 Ki 1:41–49). **4.** Son of Shimeah and nephew of David. He slew a Philistine giant (2 Sa 21:21–22). **5.** Son of Shage and one of David's warriors (2 Sa 23:32; 1 Ch 11:34). **6.** A son of Jada, grandson of Jerahmeel of Judah (1 Ch 2:32–33). **7.** A Son of Kareah. He placed himself under the protection of Gedaliah whom Nebuchadnezzar appointed governor of Jerusalem (Je 40:8). **8.** A descendant of Adin (Ez 8:6). **9.** Son of Asahel. He opposed the separation of the people from their foreign wives (Ez 10:15). **10.** A scribe in whose house Jeremiah was imprisoned (Je 37:15, 20). **11.** Son of Joiada and a high priest, also called Johanan (Ne 12:11, 22). **12.** A priest in the days of the high priest Joiakim (Ne 12:14). **13.** Son of Shemaiah (Ne 12:35).

JOPPA The name is derived from the Greek word *beauty*. The city is ancient and it has long served as the seaport of Jerusalem. In antiquity it ranked with Zoan, Damscus and Hebron. It was assigned to Dan (Jos 19:46). To this point the trees of Lebanon were floated from Tyre on the Mediterranean Sea (2 Ch 2:16). It was here that Jonah took the ship for Tarshish (Jon 1:3). Peter lived for a time in this city and it was here that he saw a vision (Ac 10:5–16).

JORDAN (the descender) The famous river of Palestine. It rises in the lower slopes of Mount Hermon and runs almost directly south. At Lake Huleh it is only a few feet above sea level. From this marshy region it continues to the Sea of Galilee where it is almost 700 feet below the level of the Mediterranean. Ninety miles farther south, where it empties into the Dead Sea, the Jordan reaches a depth of 1,292 feet below sea level. In its course the river receives two tributaries from the east, the Yarmuk and the Jabbok. The Jordan's tributaries from the west are unimportant. The river is small in normal times but becomes a torrent in the rainy season (Jos 3:15). It is not navigable though small craft have been known to descend it. At several points between the Sea of Galilee and the Dead Sea the river can be forded.

JOSEPH (may he add) **1.** The eleventh son of Jacob. His mother, Rachel, was Jacob's favorite wife, and he was Jacob's favorite son. Out of jealousy his brothers caused him to be sold as a slave and carried into Egypt (Ge 30:22–24, 37:2–36). Because he was able to interpret Pharaoh's dream, he was placed in a high position in Egypt and made responsible for preparing the country against the famine. Later, after he met his brothers, he brought his family to Egypt so that they could weather the famine. In his high position Joseph was able to preserve many Israelites from the famine (Ge 39:1–48:22). He lived in Egypt until his death at the age of one hundred and ten (Ge 50:26). **2.** Father of Igal, the spy from the tribe of Issachar (Nu 13:7). **3.** A son of Asaph (1 Ch 25:2, 9). **4.** An ancestor of Christ (Lu 3:30). **5.** A son of Bani. He put away his foreign wife in the time of Ezra (Ez 10:42). **6.** A priest, head of the family of Shebaniah. **7.** The father of Semei who lived after the Exile; an ancestor of Jesus (Lu 3:26). **8.** Son of Mattathias, ancestor of Jesus (Lu 3:24–25). **9.** The husband of Mary, the mother of Jesus (Ma 1:16; Lu 3:23). When Augustus issued his decree that all should be enrolled, or taxed, Joseph and Mary went to Bethlehem. At that time Jesus was born (Mi 5:2; Lu 2:4, 16). After the death of Herod, they returned to Nazareth from Egypt (Ma 2:22–23). He was a carpenter (Ma 13:55), as was his foster-son Jesus (Mk 6:3). At the beginning of our Lord's work Joseph was evidently alive (Ma 13:55) but probably died prior to the crucifixion since when Jesus was on the cross he committed his mother to the care of John (Jo 19:26–27). **10.** Joseph of Arimathaea. He was a member of the Sanhedrin and, like Nicodemus, was a secret disciple of Jesus. He took a positive stand regarding his Lord by going boldly to Pilate and asking for the body of Jesus, and this being granted, had the body placed in a new tomb which belonged to him (Ma 27:58–60; Mk 15:43–46). **11.** A Christian called Barsabas, i.e., son of Sabbas. He was of the company of Jesus during his labors (Ac 1:21, 23). **12.** The personal name of Barnabas; called Joses in the Authorized Version (Ac 4:36).

JOSHUA 1. The son of Nun. His name was changed by Moses from Oshea to Joshua (Nu 13:8, 16). He was the commander of the Israelites in their first battle and defeated the Amalekites at Rephidim (Ex 17:8–16). He was with Moses on Sinai (Ex 24:13, 32:17). He was the representative of Ephraim when the twelve spies were sent to Canaan and he and Caleb strove to persuade the people to go and occupy the land (Nu 13:8, 14:6–9). The Lord rewarded their loyalty, allowing them to settle in the land. At the end of the wandering, by divine direction, Moses placed Joshua before the high priest and publicly ordained him as his successor (Nu 27:18–23; De 1:38, 31:14, 23). His leadership of Israel is recorded in the book that bears his name. **2.** A native of Beth-shemesh. He owned the field through which was driven the cart that carried the ark from the land of the Philistines (1 Sa 6:14). **3.** The governor of Jerusalem at the time King Josiah was engaged in his reform work (2 Ki 23:8). **4.** The high priest during Zerubbabel's governorship of Judah. In Ezra and Nehemiah he is called Jeshua (Ez 3:2, 8–9; Ne 12:1, 7, 10, 26; Hag 1:1, 12, 14, 2:2–4; Ze 3:1–9).

JOSIAH (Jehovah heals) **1.** Son of Amon, king of Judah, whom he succeeded as king in about 639 B.C. at the age of eight. In his youth he was doubtless under the influence of Hilkiah, the high priest. In the twelfth year of his reign he instituted a reform program (2 Ki 22:1–2; 2 Ch 34:1–7, 33). Josiah was killed at Megiddo in a battle with the Egyptians (2 Ki 23:29–30). **2.** A son of Zephaniah (Ze 6:10).

JUBAL (stream) The son of Lamech. He was the inventor of musical instruments (Ge 4:21).

JUBILEE (ram's horn, trumpet) The Jubilee or Jubile occurred every fiftieth year and was ushered in on the Day of Atonement by the blowing of trumpets. It was observed by the liberating of all Hebrew slaves, by restoring all alienated land to its orignal owners, and by allowing the land to lie fallow (Le 25:8–17).

JUDAEA, JUDEA Its northern boundary extended from Joppa on the Mediterranean to a point on the Jordan about ten miles north of the Dead Sea. Its southern boundary extended from about seven miles southwest of Gaza to the southern portion of the Dead Sea.

JUDAH 1. The fourth son of Jacob. His mother was Leah, Jacob's first wife. His two sons by his Canaanite wife, Er and Onan, were slain for their sinfulness by divine judgment (Ge 38:1–10). The mother of his two sons Pharez and Zarah was Tamar, the widow of Er (Ge 38:11–30, 46:12; Nu 26:19). Through Pharez Judah became the ancestor of David (Ru 4:18–22) and of Jesus in the Davidic line (Ma 1:3–16). In Jacob's dying prophetical vision Judah was the "Shiloh Prophecy" (Ge 49:10). 2. Tribe of Judah. It consisted of five tribal families (Nu 26:19–21; 1 Ch 2:3–6). In the early period of the wandering Nahashon, son of Amminadab, was the prince of the tribe (Nu 1:7, 2:3, 7:12–17, 10:14). The tribe occupied the large part of southern Palestine. Its western boundary was the Mediterranean and its eastern the Dead Sea. From north to south the length of its territory was about fifty miles. The division of the kingdom occurred in 931 B.C. Ten of the tribes revolted under Jeroboam and formed the kingdom of Israel which existed from 931 to 722 B.C., while Judah continued until 586 B.C. 3. A Levite (Ez 3:9). 4. A Levite who returned with Zerubbabel

(Ne 12:8). **5.** A Levite who renounced his foreign wife (Ez 10:23). **6.** Son of Hassenuah, a Benjamite (Ne 11:9). **7.** One who officiated when the wall of Nehemiah was dedicated (Ne 12:34).

JUDAS The Greek form of the Hebrew Judah. **1.** Judas son of Jacob (Ma 1:2–3). **2.** An ancestor of Jesus who lived prior to the Exile (Lu 3:30). **3.** Judas of Galilee. In the days of the enrollment he instigated a revolt and was slain, and his followers were scattered (Ac 5:37). He gave rise to the party known as zealots who had much to do with the starting of the war that resulted in the destruction of Jerusalem in A.D. 70. **4.** Judas Iscariot. His father was Simon Iscariot. His surname distinguished him from another apostle named Judas (Lu 6:16; Jo 14:22). He seemed to follow Jesus to gain a position of power and wealth in an earthly kingdom. He had charge of the funds of the band, and John declared that he was a thief (Jo 12:6). He bargained with the chief priests to betray Jesus, the compensation being a little less than what was ordinarily paid for a slave. At the Last Supper he was declared by our Lord to be the traitor and that night earned his fee in the garden of Gethsemane (Ma 26:47–50). When he awoke to the enormity of his guilt, he confessed to the chief priests the sinfulness of his act and returned the money. His last act was to hang himself (Ma 27:3–5; Ac 1:18). **5.** An apostle, distinguished from Judas Iscariot (Jo 14:22). He was called Thaddaeus (Ma 10:3; Mk 3:18), as well as Lebbaeus. **6.** One of the four brothers of Jesus (Ma 13:55; Mk 6:3), probably Jude the author of the Epistle of Jude. **7.** A man of Damascus with whom Paul remained following his conversion (Ac 9:11). **8.** Judas surnamed Barsabas. A prominent man in the Church of Jerusalem (Ac 15:22, 27, 32).

JUDE An English form of Judas. He was the author of the Epistle of Jude and was a brother of James.

JUDGE A civil magistrate invested with authority to hear and decide disputes. Moses originally acted as the only judge in Israel (Ex 18:13–26). When the monarchy was established, the king became the supreme judge in civil affairs (2 Sa 15:2; 1 Ki 3:9, 28, 7:7). Six thousand officers and judges were appointed by David (1 Ch 23:4, 26:29).

JUSTIFICATION This doctrine sets forth the judicial act of God, by which sinners, meeting the divine terms, are released from condemnation and restored to divine favor. Justification denotes the change effected in man's relation to God, while regeneration signifies the change wrought in man himself by the Holy Spirit. Justification is also to be distinguished from adoption, the latter not a judicial act but the act of God as Father in which the sinner by grace is restored to God in a filial relationship (Ro 5:1–2, 8:29; 2 Co 5:17, 21; Ga 4:6; Ep 2:5).

JUSTUS (just) **1.** The surname of Joseph, also called Barsabas, one of two persons considered by the apostles to fill the place of Judas Iscariot (Ac 1:23). **2.** A disciple at Corinth with whom Paul lodged and in whose house Paul preached (Ac 18:7). **3.** A Jewish Christian, also called Jesus (Col 4:11).

K

KADESH (holy place) An ancient town with a water supply located in the wilderness of Paran or the wilderness of Zin (Nu 13:3, 26, 20:1, 27:14). It was situated on the southern border of Judah about eleven days journey north of Sinai. Abraham was here for a time (Ge 20:1). Twice the Israelites camped here. From this point Moses sent ambassadors to the king of Edom requesting permission to pass through his land (Nu 20:14, 16, 22; Ju 11:16–17).

KIDRON (dark, gloomy) A ravine between Jerusalem and Mount of Olives beginning a short distance northeast of the city. Passing beyond the city to the south, it follows a twisting course to the Dead Sea. During the hot season there is no water in it. It is crossed in going from Jerusalem to Bethany and Jericho (2 Sa 15:23). At the south of the city the valley was used for burying purposes (2 Ki 23:6).

KING The head of a kingdom, such as Pharaoh (Ge 12:15), Nebuchadnezzar and others, who exercised the chief rulership over a state. But one might be king of one city only (Ge 14:2, 20:2), as in the case of thirty-one kings conquered by Joshua within Palestine (Jos 12:7–24). In the time of the judges the nations about Palestine were ruled by kings. The Israelites then demanded that a monarchy be established. This, however, did not abolish the theocracy. The king was required to be the vicegerent of Jehovah who was the divine sovereign of Israel. The king came to the throne appointed by one higher in authority (1 Sa 16:1, 13; 2 Ki 24:17), by the people (1 Sa 18:8; 2 Sa 5:1–3; 2 Ki 23:30), by inheritance (1 Ki 9:36), or by usurpation (1 Ki 15:27–28). It is one of the titles of God (Ps 10:16), the King of kings (1 Ti 6:15). In Rev 19:16, Christ is called the King of kings.

KINGDOM The universe is the kingdom of God over which he exercises rulership (Ps 22:28, 145:13; Ma 6:13). In Daniel's man-image, God will set up an everlasting kingdom (2:44). The kingdom of grace distinct from the kingdom of the world is called the kingdom of heaven and the kingdom of God. Its character is illustrated by our Lord's parables (Ma 13:24, 31, 33, 44; Mk 4:11, 26; Lu 14:15). It is a spiritual kingdom (Jo 18:33–37), the spiritual commonwealth of God's children, and exists in the visible Church

of Christ, but is far more comprehensive than the Church.
There will be a kingdom of Christ on earth following more
specifically the Church age, a kingdom age of the glorious
and universal reign of Christ the King as predicted by the
prophets (Is 2:4, 9:7, 11:9; Da 2:44; Hab 2:14; Re 20:4, 6).

KISS In patriarchal times and later a kiss was a common
form of salutation. Children were kissed by their parents
(Ge 31:28, 55, 48:10), children kissed parents (Ge 27:26–27;
1 Ki 19:20), and brothers kissed each other (Ge 45:15;
Ex 4:27), as did other relatives (Ge 29:11; Ru 1:9). Between
friends of the same sex it was the usual form of greeting
(1 Sa 20:41; Ac 20:37). When a guest entered a house, it was
customary for the one receiving to kiss the guest (Lu 7:45).
Paul's injunction was to greet each other with a holy kiss
(Ro 16:16; 2 Co 13:12). There was nothing unusual about
Judas kissing Jesus (Ps 2:12; Ma 26:49; Lu 22:47–48).

KORAH (ice) **1.** A son of Esau. His mother was
Aholibamah (Ge 36:5, 14). **2.** A son of Eliphaz and grandson
of Esau (Ge 36:16). **3.** Son of Hebron of the family of Caleb
(1 Ch 2:43). **4.** A Levite of the family of Kohath, of the house
of Izhar (Nu 16:1). He, with Abiram, Dathan, and On,
conspired against Moses and Aaron. Moses ordered the
people to leave the locality where Korah, Dathan, and
Abiram had their tents. At that spot the earth opened and
swallowed the conspirators (Nu 16, 26:10). Fire then
destroyed those that offered incense (Nu 16:35)

L

LABAN (white) **1.** Son of Bethuel and grandson of
Nahor, the brother of Abraham. He lived at Haran in
Padan-aram (Ge 24:10, 15, 28:5, 10). Jacob stayed with him

after fleeing the fury of Esau. Eventually Jacob married his two daughters, Leah and Rachel (Ge 29:16–28). On Mount Gilead Laban made a covenant with Jacob (Ge 29–31). **2.** A place in the Sinaitic peninsula (De 1:1), thought by some to be the same as Libnah (Nu 33:20).

LACHISH (impenetrable) A city in the lowland of Judah (Jos 15:33, 39) which was taken by Joshua (Jos 10:3–35, 12:11). Amaziah, king of Judah, fled to this city and was slain by conspirators (2 Ki 14:19; 2 Ch 25:27). It was besieged by Sennacherib (2 Ki 18:14, 17) and by Nebuchadnezzar (Je 34:7). Excavations have restored the wall of the ancient city and other things that belong to the period of Judah from Rehoboam to Manasseh.

LAMB Lambs were used both as food and as sacrificial offerings. A lamb was used as a burnt offering every morning and evening. Four were used on the Sabbath (Nu 28:3– 4, 9). Seven lambs were offered on the first of the month and lambs were also sacrificed on the day of atonement and on all high feast days (Nu 28:11, 19, 27, 29:2, 8, 13). Sacrificial lambs were generally male, and without blemish (Ex 12:5). The gentleness of the lamb has caused it to become a symbol of innocence and uncomplaining submissiveness. Christ is called the Lamb of God (Jo 1:29, 36), also the Lamb (Re 5:6).

LANGUAGE See TONGUE.

LAODICEA A city of Asia Minor, the chief city of the province of Phrygia, and a commercial and medical center. Paul's disciple Epaphras labored here (Col 4:12–13), and Paul sent greetings to this city (Col 2:1). It was one of the seven churches of Asia (Re 1:11, 3:14–22).

LAVER A basin for washing. The laver of the tabernacle was made of brass (copper) and placed between the tabernacle and altar. It rested upon a metal base, the base and laver being made of the mirrors of the women (Ex 38:8). Before serving at the altar or in the sanctuary, the priests washed their hands and feet in the laver which symbolized holiness in God's service (Ex 30:17–21; Le 8:11). The Solomonite Temple had ten lavers (1 Ki 7:23–26, 38), sometimes called the brazen sea.

LAW   The word *law* is the usual rendering of the Hebrew word *Torah*, meaning instruction. The expression "the law" sometimes denotes the whole of the Old Testament (Jo 12:34, 15:25) but much more frequently is applied to the Pentateuch (Jos 1:8; Ne 8:2–3, 14; Ma 5:17; Lu 16:16; Jo 1:17). The law of Moses, which God revealed through Moses (Ex 20:19–22; Ma 15:4), consists of the legislation of Exodus, Leviticus, Numbers, and Deuteronomy. The Ten Commandments, or the Moral Law, constitute the fundamental law of the theocracy.

LAYING ON OF HANDS   The Levites were dedicated to divine service by having the Israelites lay their hands upon them (Nu 8:5–20). Timothy was dedicated to the ministry when the hands of the presbytery were laid upon his head (1 Ti 4:14). The hands of the offerer were laid on the sacrificial animal (Le 1:4, 16:21).

LAZARUS   (a form of Eleazar) **1.** A resident of Bethany, the brother of Mary and Martha, and the subject of Jesus' greatest miracle, the raising of a dead person (Jo 11:1–46). **2.** The beggar in the parable of the rich man and Lazarus (Lu 16:19–31).

LEAH   Laban's daughter who, by the trickery of Laban, became Jacob's first wife (Ge 29:16–35, 30:17–21).

LEAVEN Unfermented dough used to make bread rise (Ex 13:7). It had an unpleasant odor and taste. The Jews were required to keep it from all offerings made by fire (Le 2:11). It was allowed only when the offering was to be eaten (Le 7:13). It was prohibited because it was emblematic of corruption. During the Passover week no leaven was allowed in the house. It was used figuratively to denote false doctrine (Ma 16:11) and impure conduct (1 Co 5:6–8).

LEPER One afflicted with leprosy. He was not permitted to mingle with others, and in approaching people he had to cry out the warning, "Unclean! Unclean!" (Le 13:45; Lu 17:12–13). The symptoms of this fearful disease are set forth in Le 13:1–46. Beginning with a scab or bright spot, it would spread. The leper was required to come frequently to the priest, who judged the stage of the disease. If it showed signs of departing, much cleansing and sacrificing was required (Le 14:1–32).

LEVI (adhesion) **1.** Third son of Jacob by Leah (Ge 29:34) Together with his brother, Simeon, he massacred Shechem and the males of his city to punish Shechem for violating Levi's sister, Dinah (Ge 34:25–31). Jacob on his deathbed referred to this act of cruelty and predicted that Levi's descendants would be scattered (Ge 34:26, 49:7). He had three sons, Gershon or Gershom, Kohath, and Merari (Ge 46:11) and he died in Egypt at the age of 137 (Ex 6:16). See LEVITES. **2.** Son of Melchi and an ancestor of Christ (Lu 3:24). **3.** Son of Simeon and an ancestor of Christ (Lu 3:29). **4.** The first name of the apostle, Matthew (Mk 2:14–17; Lu 5:27–32).

LEVITES Descendants of Levi, son of Jacob. His sons, Gershon or Gershom, Kohath, and Merari, were each the founder of a tribal family (Ge 46:11; Ex 6:16; Nu 3:17; 1 Ch 6:16–48). Moses and Aaron were of the line of Kohath of the house of Amram. The Levites at Sinai remained true to Jehovah, and were chosen for religious services (Ex 32:26–29; Nu 3:9, 11–13, 40–41, 8:16–18). There were 22,000 Levites. The 22,000 were substituted for the first-born of the other tribes, and the remaining 273 firstborn of the other tribes were redeemed by paying five shekels apiece (Nu 3:45–51). At thirty years of age the Levites were eligible for full service in connection with the sanctuary (Nu 4:3; 1 Ch 23:3–5), although they began to assist in these duties at the age of twenty (1 Ch 23:24, 28–31). Luke notes that Jesus entered upon his public ministry, inaugurated by baptism, at thirty years of age (Lu 3:23).

LEVIATHAN A great sea-animal whose physical parts are described in the speech of Jehovah in Job 41:1–29.

LION An animal common in Palestine in Bible times and in the Scriptures it is mentioned relative to its strength (2 Sa 1:23; Pr 30:30); teeth (Joel 1:6); courage (Pr 28:1); preying nature (1 Sa 17:34; Is 11:6–7); hiding (Je 4:7, 25:38); Christ as Lion of tribe of Judah (Re 5:5).

LOCUST A winged, creeping thing two or more inches long. It has six legs, the hindmost pair used for springing. It can cut leaves and grass with its sharp jaws. It was ceremonially clean. The fleshy portion was roasted and eaten. It was the food of many people. It was eaten by John the Baptist (Ma 3:4) and is still used as food.

LORD The name of God (Ge 3:4–22). It is the Old Testament translation of the sacred name, YHWH, to which the vowels of the name Adonai had been added. See JEHOVAH. It was also a common noun meaning one in authority (Ge 45:8; Jos 13:3). Christ was also called Lord (Lu 2:11; Jo 13:1; Ac 2:36).

LORD'S DAY The expression occurs but once in the New Testament (Re 1:10) when John says "I was in the Spirit on the Lord's day." It was selected because Christ rose from the tomb on the first day of the week (Ma 28:1, 9; Lu 24:1, 15), then reappeared on the same day the following week (Jo 20:1, 26).

LORD'S PRAYER See PRAYER.

LORD'S SUPPER The designation by Paul (1 Co 11:20) of the memorial instituted by Christ on the evening before the crucifixion. Paul's statement is the earliest record of the facts. The Epistle to the Corinthians was written about A.D. 57 or 58, about 27 years after the institution of the ordinance and prior to the writing of the Gospels. Paul states he received from the Lord the particulars of this institution (1 Co 11:20–29), by which he meant that it was directly revealed to him by Christ.

LOT (a covering) A Shemite, who was the son of Haran and nephew of Abraham. He came with Abraham from Mesopotamia to Canaan (Ge 11:31, 12:5), went with him to Egypt, and returned to Canaan (Ge 13:1). When trouble arose over the matter of pasturage, they decided to separate. Lot was given the first selection as to district. He chose the Jordan valley and made Sodom his residence. When Chedorlaomer invaded the land, Lot was taken prisoner, but was rescued by Abraham and his allies (Ge 13:1–14:16). When divine judgment fell upon Sodom, Lot and his family were saved from destruction (Ge 19:1–29).

LUCIFER (brightness) The "bright star," the morning star—Venus. Isaiah likens the glory of the king of Babylon to Lucifer which he calls the "son of the morning" (14:12). In Re 22:16 Jesus describes himself as the bright, the morning star. From the time of Jerome the name has been applied to Satan, hurled from heaven. It "arises probably from the fact that the Babylonian empire is in Scripture represented as the type of tyrannical and self-idolizing power, and especially connected with the empire of the evil one in the Apocalypse." It is also held that this application of the word is "based on the erroneous supposition that Lu 10:18 is an explanation of Is 14:12."

LUKE A friend and traveling companion of Paul (Col 4:14; 2 Ti 4:11; Phile 24) who wrote the third Gospel and Acts. A Greek, he was a doctor and is often referred to as the beloved physician. He joined Paul at Troas (Ac 16:10) and remained with him about nine years.

LYDIA **1.** A woman of Thyatira. This city was noted for the art of dyeing and when Lydia settled in Philippi, she sold the dyed garments of Thyatira. She was a pious woman, a true worshipper of God. When she heard Paul she accepted the Gospel. It was in Philippi that the Gospel was first preached in Europe. Paula and Silas lodged in Lydia's home (Ac 16:14–15, 40). **2.** A region on the western coast of Asia Minor. Its capital was Sardis, and Philadelphia and Thyatira were within its bounds (Re 1:11).

M

MACEDONIA A country north of Greece. It rose to world-wide power under Philip of Macedon (359–336 B.C.) and his celebrated son Alexander the Great (336–323 B.C.). Paul received a vision to preach in Macedonia (Ac 16:9, 20:1).

MAGDALENE See MARY.

MAGI The plural of *magus*, designating a priestly caste, a tribe of Media, who retained an important place after the Medes were conquered by the Persians. They worshipped fire, the earth, water, air. They wore white robes. They claimed to have the gift of prophecy and the power to mediate between God and man. Bar-jesus was a Magus (Ac 13:6), as was Simon of Samaria (Ac 8:9). The wise men who came from the East to worship the newly born Jesus were of this religous caste (Ma 2:1).

MAGOG Descendants of Japheth (Ge 10:2). They are usually identified with the barbaric Scythians north of the Crimea. It was prophesied that their ruler, Gog, would fail in his expedition against the restored Israel (Ge 10:2–3; Eze 38:2, 39:6). The figurative expression *Gog and Magog* refers to nations which Satan will muster for the final attack on the Messiah (Re 20:8).

MANASSEH (forgetting) **1.** The elder son of Joseph and brother of Ephraim (Ge 41:50–51, 48:8–21). **2.** Tribe of Manasseh. It comprised seven tribal families, one springing from Manasseh's son Machir, and the others from his grandson Gilead (Nu 26:28–34; Jos 17:1–2). One half of the tribe was settled east of the Jordan and the other half west of the Jordan in the central section, north of Ephraim (Nu 32:33, 42; De 3:13–15; Jos 13:29–33). **3.** It is generally thought that the rendering of Manasseh in Ju 18:30 should be Moses. **4.** Son of Hezekiah. He followed his father to the throne at the age of twelve and had the longest reign of Judah (2 Ki 21:1–16). He was carried to Babylon by the Assyrian king (2 Ch 33:11). **5.** Son of Pahath-moab (Ez 10:30). **6.** A son of Hashum (Ez 10:33).

MANNA The food of the Israelites during the time of their wandering, sent to them first in the wilderness of Sin (Ex 16:1–4, 12; Ps 78:24, 105:40). It was white like coriander seed, having the taste of honey (Ex 16:31; Nu 11:8). For each member of the family a little over five pints were gathered each day and on the sixth day double that quantity, as it was not sent on the Sabbath (Ex 16:22–30). All the circumstances of the sending of the manna, together with the facts relative to manna-bearing plants of that peninsula, clearly declare that the Israelites were miraculously fed.

MARRIAGE A divine institution, the condition of the propagation of the race (Ge 1:27–28). When monogamous, it is the union of one man and one woman (Ge 2:18–24; Ma 19:5; 1 Co 6:16). It is a permanent relation dissolved only by death (Ro 7:2–3), adultery (Ma 19:3–9), or desertion (1 Co 7:15). Polygamy was discouraged by Moses (Le 18:18; De 17:17), and he restricted divorce (De 22:19, 29, 24:1). Polygamy was practiced by Gideon, Elkanah, Saul, David, Solomon, Rehoboam and others (Ju 8:30; 1 Sa 1:2; 2 Sa 5:13, 12:8; 1 Ki 11:3). Contrasted with the destructive conditions of polygamy are the pleasing pictures of the felicity of the monogamous state (Ps 128:3; Pr 5:18, 31:10–29; Ec 9:9). On the wedding day the bride was dressed in white robes (Re 19:8), adorned with jewels (Is 61:10; Re 21:2) and covered with a veil (Ge 24:65). The bridegroom, in company with friends and attended by musicians, went to the home of the bride (Ju 14:11; Is 61:10; Ma 9:15). If it was at night torches were carried (Ma 25:7). The whole party with the bride returned to the home of the bridegroom where there were music and dancing (Son 3:6–11). The marriage relation is used figuratively to express the spiritual relation between Jehovah and his people (Is 62:4–5; Ho 2:19; Ma 9:15; Jo 3:29; 2 Co 11:2; Re 19:7, 21:2, 9, 22:17).

MARTHA (mistress) Sister of Mary and Lazarus of Bethany (Jo 11:1–2). Jesus was a frequent guest at their home. Martha once complained to Jesus that Mary should do more housework but Jesus defended Mary's interest in things of a spiritual nature (Lu 10:38–42).

MARY The name of six women mentioned in the New Testament. **1.** The Virgin Mary, mother of Jesus. She was the daughter of Heli (Eli) of the lineage of David, but of the line of Nathan, the royal rights of the Solomonic line being transferred through the daughter of Jeconiah and in this manner transferred from Mary to Jesus. She lived in Nazareth and was betrothed to Joseph, a carpenter, a descendant of David (Lu 1:26–27). She was informed by the angel, Gabriel, that she would be the mother of the promised Messiah (Lu 1:32–3, 35). At the home of Elisabeth her kinswoman, she spoke her hymn of praise, "The Magnificat" (Lu 1:46–55). The angel explained to Joseph that Mary's pregnancy was in fulfillment of Isaiah's prophecy (Ma 1:18–25). The "brothers of the Lord" were doubtless the children of Mary and Joseph. There were also sisters (Mk 6:3), making Mary the mother of a large family. When on the cross, Jesus commended her to the care of John (Jo 19:25–27). **2.** Mary the wife of Clopas or Cleophas (Jo 19:25). They were the parents of James the Less, an apostle of Joses (Ma 27:56; Mk 15:40; Lu 24:10). It is the view of some that this Mary was the sister of the Virgin, but it is unlikely that two sisters would have the same name. This Mary followed the body of Jesus to the tomb (Ma 27:61) and was there on the third day with spices (Ma 28:1; Mk 15:47, 16:1; Lu 24:10). **3.** Mary Magdalene. A resident, doubtless, of Magdala, on the southwestern coast of the Sea of Galilee (Ma 27:56, 61, 28:1; Mk 15:40, 47; Lu 8:2, 24:10; Jo 19:25, 20:11–18). She was afflicted with seven demons which Jesus expelled (Mk 16:9; Lu 8:2). The old view that she was a woman of bad character is wholly groundless. It is based on the fact that the first mention of her follows the account of the sinful woman who anointed the feet of Jesus (Lu 7:36–50) which is far from proving that the same person is referred to. She was a devoted follower of her Lord (Lu 8:1–3) and was at the cross (Ma 27:56; Mk 15:40; Jo 19:25) and at the sepulchre on the third day (Mk 16:1). Mark states that Jesus, after his resurrection, appeared first to her (Mk 16:9). **4.** Mary of Bethany, sister of Martha and Lazarus (Jo 11:1, 12:1). She was a woman of deep spiritual appreciations (Lu 10:38–42). **5.** Mary the mother of Mark. She was a Christian woman, and it was at her house that the disciples met for prayer at the time of the imprisonment of Peter by Herod Agrippa I (Ac 12:12). It is believed that the early Christians of Jerusalem made her house one of their meeting places. **6.** A Christian woman at Rome who was, according to Paul in Ro 16:6, an active Christian worker.

MATTHEW (gift of Jehovah) A publican or tax gatherer who, before he was called by Jesus to discipleship, was called Levi, the son of Alphaeus. (Ma 9:9; Lu 5:27).

MATTHIAS A follower of Christ closely associated with the apostles. While the apostles were waiting for the advent of the Holy Spirit, the question arose regarding the filling of the place of Judas. Lots were cast and the lot fell to Matthias (Ac 1:21–26).

MEAL OFFERING See OFFERINGS.

MEGIDDO (place of troops) This town was in the territory of Issachar but was assigned to Manasseh. The Canaanites were allowed to remain (Jos 17:11; Ju 1:27). It was in the nearby plain that Josiah lost his life in his conflict with Pharaoh-necho (2 Ki 23:29; 2 Ch 35:22, 25; Ze 12:11).

MELCHIZEDEK (king of righteousness) The king-priest of Salem, which was probably Jerusalem (Ge 14:18). He is described as being without parents. But this may mean that his genealogy was not recorded (He 7:1–3). When he met

Abraham, he refreshed him with bread and wine, received tithes from him, and blessed him (Ge 14:17–20). The endless priesthood of the Messiah, the Lord Jesus Christ, is declared to be after the order of Melchizedek in the Old Testament (Ps 110:4; He 7:15–17).

MEPHIBOSHETH (destroyer of shame) **1.** Son of King Saul and Rizpah. He was slain by the Gibeonites during the harvest (2 Sa 21:8–9). **2.** Son of Jonathan. When Saul was defeated at Gilboa and Jonathan fell in battle, Mephibosheth's nurse fled with the child who was five years old. She let him fall and he was crippled in both feet (2 Sa 4:4). He is called Merib-baal in 1 Ch 8:34, 9:40.

MERCY SEAT The lid of the ark of the covenant, made of pure gold. Upon it were the two cherubim facing each other with their outstretched wings extending over the mercy seat. Between the cherubim the glory of God was exhibited (Ex 25:17–22, 30:6; Nu 7:89). The mercy seat signified atonement (Ex 26:34; He 9:5).

MERODACH The god Marduk, the patron deity of Babylon (Je 50:2); also known as Bel.

MESHACH The name given one of the companions of Daniel (Da 1:7, 2:49, 3:13–30).

MESOPOTAMIA (a land between rivers). The Greek name for the country located between the Euphrates and Tigris rivers (Ge 24:7–10).

MESSIAH (anointed one) The anticipated king and deliverer of the O.T.; Jesus fulfilled the promise with his coming. The term was originally applied to one anointed with holy oil, as high priest or king. Isaiah foretold the coming of a child, Immanuel, whose name would be the

Lord's pledge of salvation for his people (Is 7:14–17). The Messiah was next identified with a descendant of David and his reign was declared to be everlasting (Is 9:6–7). Micah predicted that he would be born in Bethlehem (Mi 5:2). Many of the Psalms (as Ps 2) are Messianic. Jesus acknowledged himself to be the Christ or Messiah (Mk 14:61–62).

METHUSELAH The son of Enoch of the line of Seth and an ancestor of Jesus (Ge 5:21–27). The oldest man in the Scriptures, he lived to be 969 years old.

MICAH **1.** A Morasthite who was one of the minor prophets. A contemporary of Isaiah, he prohesied during the reigns of Jotham, Ahaz, and Hezekiah (Mi 1:1, 3:1–4, 11). **2.** A Levite, a Kohathite of the house of Uzziel (1 Ch 23:20, 24:24–25). **3.** An Ephraimite who stole his mother's money but returned it. Part of it then was used to make an image. Micah appointed a Levite, Jonathan, to act as his personal priest (Ju 17:13). **4.** A Reubenite who lived before the Exile (1 Ch 5:5). **5.** Son of Merib-baal (1 Ch 8:34–35, 9:40–41). **6.** Father of Abdon, prior to the reign of Josiah (2 Ch 34:20); called Michaiah in 2 Ki 22:12. **7.** A descendant of Asaph (1 Ch 9:15).

MIRACLE A sign, a special manifestation of God. They set forth God's character, and are used to accredit his messengers. Used only on specific and necessary occasions, for instance during such periods as the time of Moses and Joshua, of the divided kingdom, and of the Exile. Our Lord referred to his miracles in support of his divine claims, consequently more belong to this period than to all the others combined. The miracles of the Bible cannot be explained away. To accept the Scriptures, Christ, and his claims is to accept the miraculous.

MIRIAM (rebellion) **1.** Sister of Aaron and Moses (Ex 15:20; Nu 26:59) When the Israelites passed through the Red Sea, she took a timbrel and sang a song of triumph (Ex 15:20–21). In a spirit of jealousy, she and Aaron spoke against Moses because of his marriage to a Cushite woman. Miriam was smitten with leprosy. Moses interceded for her and she was healed (Nu 12:1–16; De 24:9). She was buried in Kadesh (Nu 20:1). **2.** A man or woman named in the genealogy of Judah (1 Ch 4:17).

MOAB, MOABITES **1.** Son of Lot by his elder daughter (Ge 19:37). **2.** Descendants of Lot's son. They were closely related to the Ammonites who were the descendants of Lot's son, Ammon (Ge 19:37–38). By the time of the Exodus they had become numerus and were in possession of the district from the plain of Heshbon to the wadi Kurahi, east of the Jordan. Moses was forbidden to attack them because the Lord gave the land to the children of Lot (De 2:9). It was on the plain of Moab the Israelties had their last encampment (Nu 22:1). Eglon, king of Moab, invaded Palestine and oppressed the people until they were delivered by Ehud (Ju 3:12–30; 1 Sa 12:9). Ruth the Moabitess married Boaz of Bethlehem and became an ancestress of Jesus.

MOLECH An Ammonite deity (1 Ki 11:7) who was also called Milcom (1 Ki 11:5, 33) and Malcam (Je 49:1–3; Zep 1:5).

MOLTEN SEA, BRAZEN SEA A great basin made of brass which stood in the court of Solomon's Temple (1 Ch 18:8). It was decorated with flower-like ornaments. It was placed on the backs of twelve bronze oxen, had an estimated capacity of 16,000 gallons, and served the priests as a place for washing (1 Ki 7:23–26, 39; 2 Ch 4:2–6).

MONEY As early as 650 B.C. money made of an alloy of gold with silver was made in Lydia. In the other regions of Asia Minor and Egypt money was used in bars and other forms, the value being determined by weight (Ge 23:16, 43:21). Shekel denoted weight. The right to coin money for his nation was granted Simon Maccabaeus in 140 B.C.

MONEY CHANGER One who exchanged foreign for native money or who changed money into different denominations. Jesus rebuked them and cast them from the Temple (Ma 21:12–13; Mk 11:15–17; Lu 19:45–46; Jo 2:13–16).

MOON One of the celestial bodies. It was worshipped as a god by many ancient people including the Egyptians, Assyrians, and Babylonians. Some Hebrews worshipped the moon (Je 19:13; Zep 1:5) despite the fact that it was forbidden (De 17:3–5). The most famous temple to the moon god was in the city of Ur of the Chaldees. The moon served as a measure for marking off months and in regulating feasts (Ge 1:14; Ps 104:19).

MORDECAI (little man) **1.** The son of Jair, a descendant of Kish, a Benjamite (Es 2:5). His people were carried to Babylonia in the second stage of the captivity. He was a close relative of Esther whom he reared as his foster-daughter (Es 2:7). **2.** A Jew who returned to Jerusalem (Ez 2:2; Ne 7:7).

MOSES (drawn out) This great leader and lawgiver of the covenant people was a Levite of the family of Kohath, of the house of Amram (Ex 6:18, 20). He was the brother of Aaron, the head of the priestly family, and also the brother of Miriam. It was probably she who watched over the infant Moses on the Nile. The first mention of him is in connection with the incident in the bulrushes of the Nile when as a baby he was found by Pharaoh's daughter (Ex 2:10). At the age of 40 he killed an Egyptian and as a result fled to the region of Horeb. There he lived with Jethro, priest of Midian, and later married his daughter, Zipporah, who bore him two sons (Ex 2:11–22, 18:1–4; Ac 7:23–29). After forty years, the Lord bid him to liberate his people from Egypt (Ex 3:1–10; Ac 7:30–36). He obeyed, and through the plagues of Egypt, the difficulties of the Exodus, and forty years of wandering, to his death and burial on the mountains of Moab (De 34:1–7), his influence continually increased.

MOUNTAIN The two highest mountains in or near Palestine are Hermon and Lebanon (De 3:8, 25). Mountain is used figuratively denoting things of a difficult or dangerous nature (Je 13:16), perpetuity and stability (Is 54:10; Hab 3:6), obstacles (Ze 4:7; Ma 21:21).

MOURNING The Oriental expressed his grief in a very noticeable manner, by tearing his garments (2 Sa 13:31; Joel 2:13), putting on sackcloth, and sprinkling dust or ashes on his head (2 Sa 15:32; Joel 1:8), by removing from his person anything of an ornamental nature (2 Sa 14:2, 19:24; Ma 6:16–18). Professional mourners, mainly women, were sometimes employed (Je 9:17–18; Ma 9:23; Ac 9:39). There was an extended period of mourning. They mourned for Aaron and Moses thirty days (Nu 20:29; De 34:8) and for Saul seven days (1 Sa 31:13).

MURDER After the flood a law was announced that "Whoso sheddeth man's blood, by man shall his blood be shed" (Ge 9:6). The murderer could be put to death by the avenger of blood (Nu 35:19) unless he reached a city of refuge.

MYRRH An aromatic gum resin of brownish color obtained from certain trees of Arabia and East Africa. It was used to perfume beds and clothing (Ps 45:8; Pr 7:17; Son 3:6). The anointing oil of the priests contained myrrh (Ex 30:23). Mixed with wine it was offered to Jesus when he was on the cross (Mk 15:23) and later was used to anoint his body (Jo 19:39).

MYSTERY The use of the word in the New Testament denotes the secret or hidden purpose of God in the salvation of Christ to be fully revealed in due time (Ro 16:25; 1 Co 2:7; Ep 1:9, 3:9; Col 1:26). The "mysteries of the kingdom of heaven" (Ma 13:11; Mk 4:11; Lu 8:10) are God's secret purposes relative to his kingdom. They are no longer secret to him who by the Spirit of God has become a citizen of the kingdom of grace.

N

NAAMAN (pleasantness) **1.** Son of Bela (Nu 26:40). **2.** A Syrian, commander of the army of Ben-hadad, king of Damascus (2 Ki 5:1–19). **3.** A son of Benjamin (Ge 46:21).

NABAL (foolish) A resident of Maon. He had large flocks of sheep and goats. David had protected his property and that of others from thieves. When David was persecuted by Saul, he sent ten of his band to Nabal asking for help. Nabal refused (1 Sa 25:1–42).

NABOTH A man of Jezreel, owner of a vineyard that Ahab, king of Israel, wanted to buy. Jezebel, wife of Ahab, had Naboth and his sons put to death (2 Ki 9:26) and Ahab seized the vineyard. The judgment of God was pronounced against them (1 Ki 21:1–24, 22:34–38; 2 Ki 9:30–37).

NAHUM (compassionate) One of the minor prophets, called the Elkoshite (Na 1:1).

NAOMI (pleasant) The wife of Elimelech and mother of Mahlon and Chilion (Ru 1–4).

NAPHTALI (my wrestling) **1.** Son of Jacob by Bilhah, Rachel's maid. Rachel wrestled in prayer for a son, hence the name (Ge 30:8). **2.** The tribe descended from the four sons of Naphtali (Ge 46:24; Nu 26:48–49).

NATHAN (he has given) **1.** Son of Attai of the house of Jerahmeel, family of Hezron of Judah (1 Ch 2:36). **2.** A son of David born in Jerusalem (2 Sa 5:14). He was the father of Azariah and Zabud (1 Ki 4:5) and an ancestor of the family of Jesus (Lu 3:31). **3.** An eminent prophet in the reign of David and Solomon. He was divinely used to tell David that not he but his son would build the Temple (2 Sa 7:1–17; 1 Ch 17:1–15) and to rebuke him for his sin with Bathsheba (2 Sa 12:1–15). **4.** Father of Igal, a warrior of David (2 Sa 23:36). He lived in Zobah in Syria. **5.** One sent by Ezra at the river Ahava to secure Levites for the sanctuary in Jerusalem (Ez 8:16). **6.** A son of Bani; he renounced his foreign wife (Ez 10:39).

NATHANAEL (given of God) One of the apostles who was probably the same as Bartholomew (Jo 1:45–51).

NAZARENE A native or inhabitant of Nazareth (Ma 2:23, 26:71; Mk 16:6). Jesus was so designated. The town and its people were held in low esteem (Jo 1:46).

NAZARETH (perhaps germ, offshoot) A town on an elevation in Galilee, not mentioned in the Old Testament. It is north of the plain of Esdraelon, about twenty miles southwest of Capernaum. The fountain of the Virgin supplies the town with water. It was the home of Joseph and Mary, and of Jesus until he entered upon his public ministry at the age of thirty (Ma 2:23; Lu 2:39, 4:16).

NAZARITE (separated) The word is derived from the verb that denotes to separate and signifies that a person, male or female, is especialy consecrated to God. The Nazarite took a vow by which his life, for a certain time, would be devoted to the Lord. The law forbid the Nazarite to drink fermented juice or cut his hair. He was to devote his body to God and keep himself ceremonially clean (Nu 6:1–21; De 15:19). When the time specified by his vow had expired, he presented himself to the priest. Offerings were made, his hair was shaved off and burned, and he was permitted to drink wine (Nu 6:1–21).

NEBUCHADNEZZAR Son of Nabopolassar and most famous of the Babylonian kings. In 625 B.C., his father founded the New Babylonian Empire which became one of the first of the world empires. In the battle of Carchemish the forces of Nabopolassar were under the command of his son by whom the Egyptians were defeated. This was in 605 B.C. (2 Ki 24:7; Je 46:2). In that year, upon the death of his father, Nebuchadnezzar ascended the throne. In Biblical history he is linked with three great prophets, Jeremiah, Ezekiel, Daniel. In 606 B.C., in the reign of Jehoiakim, he invaded Palestine, placed it under tribute (2 Ki 24:1), and carried away some of the people, one of whom was Daniel. In 597 B.C., he returned and carried to Babylon the king, Jehoiachin, and many of the people, one of them Ezekiel. He placed Zedekiah on the throne (2 Ch 36:6–10).

NEHEMIAH (Jehovah consoles) **1.** One who returned with Zerubabel from Babylon (Ez 2:2; Ne 7:7). **2.** Son of Azbuk. He ruled part of the district of Bethzur and labored on the wall under Nehemiah (Ne 3:16). **3.** Son of Hachaliah

(Ne 1:1), a Jewish statesman, patriot, and reformer of the period of the Exile. While at the Persian capital, Nehemiah requested permission of Artaxerxes, the king, to go to Jerusalem, because of reports reaching him concerning the poor state of affairs there. The permission was granted. His first task was to rebuild the wall of the city. This was completed in two months by the inhabitants (Ne 2:10–6:15). He then turned his attention to religious reform. He had the book of the law read publicly, the Feast of the Tabernacles observed, the new walls dedicated, and a covenant to observe all obligations signed (Ne 8–10).

NEPHILIM See GIANT.

NEW BIRTH See REGENERATION.

NEW MOON See MOON.

NEW TESTAMENT The book that is the foundation of the Christian religion. Together with the Old Testament it comprises the Bible. It is the new covenant (2 Co 3:14) of which Christ is the Mediator (He 9:15).

NICODEMUS (victorious) Nothing is known of his family. He was a Pharisee and member of the Sanhedrin. Jesus, by his works, satisfied him as to his divine character. Our Lord told him of the nature, necessity, and agency of the new birth which comes by faith in Christ and regeneration by the Spririt (Jo 3:1–21; 7:50–52).

NICOLAITANS It is probable that this sect or party followed the teachings of one called Nicolaus. They taught that it was the right and liberty of Christians to eat meat offered to idols and to indulge in other forms of heathenism (Re 2:6, 14–15). This was contrary to and in defiance of the action of the Council at Jerusalem in A.D. 50 (Ac 15:29).

NICOPOLIS (city of victory) There were several cities having this name but the one where Paul expected to spend the winter and where he wrote the Epistle to Titus was most likely the Nicopolis of Epirus, about four miles from Actium (Tit 3:12).

NILE The one great river of Egypt (Is 23:3). The land promised to Abraham for his posterity was from the river of Egypt to the river Euphrates (Ge 15:18). In connection with sojourn of the Israelites in Egypt, the Nile is frequently mentioned. Its waters were turned to blood by the Lord when the Pharaoh refused to allow Moses to lead the Israelites out of Egypt (Ex 7:20).

NIMROD The son of Cush (Ge 10:8–10; Mi 5:6) and a mighty hunter. He was the founder of the Assyrian empire and several Babylonian cities.

NINEVEH The capital of the Assyrian empire (Ge 10:11–12; Jon 1:2, 3:3). It stood on the eastern bank of the Tigris.

NOAH (rest) **1.** Son of Lamech in the line of Seth; an ancestor of Jesus (Ge 5:28–29). He was divinely instructed to build an ark on which he, his family, and two of each kind of animal were to survive the flood planned by the Lord to rid the world of wickedness (Ge 6:14–8:19). After the flood he became the originator of vine culture and the discoverer of the art of wine making (Ge 9:20–27). **2.** A daughter of Zelophehad of the tribe of Manasseh (Nu 26:33).

NUMBER That the Hebrews used letters for figures is quite evident from Maccabaean coins after the Exile and there is no evidence that they used figures before that time. The letters of the alphabet were employed for coinage purposes, aleph, the first letter of the alphabet, being used for one, beth the second letter for two, and so on. Seven was a sacred number (Ge 2:2, 4:24, 21:28). See SABBATH. Ten was a complete number–ten commandments (Ex 20:3–17, 34:28). Forty as a round number was much in use (Ex 24:18; 1 Ki 19:8; Jon 3:4; Ma 4:2).

O

OATH An oath was taken declaring a statement to be true, or to assure the keeping of a promise (Ge 21:23, 31:53; Ga 1:20; He 6:16). When God made his promise, he confirmed it by an oath (He 6:13–20). When an oath was taken, the hand was lifted upward, calling upon God to witness (Ge 14:22; Re 10:5). At times the hand was placed under the thigh of the person to whom the promise was made, probably indicating that the oath would be kept by his descendants (Ge 24:2, 47:29). Walking between the parts of a slain animal signified that the fate of the animal was to fall upon the one who broke the covenant (Ge 15:8–18). Swearing by a false god was prohibited (Jos 23:7). Jesus and James warned against frivolous oaths (Ma 5:34–37; Ja 5:12).

OFFERINGS There were offerings to God prior to the time of Moses and the Mosaic system (Ge 4:3, 8:20, 31:54, 35:14). After the law was given through Moses, the priests offered several kinds of sacrifices on altars, first in the Tabernacle, or tent of meeting, and later in Solomon's temple. The burnt offering was the sacrifice of a herd animal or a bird, brought by the Israelites as a dedication to God. The meal offering (A.V. meat) was flour, oil, frankincense, and/or salt, with no yeast, offered to express thankfulness. The peace offering was an animal sacrificed to signify fellowship with God. The sin offering, an animal, and the trespass offering, a bird, were to atone for sin committed by the offerer. All the animals had to be without blemish or defect (Le 1:3, 10, 3:1). Part of the offerings were burnt, and part went to provide the priests and Levites with food. Christ's death on the cross fulfilled and ended the sacrificial system, which could never really take away sins (He 9:22–28, 10:1–22).

OINTMENT A preparation, usually perfumed oil, used chiefly for anointing. It was used on the skin and hair (Es 2:12), as a cosmetic (Ru 3:3; Ec 9:8), and in connection with burial (Mk 14:3, 8; Lu 23:56; Jo 12:3, 7). On several occasions Jesus was anointed with ointment (Ma 26:6–13; Lu 7:36–50). The fragrant oil of the holy ointment used in the tabernacle was prepared by special formula (Ex 30:25–28, 34–36). See PERFUME.

OLD TESTAMENT It consists of 39 of the 66 books of the Bible, and is divided into four sections: The Pentateuch, first five books; twelve historical books, from Joshua to Esther; five poetical books, from Job to Song of Solomon; seventeen prophetical books, from Isaiah to Malachi. It was originally written in Hebrew except for a few portions which are in Aramaic (Ez 4:7–6:18, 7:12–26; Da 2:4–7:28).

OLIVES, MOUNT OF, OLIVET A place where olive trees grew. This hill, which consists of four peaks, is separated from Jerusalem by the Kidron valley and to its summit from Jerusalem was a Sabbath-day's journey (Ac 1:12). In the prophetical vision of Zechariah Jesus will stand upon this mount when he returns to the earth (Ze 14:4) as he often went to this mount during his labors (Lu 21:37, 22:39; Jo 8:1). On the western slope is the garden of Gethsemane. See GETHSEMANE.

OMEGA The last letter of the Greek alphabet. It is used figuratively (Re 1:8, 11, 21:6, 22:13).

OMRI **1.** A son of Becher of Benjamin (1 Ch 7:8). **2.** A descendant of Judah of the family of Perez (1 Ch 9:4). **3.** Son of Michael and prince of Issachar in the reign of David (1 Ch 27:18). **4.** The sixth king of Israel and the founder of the fourth dynasty (1 Ki 16:15–20).

ONESIMUS (profitable) A slave of the Christian, Philemon of Colossae, who ran away fom his master to Rome. There he met Paul who converted him to Christianity. The Epistle to Philemon was written on behalf of the slave.

ONYX A precious stone (Eze 28:13), one of which was on the breastplate of the high priest (Ex 28:20). It is a variety of quartz.

P

PALESTINE The land of the Israelites, only once called Palestine (Joel 3:4). In the Revised Version it is always Philistia. In the Old Testament the name signifies the land of the Philistines. It was called Canaan by the Hebrews in distinction from Gilead, east of the Jordan. When taken by Joshua, it became known as the land of Israel (1 Sa 13:19; Ma 2:20). It is called the Land of Promise (He 11:9) and the Holy Land (Ze 2:12), the designation during the Middle Ages. As occupied by the Israelites, the land extended from Mount Hermon on the north to Kadesh-barnea on the south and from the sea on the west to the Jordan and the region east of the river occupied by Reuben, Gad, and half-tribe of Manasseh.

PALM A tall, straight tree (Song 7:7–8; Je 10:5). Parts of it were used in various portions of the Temple (1 Ki 6:29,

32, 35). The palm leaf was emblematic of peace, also of victory (Jo 12:13; Re 7:9). The Israelites found palm trees at Elim (Ex 15:27).

PARABLE A story or fable for the illustration of moral or religious truth. It is not to be confused with a simile, metaphor, or figures of speech. John's Gospel makes use of the latter but not of parables in the proper use of the word. In the discourse on the Good Shepherd the word parable is used (Jo 10:6) but it is not the word for parable commonly used by the Synoptic Gospels. In order to make the truths of the kingdom more intelligible and impress them upon the memory, Jesus clothed them in images and narrative form.

PARACLETE (advocate) One who pleads another's case before a judge. Jesus applied the term to the Holy Spirit, sometimes translated *comforter* (Jo 14:16, 26, 15:26, 16:7–11).

PARADISE (a park) A word used to denote Heaven. It is the place of the just and the righteous (Lu 23:43; 2 Co 12:4; Re 2:7). It is also called Abraham's bosom (Lu 16:22–23).

PARENTS While the fifth commandment sets forth the duty of children to parents, the obligations parents sustain to their children are clearly taught. The child should be trained to fear the Lord, and the parent to refrain from provoking their children unnecessarily (De 6:7; Ep 6:4).

PASSOVER (passing over) The first of the three annual Hebrew festivals at which all the men had to appear at the sanctuary (Ex 12:43, 13:3–10; De 16:1), and one of the feasts in memory of past events. The first passover and instructions about keeping it (Ex 11:4–7, 12:1–51, 13:3–16; Le 23:5–8). Christ is the perfect fulfillment of the passover

(1 Co 5:7). The paschal lamb was required to be without physical blemish, and Christ was perfect spiritually (Ex 12:5; He 4:15; 1 Pe 1:18–19). The bones were not to be broken (Ex 12:46; Jo 19:36). The passover was eaten with unleavened bread (Ex 12:18; 1 Co 5:8).

PATMOS A rocky island in the Grecian Archipelago, one of the Sporades, off the southwestern coast of Asia Minor. It is a barren island about thirty miles in circumference. To this island the apostle John was banished in the reign of Domitian. It was here he received the visions related in the Book of Revelation (Re 1:9).

PATRIARCH The founder of a family or a race. In the New Testament the term is applied to Abraham, the head of the Messianic nation (He 7:4), to the sons of Jacob (Ac 7:8–9), to Jacob, the father of Israel, and to David (Ac 2:29). It applies to the heads of families of the age prior to the time of Moses so that the Patriarchal Era was the period prior to the institutions of Sinai.

PAUL (little) The great apostle to the Gentiles. His Hebrew name was Saul which he retained until the time of his visit to Paphos where Serguis Paulus was converted. He was of the tribe of Benjamin, a native of Tarsus, the chief city of Cilicia (Ac 9:11, 21:39, 22:3; Ph 3:5). In this intellectual center, the seat of a famous school of philosophy, he was reared under Grecian influences. Like other Jewish boys he was taught a trade, that of tent making (Ac 18:3). In Jerusalem he was trained in the Scriptures by one of the most learned and distinguished rabbis of the day, Gamaliel, grandson of the famous Hillel. When Paul was on a journey to Damascus where he was planning to persecute the Christians, the voice of Jesus spoke to him from a bright light and he was converted (Ac 9:1–25). Later he participated in three great missionary journeys extending from Jerusalem and Antioch westward through Cyprus and Asia Minor, and even into Europe. Among his travelling companions at various times were Barnabas, John Mark, Silas, and Luke. One of his journeys took him to Rome, where he was imprisoned. He is believed to have suffered martyrdom in Rome late in the reign of Nero (about A.D. 67). Thirteen letters written by Paul during his lifetime, under the Spirit's inspiration, are preserved in the New Testament.

PEACE OFFERING See OFFERINGS.

PENTATEUCH The first five books of the Old Testament. The Israelites called it the law (Jos 1:7; Ma 5:17), the law of Moses (Ez 7:6; Lu 2:22), the book of the law, and the book of Moses (Jos 1:8; 2 Ch 25:3–4). In the Hebrew manuscripts they are considered one book.

PENTECOST See WEEKS, FEAST OF.

PENUEL (face of God) **1.** A place east of the Jordan, the site unknown, where Jacob wrestled with the angel and saw God face to face on his way back to Canaan from Padanaram (Ge 32:30–31). **2.** Son of Hur of the tribe of Judah (1 Ch 4:4). **3.** Son of Shashak of Benjamin (1 Ch 8:25).

PERFUME A sweet-smelling substance which consisted of various spices such as cassia, aloes, myrrh, spikenard, frankincense, and cinnamon. The extract was carried in bottles. In the sanctuary it was used as incense (Ex 30:22–38).

PERSIA A territory bounded on the north by Media, on the south by the Persian Gulf, on the west by Elam, on the east by Carmania. Persia became the second world empire after Babylon in Daniel's vision. The Jews returned to Israel under the decree of Cyrus, the Persian ruler. See CYRUS.

PETER (rock) His name was formerly Simon, the son of Jonas (Jo 1:42, 21:15–16). He was a native of Bethsaida (Jo 1:44) but later dwelt at Capernaum (Ma 8:14; Lu 4:38). His brother, Andrew, a disciple of John the Baptist, brought him to Jesus, whose disciple he became (Jo 1:40). He became associated with Jesus (Ma 4:19; Mk 1:17; Lu 5:10) and then became an apostle (Ma 10:2; Lu 6:13–14). He was a man of great earnestness, was self-assertive and impulsive, and had the qualities of leadership. In the lists of the apostles his name is always first (Ma 17:1; Mk 5:37, 9:2, 13:3; Lu 8:51, 9:28). In the fishing industry he was in partnership with Zebedee and his two sons on the Sea of Galilee (Ma 4:18; Mk 1:16; Lu 5:3) and, with James and John, he responded without hesitation to the call of Christ. He, with James and John, beheld the marvelous transfiguration of Christ (Ma 17:1–2) and they were again his companions in the scene of Jesus' agony in Gethsemane (Ma 26:36–37). Peter denied knowing Jesus but was restored (Ma 26:69–75; Jo 21:15–19) In the early church Peter was an instrumental preacher and miracle-worker (Ac 1:15, 2:14, 38, 3:6, 12, 4:13, 5:3, 15, 8:14, 20, 9:34, 40, 10:17, 11:4, 12:5, 11, 15:7, 34). He authored the two Epistles of Peter.

PHARAOH The general title of the kings of Egypt. There were several who figure in Biblical history. **1.** The Pharaoh of the time of Joseph. That he was a Pharaoh of the Hyksos dynasty is supported by strong evidence. **2.** The Pharaoh of the oppression. The Hyksos kings were expelled by Amasis, a Theban prince who founded the eighteenth dynasty. It is the view of many that Rameses II, third king of the nineteenth dynasty, was the oppressor of the Israelites. He was a great warrior. In his war with the Hittites he was forced to make a treaty of peace. **3.** The Pharaoh of the Exodus. He is believed to have been Meneptah II, the thirteenth son of Rameses II. **4.** Shishak and So. **5.** Tirhakah. He was the last king of the Ethiopian dynasty. He was defeated by

Esarhaddon, king of Assyria, in 671 B.C., and was later defeated by Ashurbanipal who captured Thebes. **6.** Necho son of Psammeticus I.

PHARISEES (separated) There were three Jewish sects—Pharisees, Sadducees, Essenes (Ac 26:5). This sect arose prior to the period of the Maccabees when there was a tendency on the part of the Jews to adopt Grecian customs. In opposition to this the Pharisees conformed in the strictest manner to the Mosaic institutions. They were first known by this name in the time of John Hyrcanus. They were distinguished from the Sadducees in their doctrinal beliefs in holding to the doctrine of the resurrection and immortality of the soul, the doctrine of future reward and punishment (Ac 23:8), foreordination consistent with freedom of action. But conformity to the law was the essential characteristic of their religion. In addition to the Mosaic law they adhered strongly to traditions of the elders. This was denounced by Christ because it nullified the Scriptures (Ma 15:2–3, 6). They were denounced by John the Baptist as well as by Christ for their observance of letter of the law instead of the spirit of it (Jo 8:1–11).

PHILEMON (affectionate) A Christian of Colosse to whom Paul wrote a letter about Philemon's slave Onesimus.

PHILIP (lover of horses) **1.** One of the Twelve Apostles. He lived in Bethsaida on the Sea of Galilee. He met Jesus beyond the Jordan and was called to be his disciple. Later, he brought Nathanael to Jesus (Jo 1:43–48). It was to him certain Greeks expressed their desire to see Jesus (Jo 12:20–21). **2.** Philip the Evangelist. He was one of the seven deacons of the early church (Ac 6:5). When the disciples were dispersed by persecution, he preached in Samaria (Ac 8:4–8, 21:8). He was then divinely directed to go to Gaza where he taught and baptized the eunuch (Ac 8:26–39) and went on to Caesarea (Ac 8:40). His four daughters had the gift of prophecy (Ac 21:8–9). **3.** Son of Herod the Great and half-brother of Herod Antipas (Ma 14:3; Lu 3:1).

PHILIPPI An important inland city on the border of Macedonia (Ac 16:12, 20:6; Ph 1:1).

PHILISTINES A non-Semitic people, doubtless the Caphtorim who came in the twelfth century B.C. from Caphtor, dispossessed the Avim, and occupied their territory—the Maritime Plain of Palestine (De 2:23; Je 47:4; Am 9:7). These formidable opponents of Israel, particularly from the time of the judges to David, are not mentioned by name in the New Testament. Against them Samson waged a single-handed contest (Ju 14–16). When the elders of Israel, fearful of defeat, sent the ark to the camp, the Philistines captured it but returned it when a plague broke out among them (1 Sa 4–6). The famous stone, called Ebenezer, was set up by Samuel in commemoration of a victory over them (1 Sa 7:11–12). Jonathan won signal victories over them at Geba and Michmash (1 Sa 13:1–3, 14:1–23). Saul fought them valiantly but was defeated at Mount Gilboa where he and three sons died in battle (1 Sa 31). David defeated and reduced them to vassalage (2 Sa 5:22, 25, 8:1) though twice previously he had sought refuge among them and had been granted possession of Ziklag (1 Sa 21:10–15, 27:6). Hezekiah and Uzziah waged successful war against them (2 Ki 18:8; 2 Ch 26:6–7).

PHOENICIA A narrow strip of land on the Mediterranean that in the time of Christ extended about sixteen miles south of Carmel. The ancient Hebrews called the inhabitants Canaanites. They traced their origin to the region of the Persian Gulf. They spoke the Semitic language. Their two chief cities were Tyre and Sidon. In one of his withdrawals Jesus came into the borders of Tyre at Sidon (Ma 15:21;

Mk 7:24, 31). On their way from Antioch to Jerusalem Paul and Barnabas passed through the area (Ac 15:3).

PHYLACTERY A small case made of leather and worn by Jewish men on the forehead and the left arm. The forehead case contained four compartments, each of which held parchment inscribed with scriptural quotations from Ex 13:1–10, 11–17; De 6:4–9, 11:13–21. The arm case had only one compartment which held the same passages. Jesus rebuked the Pharisees for their ostentatious display in wearing unnecessarily large phylacteries (Ma 23:5).

PILATE, PONTIUS He was appointed by the Emperor Tiberius to be procurator of Judea in 26 A.D. (Lu 3:1). Pilate was obstinate and merciless, a hard, cruel man. When duty conflicted with personal interests, the claims of duty were disregarded, as in the case of Jesus. His liberation would have increased Pilate's unpopularity (Ma 27; Lu 23). For his unbridled cruelty he was finally summoned to Rome, banished, and at last took his own life.

PLAGUE A punitive affliction brought about because of sin. It was a judgment that might take any one of several forms. The first of these was the affliction of Paraoh in connection with Abraham and Sarah (Ge 12:17); then the ten plagues of Egypt (Ex 7:8–12:31).

PONTIUS See PILATE.

POOR The impoverished, for whom the Mosaic law made ample provision. The poor laws were very explicit. Cancellation of considerable indebtedness was required in years of Jubilee (Le 25, 27:14–25). A hungry person was permitted to satisfy his immediate needs in the field or vineyard of another (De 23:24–25). The poor by law gleaned after the reapers and cut and gathered what was left standing in the fields. Also, the fruit left on the branches was the property of the poor (Le 19:9–10, 23:22; De 24:19–21). The poor should be remembered on joyous occasions and at the time of sacrificial feasts (De 16:11, 14). Injustice toward the poor was denounced by the prophets (Is 1:23, 10:2; Eze 22:7, 29; Mal 3:5).

POTIPHAR A captain of Pharaoh in whose home Joseph was a slave (Ge 39:1–20).

PRAETORIUM The official residence of a Roman governor. The palace of Pilate at Jerusalem to which Jesus was taken after his capture was so designated (Ma 27:27; Mk 15:16).

PRAYER The most direct expression of the religious nature in its communion with God. The Bible cites many examples of prayer. (Ge 4:26, 20:17, 25:21; Ex 32:11). Prayer expresses the innate conviction of the soul of the personality of God. It is instinctive with man, but rationally grounded in the Word of God. Some of the great prayers in the Old Testament are the intercessory prayers of Abraham and Moses (Ge 18:23–32; Ex 32:11–14; Nu 14:13–19); the great penitential prayer of David (Ps 51); the prayer of Solomon for wisdom (1 Ki 3:5–9); Solomon's prayer of dedication of the Temple, one of the greatest prayers of the Bible (1 Ki 8:23–53); and the prayer of Daniel (Da 9:3–19). Jesus was often in prayer (Lu 5:16). He taught his disciples how to pray using the Lord's prayer (Ma 6:5–15), prayed for Peter (Lu 22:31–32), prayed for his disciples and all believers (Jo 17), anguished in Gethsemane before his betrayal and death (Lu 22:41–44), and prayed for his murderers as he died (Lu 23:34). Stephen also prayed for his murderers (Ac 7:59–60). Jesus contrasted the Pharisee's and the publican's prayers (Lu 18:11–14). Paul prayed for the churches

(Ep 1:15–23, 3:14–19; Ph 1:3–7). Believers are instructed to pray (Ps 32:6; Lu 18:1; Ep 6:18; 1 Th 5:17; Ja 5:13, 16; 1 Pe 4:7).

PREDESTINATION See ELECTION.

PRIEST Prior to the Mosaic institution of priesthood, the functions of priest were exercised by individuals, as in the case of Abel and Cain. The natural head of a body of people stood in this relation, as in the case of the patriarchs. At Sinai the office was instieud in the most solemn manner. The tribe of Levi was set apart for religious service. The priesthood was made hereditary in the family of Aaron (Ex 28:1, 40:12–15; De 10:6; 1 Ki 8:4; Ez 2:36). When Aaron died, his oldest living son, Eleazar, succeeded him in the high priesthood (Nu 20:25–28; De 10:6) and he was succeeded by his son Phinehas (Ju 20:28; 1 Ch 6:4, 50).

PRISCA, PRISCILLA The wife of Aquila (Ac 18:1–3, 18, 26; Ro 16:3; 2 Ti 4:19). See AQUILA.

PRISON A place for the confinement of criminals. Prisons had no place in the penal system of the ancient Hebrews. Joseph's imprisonment was in Egypt and Samson's was in Philistia (Ge 39:20, 23, 40:3, 5; Ju 16:21, 25). From the time of Jeremiah, mention is made of dungeons and pits in the sense of prisons (Je 37:16, 38:6; Ze 9:11). In New Testament times the prisons were patterned after Greek and Roman models. There were prison rooms in the palace of Herod, and in the palace at Caesarea (Ac 12:6, 10, 26:10).

PROPHET A divinely inspired minister of Jehovah; originally called a seer (1 Sa 9:9). Abraham, Aaron, and others were considered prophets but it was not until Samuel that prophecy came into its own. In the period from Samuel to Elisha the so-called schools of the prophets were established in important commercial centers. Until the period of the Exile the prophets were advisers to kings. In this capacity they never hesitated to administer a deserved rebuke to the monarch. In their writings the prophets consistently attacked unrighteousnes, self-indulgence, and greed. They stood for monotheism and sometimes they predicted future events. Prophecy reached its peak with the Messianic prophecy. Prophets and prophecy are mentioned in the New Testament. Jesus was a prophet (Ma 13:57, 21:11; Lu 13:33).

PROPHETESS A woman divinely called to prophesy. Such were Miriam (Ex 15:20–21; Nu 12:2; Mi 6:4), Deborah (Ju 4:4–6, 14), Huldah (2 Ki 22:14–20), and the daughters of Philip the evangelist (Ac 21:9).

PROSELYTE A New Testament term designating a convert to Judaism (Ac 6:5, 8:27).

PROVINCE An administrative district either within or without the confines of the controlling nation. The provinces of the Bible were usually subject to Babylonia, Persia, or Rome. The word also denotes the divisions of the Babylonian and Persian empires (Ez 2:1; Ne 7:6; Es 1:1, 2:3; Da 2:49, 3:1, 30).

PUBLICAN A member of a company to which the Romans auctioned off the right to collect taxes. They were required to give security for the amount the government should receive. They sold to others certain portions of the revenue. Publicans were engaged to do the actual collecting of the customs. The system afforded opportunity for extortion, though doubtless there were some exceptions (Lu 3:12–13, 19:8). A Jewish publican was a social outcast, looked upon with contempt, for raising taxes for a foreign and heathen government. Zacchaeus, a Jew, had charge of the revenues of Jericho (Lu 19:1–2) and Matthew had charge of the customs of Capernaum (Ma 9:9; Mk 2:14; Lu 5:27).

PUNISHMENT It is inflicted to maintain the majesty of the law that has been violated, and should be proportionate to the crime committed. This is the basic purpose of punishment. Under the Hebrew theocratic system capital punishment was inflicted for certain offenses, such as the breaking of the Sabbath (Ex 31:14–15, 35:2), blasphemy (Le 24:10–16), sacrificing to idols (Ex 22:20; Le 20:2; De 13:6–17, 17:2–7). Under the theocracy such offenders were guilty of treason. The same penalty was inflicted for various forms of unchastity (Ex 22:19; Le 20:10; De 22:21–27). Conjugal relations of a less heinous nature were punished by cutting off the offenders from their people, or being deprived of children (Le 20:17–21). Death was by stoning and in some cases the body was hanged and then burned. In the case of chastisement, the stripes could not exceed forty (De 25:3). One who testified falsely must suffer the penalty of the crime of the one accused (De 19:16, 19). The Hebrew laws were severe, but not cruel.

PURIFICATION The process by which a person ceremonially unclean was made clean again. Contact with a dead body, for example, rendered one unclean under the Mosaic law and purification by the ashes of a heifer was necessary (Nu 19). Purification for certain bodily disorders was required in the form of cleansing and offering of a burnt offering (Le 15; Nu 5:2–3). If one came in contact with a person in that condition, a bath was required and he remained ceremonially unclean until evening (Le 15:5–11). Following childbirth, the mother was placed under rigid requirements not to touch a hallowed thing or to enter the sanctuary (Le 12:8; Lu 2:21, 24). The leper was sprinkled with the blood of a bird by the priest, and after washing and cutting the hair he appeared at the sanctuary with his offering of lambs and was sprinkled with the blood of the offering (Le 14).

PURIM An annual Jewish festival celebrating the deliverance of the Jews in Persia from the destruction planned by Haman. The event is narrated in the Book of Esther.

Q

QUEEN The wife of a king, or a woman reigning in her own right. If a son followed the father on the throne, the widow continued to hold an influential position (2 Ki 10:13). Athaliah usurped the throne of Judah and reigned for six years (2 Ki 11:1–13).

QUIRINIUS A Roman who was governor of Syria (A.D. 6). He was in charge of the enrollment and the taxing that caused Joseph and Mary to go to Bethlehem just prior to the birth of Christ (Lu 2:1–5).

R

RABBI A title of respect given by the Jews to their teachers (Ma 23:7; Jo 1:38). It was also applied to doctors and other learned persons. It was often used for Jesus (Jo 1:38, 49, 3:2, 6:25, 20:16) and once for John the Baptist (Jo 3:26).

RACHEL (ewe) Laban's younger daughter whom Jacob loved when he first met her in Mesopotamia. To secure her as his wife he worked for seven years for Laban, who then tricked him into marrying Leah, the older daughter. After this, he served another seven years to marry Rachel (Ge 29:1–30). She had two sons, Joseph and Benjamin, but died giving birth to the latter in Canaan. Benjamin was the only one of Jacob's twelve sons to be born in the Land of Promise. Rachel's burial place is near Bethlehem (Ge 30:22–25, 35:16–18).

RAHAB A woman who lived in Jericho, whose house was on the wall. When Joshua sent spies to the city she concealed them and enabled them to escape by lowering them by a cord on the outside of the wall (Jos 2:1–24). She and her family were spared when the city fell, and they became part of the chosen people (Jos 6:22–25; He 11:31; Jam 2:25).

RAINBOW A beautiful arc exhibiting the colors of the spectrum, formed opposite the sun by the refraction and reflection of the sun's rays on raindrops or mist. In Genesis, God tells Noah that the rainbow is the symbol of the covenant between God, Noah, and every living creature (Ge 9:12–17; Re 4:3).

RAM A male sheep. One of the clean animals the Jews were permitted to eat (Ge 31:38). They were used as burnt or peace offerings (Ge 22:13; Le 1:10, 8:18) and also as a sin offering (Le 5:15, 6:6). The skin of the ram was used for covering the tabernacle (Ex 26:14).

RAMESES **1.** A town in the district of Goshen in Egypt, a section of great fertility, where Joseph settled his people (Ge 47:11), probably the treasure city built for Rameses II by the enslaved Israelites (Ex 1:11). From this place the Israelites marched to Succoth at the time of the Exodus (Ex 12:37). **2.** Rameses, Egyptian king. See PHARAOH.

REBEKAH, REBECCA (a noose, or figuratively speaking, a maiden who ensnares men by her beauty). Daughter of Bethuel and sister of Laban. The servant of Abraham was sent to Mesopotamia to secure a wife for Isaac. He met

Rebekah at a well and was impressed by her beauty. In her home he explained his mission and she agreed to return with him to Canaan. She became the wife of Isaac and the mother of Esau and Jacob (Ge 24:1–67). Jacob was her favorite. With him she contrived to deceive Isaac and secured for Jacob the blessing (Ge 25:28, 27:1–28:5).

RECONCILIATION To establish a state of peace between two persons, or between God and man by the atoning work of Christ. The latter is the Biblical sense of the term. It embraces two ideas, the first of which is that of God being reconciled to man. It denotes that necessary attitude of opposition to sin on the part of God, and that in order to pardon and receive the sinner, the demands of justice and holiness must be met. God made this possible by sending his Son that sinners might be reconciled to God (Jo 3:16; Ro 5:6–21). Reconciliation is made possible because of the death of Christ on the cross. Christ in heaven intercedes in behalf of man (He 7:25). The second idea is that of man when man accepts the provision God has made for his salvation; at that moment there is a cessation of his enmity to God. It should be noted that there are some who feel that reconciliation in the N.T. refers only to the latter idea (2 Co 5:18–21).

REDEMPTION It denotes release, freedom, by the payment of a price. When the Levites were set apart for the service of the sanctuary, all others were redeemed in the person of the firstborn. For this redemption and the redemption price see LEVITES. The need for redemption certainly implies bondage—to the curse and dominion of sin (Ga 3:13) and to its penalty of death (Ac 26:18; He 2:14–15). To effect this redemption Christ is man's Redeemer. He paid the redemption price, his atoning work, the price paid for human redemption. By this we are made free, redeemed from the curse of the law upon sin. When we accept him,

Satan's power and dominion are broken, we have the power to lead a new, a holy, a free life, and death has lost its sting and terror. This redemption embraces not only the soul but also the body (Ro 8:15–23; 1 Co 15:55–57; Ep 1:7; 2 Ti 2:26; He 2:9). See ATONEMENT.

RED SEA To the Hebrews it was known as the "Sea of Weeds." It was crossed by the Israelites when they escaped from the Egyptians (Ex 14:16; Nu 33:8; De 11:4; Ac 7:36).

REGENERATION Being born again (Jo 3:6; 1 Pe 1:23), born of God (1 Jo 5:1, 4), and born of the Spirit (Jo 3:6) are some of the terms used in the Scriptures to express the idea of regeneration. Nicodemus was told by Jesus that man must be born again to see the kingdom of God (Jo 3:1–16). We are justified by or through faith, but we are not regenerated by faith, or by any external act, such as baptism, but by the agency of the Holy Spirit by which our nature is renewed, i.e., made new. It is this divine agency so clearly emphasized by the Scriptures (1 Pe 1:23; 1 Jo 3:9, 4:7, 5:1). Furthermore, regeneration is not to be confused with sanctification. The new nature originated and effected by the Holy Spirit (regeneration) is now by the operations of the Spirit developed in its growth in grace in which the spiritual life is brought to perfection (sanctification). The one is the beginning of the new life, the other the development and consummation of it. See SALVATION. The regenerated man becomes a new creature (2 Co 5:17) with new power (Ac 1:8) and with spiritual attitudes (Ga 5:18–25; Ep 4:22–32; Col 3:8–24; 1 Pe 3:8–18; 2 Pe 1:5–8; 1 Jo 3:9–17, 4:7, 20–21, 5:1–8). See HOLY SPIRIT.

REHOBOAM (the people enlarged) Son and successor of Solomon. His mother was Naamah, an Ammonitess. The Ammonites were the descendants of Lot, and therefore of the line of Arphaxad, of Shem, the line that through Abraham brought forth the Messiah (1 Ki 14:31). When Rehoboam assumed the throne, the representatives of the tribes asked him to lessen their tax burdens. The king countered with a plan to tax them even more. As a result ten tribes withdrew from the nation. Rehoboam later prepared an army in order to subjugate them but he was forbidden to do it by the prophet, Shemiah. Rehoboam reigned for seventeen years during which time his country was invaded by Shishak of Egypt who seized Jerusalem and other cities. Rehoboam and his nation reverted to idolatry (1 Ki 11:43–15:6; 2 Ch 9:31–13:7).

REMNANT The portion of Israel which was preserved to form a renewed Israel—one which would replace the nation upon which judgment had fallen (Is 4:2–6, 10:20–23, 12:6; Je 23:3, 32, 36–44; Am 9:8–15; Mi 4:6–8, 8:12).

RESURRECTION The doctrine of the reunion of body and soul which have been separated by death. This doctrine is not explicitly dealt with in the earlier portions of the Old Testament. There are allusions to it in Ps 49:14–15; Is 26:19–20; and Eze 37, while Da 12:2 states it directly. In the time of Christ it was a doctrine of the Jews, but denied by the Sadducees (Ma 22:30; Lu 20:39; Jo 11:24; Acts 23:6, 8). It was specifically taught by the apostles (1 Co 15; Ph 3:20–21; 1 Th 4:14; Re 20:6–14). The Scriptures clearly teach that the body shall rise again having its identity preserved; that it will be a glorious body, like the glorified body of Christ, and will endure with the soul through all eternity; and that the resurrection of Christ is the first fruits of the resurrection, the guarantee of our resurrection in the likeness of his body. In the book of Revelation, the Bible distinctly teaches the doctrine of two resurrections. The first is to occur at the first stage of Christ's second coming (1 Th 4:13–17). Those rising in this resurrection are designated "the dead in Christ," and immediately following that will be the translation of living saints. There is nothing ambiguous about this language. This is supported by our Lord's statement that the reward of the righteous will occur at "the resurrection of the just" (Lu 14:14), which clearly implies there will be another resurrection, that of the unjust. The second resurrection, that of the lost, will not occur until the thousand years have expired. Revelation states, "Blessed and holy is he who has part in the first resurrection" (Re 20:4–6). This period of a thousand years is mentioned, in different connections, six times in this chapter. However that may be interpreted, two resurrections are distinctly taught. The postmillennial doctrine teaches there will be but one resurrection, at the end of the world, a general resurrection, and a general judgment.

REUBEN (behold a son) **1.** The eldest son of Jacob by Leah, Jacob's first wife (Ge 29:31–32, 35:23, 46:8). It was Reuben who saved the life of his brother, Joseph, when the other brothers wished to kill him. Reuben suggested putting him in a pit, for he planned to return Joseph to his father when the other brothers left the scene. However, before Reuben was able to rescue him, Joseph was sold to the Midianites (Ge 37:21–29). Reuben had four sons: Hanoch, Phallu, Hezron, and Carmi (Ge 46:8–9; Ex 6:14; 1 Ch 5:3). Because of his conduct with Bilhah, his father's concubine, he forfeited his birthright (Ge 35:22, 49:3–4). **2.** The tribe of Reuben had an inconspicuous place in Israelite history. The request of the Reubenites and Gadites that they have assigned them the district east of the Jordan was granted on condition that they would do their part in the taking of the land. This they did (Nu 32:1–42; Jos 4:12, 18:7).

RIVER OF EGYPT **1.** The Nile (Ge 15:18). This and the Euphrates are designated as the bounds of the Land of Promise, the inheritance of the chosen people. **2.** The desert stream, called the river of Egypt (Nu 34:5; 1 Ki 8:65; 2 Ki 24:7).

ROCK The translation of several Greek and Hebrew words meaning both a solid piece of stone and a cliff or crag. It might serve as a dwelling or a place of refuge (Job 30:6; Je 4:29). Many rocks were given names; for example, the rocks of Oreb, Etam, and Rimmon (Ju 7:25, 15:8, 20:45, 21:13). The word was often used figuratively to denote the strength of God, the church, and faith (De 32:4, 31, 37; 2 Sa 22:2–3; Ps 18:1–2, 62:7; Is 17:10; Ma 16:18). Peter's name meant "rock" (Ma 16:18). Christ, as a fulfillment of a type, was called the Rock (1 Co 10:4).

ROME The capital and chief city of Italy. It was founded on the Tiber River in 753 B.C., allegedly by Romulus and Remus. Eventually the city dominated much of Europe, Asia, and north Africa. It was first a kingdom, then a republic, then an empire. Tiberius was on the throne during the time of Christ's ministry and at the time of his death (Lu 2:1, 3:1–2). Under Nero the persecution of the Christians was instituted. This continued until the reign of Constantine, who made Christianity the state religion in A.D. 313.

S

SABBATH (rest) The day on which labor ceases. It occurs on the seventh day of the week because, according to Genesis, that was the day on which the Lord rested after creating the world (Ge 2:1–3). Other sacred days and periods were also called sabbaths such as the Day of Atonement, the sabbatical year and the year of jubilee. From the flood to the Exodus the Sabbath is not definitely mentioned, but before reaching Sinai and before the giving of the Decalogue containing legislation regarding the Sabbath, it appears in the record in connection with the manna in the wilderness of Sin (Ex 16:23–26). It was at Sinai that the law was first announced relative to maintaining the sanctity of the Sabbath. It was the fourth commandment (Ex 20:8–11, 31:16–18; De 5:15). It was to be a holy convocation for divine worship (Le 23:3) and a sign indicating that the Israelites were sanctified by Jehovah (Ex 31:13). When the Jews were restored to their land after the Exile and their Mosaic institutions were re-established by Ezra and Nehemiah, they covenanted to keep the Sabbath. When traders brought their wares from Tyre to be sold in Jerusalem on the Sabbath, Nehemiah put a stop to it (Ne 10:31, 13:15–22). In the time of Christ the Pharisees applied the law regarding Sabbath observance in the most scrupulous manner with the result that they missed the whole spirit and purpose of the Sabbath. In opposition to them, in the performance of works of necessity and mercy, our Lord stated that the Sabbath was made for man, that the Son of man is not the slave but the lord of the Sabbath. The day of the holy convocation was not the weekly Sabbath, but the day after the passover, a rest day on which no laborious work was performed. (Mk 2:27; Lu 13:14, 14:3, 5; Jo 5:10).

SABBATICAL YEAR A year-long Sabbath every seven years in which no work was done. The land was not cultivated during this year and all debts were canceled. It was designed to be a year of quiet religious contemplation.

SACKCLOTH A coarse dark cloth made of goat's hair (Is 50:3; Re 6:12), the garment of mourners (2 Sa 3:31; 2 Ki 19:1–2), often of prophets (Is 20:2). It had the appearance of a sack and was usually worn over the other garments (Jon 3:6), sometimes underneath (1 Ki 21:27; Job 16:15; Is 32:11).

SACRIFICE See OFFERINGS.

SADDUCEES (of Zadok?) One of the Jewish religious parties in existence at the time of Christ. This sect did not believe in the resurrection and a future state of the soul, nor did it believe in the theory of reward or punishment after death. In these beliefs it was opposed by the Pharisees, another important Jewish religious party. Politically the Sadducees, who took their name from Zadok, a high priest in the reign of David, favored the policies of Rome in the government of Palestine. For about 200 years prior to the fall of Jerusalem in A.D. 70, most of the high priests were drawn from this party of the priesthood. John the Baptist once called both the Sadducees and the Pharisees a generation of vipers (Ma 3:7) and Jesus warned his disciples against their doctrines (Ma 16:1–12). Paul once caused division in the ranks of both groups by bringing up the issue of the resurrection of the soul (Ac 23:6–10).

SALEM (peaceful) The abbreviation of Jerusalem (Ps 76:2). See JERUSALEM and MELCHIZEDEK.

SALOME (peace) **1.** Daughter of Herodias and Philip. Her mother left Philip for his half-brother, Herod Antipas, the man who imprisoned John the Baptist. Salome so delighted Antipas with her dancing that he offered to grant her any wish. Her mother instructed her to ask for the head of John the Baptist. Her request was granted (Ma 14:6). **2.** Wife of Zebedee and mother of James and John (Ma 27:56; Mk 15:40, 16:1).

SALUTATION The Hebrews saluted each other with such expressions as "God be gracious unto you" (Ge 43:29), "Blessed be you of the Lord" (Ru 3:10; 1 Sa 15:13), "The Lord bless you" (Ru 2:4). At parting, such expressions as "Go in peace," or "Farewell" (1 Sa 1:17, 20:42; Mk 5:34; Ac 15:36) were in use. Paul's letters began with salutations of an extended nature as Ro 1:1–7; and in a briefer form as "Grace unto you and peace." Letters were also closed with salutations from himself in which others would join (1 Th 1:1, 5:26–28).

SALVATION The general idea of various Hebrew and Greek words is that of deliverance, safety, being saved, a state of security being effected. In the Old Testament God's people are delivered by him from foes and from the devices of the wicked (Ps 37:40, 59:2, 106:4). It is also expressed in sins being forgiven, in prayers being answered (Ps 51:12, 69:13, 79:9). The prophets spoke about one through whom salvation would be brought to a lost race in need of spiritual deliverance. He is the Messiah of the prophets. This is the thought of the New Testament doctrine of salvation—deliverance from the state and consequences of sin by the saving work of Christ alone (Ma 1:21; Ac 4:12; He 2:10, 5:9), made efficacious to us by repentance and faith (Jo 3:16; He 2:3). The motive in providing such salvation is the love of God, but it is made possible by the holiness of Christ who offered himself without spot or blemish for our salvation.

SAMARIA 1. The capital of the northern kingdom of Israel. It was founded on a hill about three hundred feet high by Omri who purchased the hill from Shemer (1 Ki 16:24). Before this, Shechem had been the capital. Samaria was the scene of many of the events in the history of the northern kingdom. The city was besieged several times and was almost starved into submission by Ben-hadad (1 Ki 20:1; 2 Ki 6:8–7:20). During the reign of Ahab and his wife Jezebel, a temple was built to Baal and idolatry flourished. Because of the idolatry, the prophets threatened Samaria with destruction (Is 7:9, 28:1–4; Ho 8:5–14; Am 3:9–15). In 722 B.C. the city was captured by the Assyrians after a three-year siege. Many of the inhabitants were then deported to Mesopotamia. From then on Samaria was always under foreign control. The city had many magnificent pagan temples in the time of Jesus. **2.** The entire northern kingdom was occasionally designated by the name of its capital (1 Ki 21:1; 2 Ki 17:24; Je 31:5). **3.** The district of Samaria was one of the subdivisions of a Persian province (Ne 4:2).

SAMSON (sunlike) An outstanding judge of Israel. His father was Manoah of the tribe of Dan. Samson was born at Zorah and was a Nazarite from birth (Ju 13:1–24). He was destined to deliver his people from the oppression of the Philistines which was felt especially by Judah and Dan. Samson possessed marvelous physical strength which he used against the Philistines, but he was not correspondingly morally strong. After Samson set the foxes loose in the fields of the Philistines, the Philistines demanded that Samson be surrendered to them (Ju 14:1–15:5). He allowed himself to be bound by his cowardly countrymen who failed to realize that he was their deliverer, but breaking the bands, he slew a thousand of his foes. Samson courted a Philistine woman, Delilah, and eventually told her that the source of his strength was his long hair. While he was asleep, she cut his hair. No longer able to resist his Philistine enemies, he was taken prisoner and blinded (Ju 16:16–30).

SAMUEL (heard by God) The son of Elkanah and Hannah, a Levite family of Kohath, house of Ishar (1 Sa 1:1; 1 Ch 6:26, 35). He lived in the hill country of Ephraim, at Ramah. Following the death of Eli, Samuel the prophet became the chief religious authority in the land. Under his administration the moral and religious state of things greatly improved.

SANBALLAT A Horonite, probably a man of Beth-horon or of Horonaim in Moab. He had considerable influence in Samaria and served Artaxerxes (Ne 2:10, 19, 4:2).

SANCTIFICATION It signifies setting apart for a sacred purpose. In the Mosaic system there were sacred persons, as the high priest, sacred things, as the tabernacle, sacred seasons, as the passover and day of atonement. Sanctification is to be distinguished from justification and regeneration. Justification signifies the judicial relation of the sinner to God, and regeneration the changed nature of the sinner by the agency of the Holy Spirit. Sanctification denotes the carrying forward of that work of grace in the soul to its completeness (Ro 6:11; Ph 1:6; 1 Pe 2:24). These three states are clearly set forth in the Scriptures. A person may be justified and regenerated, but not yet be sanctified. Justification is an act, while sanctification is a process. The believer may be sanctified, living a sanctified life and have the fruits of the spirit in sanctification, and not be perfectly sanctified. This is the view held by those who declare that sanctification is imperfect in the present life. Others hold that perfect sanctification may be wrought instantaneously, and still others that while sanctification is a *work* of grace it may reach perfection in the present life.

SANHEDRIN The word is derived from the Greek word *sunedrion*, a council. It was the name of the highest Jewish governing body in the time of Christ. See COUNCIL.

SAPPHIRA (beautiful) The wife of Ananias (Ac 5:1–10).

SAPPHIRE A precious stone, a variety of corundum. It is transparent and of bluish color. It was found in Ethiopia and India. It was one of the stones of the breastplate of the high priest, and in John's vision, it was in the foundation of the New Jerusalem (Ex 28:18; Son 5:14; Is 54:11; Re 21:19).

SARAH, SARAI, SARA (a princess) The wife of Abraham; also his half sister (Ge 20:12). She was ten years younger than he. She came with him from Ur of the Chaldees (Ge 11:28–31, 17:17). In Egypt Abraham, afraid men would slay him in order to marry her, introduced her as his sister (Ge 12:10–20) and repeated it years later in Gerar (Ge 20:1–18). In both instances it brought trouble. Abraham was divinely promised an heir. Sarah, at the age of 75, thought she could not bear a child, so she urged Abraham to make Hagar, Sarah's Egyptian maid, a second wife. He did this and Ishmael was born (Ge 16:1–16). When Sarah was 89, God promised her a son (Ge 17:1–19; He 11:11–12) and Isaac was born—the child of promise. At this point her name was changed from Sarai to Sarah (Ge 17:15–22, 18:9–15, 21:1–5).

SARDIUS A precious stone found near Sardis. Finer qualities of the stone were found in Babylon, also in India and Arabia. It garnished the sixth foundation of the wall about the New Jerusalem of John's vision (Re 21:20) and was one of the stones of the breast-plate of the high priest (Ex 28:17).

SARDONYX A variety of chalcedony, which in structure is like the onyx (Re 21:20).

SARGON One of the greatest of Assyrian kings (Is 20:1). He succeeded Shalmaneser IV. Sargon brought about the fall of Samaria and carried the people into captivity c. 722 B.C.

SATAN (adversary) The term Satan is used in its generic sense, adversary, in 1 Ki 11:14: "The Lord stirred up an adversary." Satan is first mentioned by name in Job 1:6–12, 2:1. He is mentioned as a personality in Ze 3:1, and Christ called him by this name in the third temptation (Ma 4:10). He is called the devil (Ma 4:1; Mk 1:13), and as adversary he is characterized as hostile to God and man (Job 2:3; Lu 22:3) in his attempt to destroy the work of God (Mk 4:15) and to induce men to sin (Ac 5:3; 26:18). His first appearance in the history of mankind was in Eden as the seducer of Adam and Eve (Ge 3:1–6; 2 Co 11:3; Re 12:9). Christ declared he was a murderer from the beginning (Jo 8:44). He inspired Judas to betray his Lord (Jo 13:27; Lu 22:3). It is in the New Testament especially that the personality, character, and activities of Satan are set forth. He is the ruler of a kingdom, invested with powers, and he rules demons (Ma 12:24, 26; Lu 11:18; Re 12:7). He is the god of this world seeking to enslave men to serve him (Lu 22:3; Ac 26:18; 2 Co 4:4; 2 Th 2:9; Re 12:9).

SAUL **1.** A king of Edom (Ge 36:37–38). He was called Shaul in 1 Ch 1:48. **2.** The son of Kish, a Benjamite and the first king of Israel. He was a faithful worshipper of Jehovah as well as a man of considerable military ability. It was following his victory over the Ammonites at Jabesh-gilead that he was made king (1 Sa 11:1–15). Saul took his own life after the Hebrews were defeated by the Philstines (1 Sa 31:1–10). **3.** The name of the apostle Paul before his conversion (Ac 7:58).

SAVIOR One who saves, a deliverer from danger or evil. In the Old Testament God is the savior of the covenant people (Ps 106:21; Is 43:3, 11, 45:15, 21, 63:8; Je 14:8; Ho 13:4). The word applies especially to Jesus Christ who was called Savior by the angel announcing his birth (Lu 2:11), by some Samaritans (Jo 4:42), by Paul (Ph 3:20), and by others (Ac 5:31; 2 Pe 2:20; 1 Jo 4:14). See SALVATION.

SCEPTER A staff or rod which served as an emblem of authority, especially for royalty (Ps 45:6; Am 1:5; He 1:8).

Among such ancients as the Egyptians and Persians it was a rod, probably about five feet long, bearing at one end an ornamental ball or other figure.

SCHOOL In ancient Israel children were instructed in religion by their parents (Ge 18:19; De 6:7; 2 Ti 3:15). The people were instructed in the law at the feast of taberacles during the Sabbatic year (De 31:10–13). Religious knowledge was disseminated and religious life stimulated by the work of the prophets. At a later period there were schools in connection with the synagogues. Children were taught to read the Scriptures and to write. The law was taught by the scribes in the court of the Temple (Lu 2:46). Samuel was the earliest of the prophets. He dwelt at Ramah where he was the head of a community of prophets (1 Sa 19:18–20) who devoted their times to religious study (1 Sa 10:10, 19:20–23). Two hundred years later there were prophetical communities or schools of the prophets, probably established by Elijah. The members were called sons of the prophets (1 Ki 20:35, 38; 2 Ki 2:3, 5, 9:1).

SCHOOLMASTER This is the rendering of the Greek *paidagogos*, a boy leader, pedagogue (Ga 3:24–25), or a tutor (1 Co 4:15). In a Greek home a trusted slave had the care of children, to watch over them, keep them from danger and conduct them to and from school. Thus the law as a pedagogue, says Paul, led us to Christ. That is, it prepared us to see him as the Redeemer by declaring our unrighteousness and the inability of the works of the law to bring us salvation. By using types and symbols, the law revealed the plan of redemption (Ro 3:19–21, 4:15, 7:7–25).

SCRIBE A public writer. He may have been simply an amanuensis, as Baruch (Je 36:4, 18, 32). He may have acted in a secretarial capacity or as a governmental clerk (2 Ki 12:10; Ez 4:8). As one who copied the Scriptures, Ezra was the most distinctive of Old Testament scribes (Ez 7:6, 10). He also taught the statutes of the law. In New Testament times scribes were the interpreters and teachers of the law. They held the highest place among the people, many members of the Sanhedrin being of this class (Ma 16:21, 26:3). They had the respect and reverence of the people. They bitterly opposed Jesus (Ma 21:15) and he denounced them (Lu 11:44).

SCRIPTURE A term denoting the Bible as a whole or some portion of it. When regarded collectively the word is used in the plural (Ma 21:42; Lu 24:27; Jo 5:39; Ro 1:2; 2 Ti 3:15). Specific portions are indicated by the singular (Mk 12:10; Lu 4:21; Jo 19:37). See OLD TESTAMENT, NEW TESTAMENT.

SEA The word has various designations. **1.** The waters in general, the ocean (1 Ki 10:22; Ps 8:8, 24:2; Re 7:1–3, 21:1). **2.** A particular body of water. The Israelites were acquainted particularly with four seas–Red Sea, Mediterranean, Sea of Galilee, Dead Sea. The Mediterranean was called the great sea. The two lakes of Palestine, Galilee and Dead Sea, were also called seas. **3.** The word sea is also applied to large rivers like the Nile (Is 19:5; Na 3:8) and the Euphrates (Je 51:36, 42). **4.** The Brazen Sea, the great laver for priestly washings before they entered the sanctuary in Solomon's Temple, also called the Molten Sea (1 Ki 7:39; Je 52:17). **5.** The sea is used figuratively to express the roaring of hostile armies (Is 5:30), unsteadiness (Jam 1:6), and diffusing of spiritual truth (Is 11:9; Hab 2:14).

SEAL **1.** A marine animal, possibly a porpoise. Its skin, called badger's skin in the Authorized Version, was used for covering the tabernacle (Ex 35:7). **2.** A design or name of the owner inscribed into a signet ring. It was made of precious stone, metal, or clay and could also be worn about the neck. The seal, which leaves an impression in wax or clay, was used to fasten documents and letters. If the seal was unbroken it was certain the letter or document had not been opened. The seal was also used as a signature by persons who could not write (1 Ki 21:8; Ne 10:1; Da 12:4; Re 5:1).

SENNACHERIB Son of Sargon. He ascended the throne of Assyria when his father was assassinated (705 B.C.). He put down the revolt of Merodach-baladan of Babylon and placed Belibni on the throne. About twenty years after the capture of Samaria by his father, he invaded Judah and according to his account he captured 46 towns and carried away over 200,000 captives. For the disaster that overwhelmed him at Jerusalem see HEZEKIAH. Later he again captured Babylon, massacred the people, and ruined the city. He built a great palace in Nineveh, 1,500 feet long and 700 broad and brought water into the city by a system of canals. In 680 B.C. he was assassinated by two of his sons, and another son, Esar-haddon, came to the throne (2 Ki 19:37; 2 Ch 32:21).

SEPTUAGINT A Greek translation of the Old Testament made at Alexandria for Greek-speaking Jews. The oldest version of the Bible, the Septuagint was finished about the beginning of the Christian era and became the Bible of the early Christian church. It was made by seventy translators, hence its name.

SEPULCHER Caverns, both natural and artificial, were used by the Hebrews for the burial of their dead (Ge 23:9; Is 22:16; Jo 11:38). Jerusalem is the center of a great cemetery as the cliffs about the city have numerous tombs. To protect the tomb, a stone was placed against the entrance (Ma 27:60). Sepulchers were generally outside the city, often on the face of a cliff some distance from the ground. They were commonly whitewashed so they could be clearly seen and not touched, as contact with them would render one ceremonially unclean. In many instances they were shafts in the side of the cavern. There were also family burial places (Ge 49:29–31; 2 Sa 2:32; 1 Ki 13:22) and public places for the poor and strangers (2 Ki 23:6; Je 26:23; Ma 27:7).

SERAPHIM Intelligent, moral beings before the throne of God. They are described by Isaiah as having six wings (Is 6:2–7). They declare the holiness of God and that "the whole earth is full of his glory."

SERMON ON THE MOUNT The customary designation for the teachings of Jesus recorded in Ma 5–7. The mountain on which Jesus gave the sermon to his desciples has been identified with twin peaks west of Tiberias. The use of the word mountain here probably means a plateau region as opposed to the lowlands near the Sea of Galilee.

SERPENT A limbless reptile with an elongated body. Its subtlety is noted (Ge 3:1, 14). It was the agent of Satan (Jo 8:44; Re 12:9). Eve was tempted by a serpent to eat of the tree of knowledge in the garden of Eden (Ge 3:1–6).

SERVANT OF JEHOVAH One who acknowledges God and performs his will. Moses (Ps 105:26), David (Ps 132:10), and Abraham (Ps 105:6) were servants of God. The servant of Jehovah is depicted in Is 52:13–53:12 as having suffered affliction and death, thereby atoning for the sins of man. Most commentators hold that the servant here is Christ, the Messiah.

SHADRACH The name given by the Babylonian eunuch to Hananiah, one of Daniel's three companions (Da 1:7, 3:12–30).

SHEEP An animal extensively raised in Palestine for its wool, skin, meat, and milk. It was a ceremonially clean animal much used in sacrfice (Le 1:10, 4:32, 5:15, 22:21). The Hebrews in the patriarchial age were shepherds (Ge 12:16) as were their descendants who settled in Canaan after the Exodus (1 Ch 27:31). Angels appeared to certain shepherds at the time of the birth of Christ (Lu 2:8–16). Trumpets were made of the horns of rams (Jos 6:4).

SHEEPFOLD An enclosure within which sheep were herded for the night (Nu 32:16; Eze 34:14). The enclosing wall which was pierced by a gateway or door (Jo 10:1–2) might also be surmounted with thorns to provide additional protection. A watchtower often stood close by (2 Ki 17:9; 2 Ch 26:10; Mi 4:8).

SHEKEL (weight) An ancient weight and money unit introduced into Palestine from Babylonia.

SHEM (name) A son of Noah, probably the firstborn of the three sons (Ge 5:32). At the time of his birth his father was five hundred years old. At the age of one hundred, Shem entered the ark (Ge 7:7; 1 Pe 3:20). For not looking upon his father's nakedness he received Noah's blessing (Ge 9:23–37). He was six hundred years old when he died (Ge 11:11). The father of Arphaxad, he was an ancestor of Abraham and of the family of Jesus (Lu 3:36). The Semites are descended from him.

SHEOL See HELL.

SHEPHERD A herder of sheep. In biblical times he led them to pasture, to watering places, and at night to the fold. He was responsible for driving away attacking wild beasts (1 Sa 17:34–36). The patriarchs of Genesis were shepherds (Ge 13:6). Jesus called himself the good shepherd (Jo 10:14).

SHIBBOLETH (a stream) When the Ephraimites were defeated by Jephthah, the fords of the river Jordan were seized by the victors to prevent the return of the Ephraimites. To determine whether one seeking to cross belonged to that tribe he was required to pronounce the word *Shibboleth*. The Ephraimites did not give the sound of *sh* at the beginning of a word, hence those who said *Sibboleth* were put to death (Ju 12:5–6).

SHILOH (rest) **1.** A town of Ephraim, north of Bethel. It was here the tabernacle was set up thus making it the religious center until the death of Eli (Jos 18:1). Eli, the high priest, judged Israel at Shiloh until his death when the ark was captured by the Philistines (1 Sa 4:12–18). It was here that the Benjamites seized young women for wives (Ju 21:19–23). The loss of the ark signified that God had forsaken Shiloh (Ps 78:60; Je 7:12, 14, 26:6, 9). **2.** A word in Jacob's blessing of Judah (Ge 49:10). Most commentators agree that the passage is a great Messianic prophecy.

SHOWBREAD The word means literally "bread of the presence." It was placed on the table in the holy place of the sanctuary in two rows, six loaves in each row. It was changed on the Sabbath, and eaten by the priests (Ex 25:30; Le 24:5–9; Ma 12:4). According to Josephus it was unleavened. The number represented the tribes of Israel (Le 24:7).

SHULAMMITE The designation for the young woman who was the shepherd's lover in the Song of Solomon (Son 6:13).

SIGNET See SEAL.

SILAS The contracted form of Silvanus. A member of the church at Jerusalem (Ac 15:22), probably a Hellenistic Jew. He was commissioned by the Council at Jerusalem to report its decision about circumcision to the church of Antioch (Ac 15:22, 27, 32). When Paul and Barnabas disagreed regarding Mark, Silas became Paul's companion on the second journey (Ac 15:40). At Philippi they were imprisoned (Ac 16:19, 25). Silas remained with Timothy at Berea and both of them joined Paul at Corinth (Ac 18:5). In the epistles he is called Silvanus.

SIMEON (hearing) **1.** The second son of Jacob. His mother was Leah (Ge 29:33). After Shechem defiled Simeon's sister Dinah, Levi and Simeon massacred the inhabitants of the city of Shechem. Later Jacob deplored this deed (Ge 34:24–31, 49:5–7). **2.** A tribe descended from the sons of Simeon. The six sons were Jemuel, Janim, Jachin, Zohar, Shaul, and Ohad, and all but the latter founded a tribal family (Ge 46:10; Nu 26:12–14; 1 Ch 4:24). The tribe was located in the extreme south of Judah and eventually was absorbed by the tribe of Judah (Jos 19:1–2, 9). **3.** The son of Judah and an ancestor of Jesus (Lu 3:30). **4.** A devout man who had been divinely assured that he would not die until he had seen Jesus. When Jesus was but a boy, Simeon saw him (Lu 2:25–35). **5.** A prophet or teacher of Antioch, surnamed Niger (Ac 13:1). **6.** Simon Peter (Ac 15:14). See PETER.

SIMON (hearing) **1.** Simon Peter. See PETER. **2.** Father of Judas Iscariot (Jo 6:71). **3.** Simon the Zealot, called "Simon the Canaanite," one of the apostles (Lu 6:15; Ac 1:13). **4.** A kinsman of Jesus, brother of James and Jude (Ma 13:55; Mk 6:3). See BROTHERS OF THE LORD. **5.** Simon the Leper. He lived at Bethany and it is probable that Christ cured him of leprosy. It was in his house, after Lazarus had been raised to life, that Mary anointed Jesus with the spikenard. It is possible he was the husband of Martha (Ma 26:6–13; Mk 14:3–9; Jo 12:1–8). **6.** A Pharisee in whose house Christ was a guest when a sinful woman anointed his feet

(Lu 7:36–50). **7.** Simon the Cyrene, father of Alexander and Rufus (Mk 15:21). When Jesus fell under the weight of his cross on the way to Calvary, it was placed upon Simon (Ma 27:32). **8.** Simon the sorcerer, usually called Simon Magnus. A magician of Samaria, he was converted to Christianity by the preaching of Philip. He was severly rebuked by Peter when he offered to purchase the wonder-working power of the Holy Spirit (Ac 8:9–24). **9.** Simon the tanner. He lived at Joppa. He was a Christian (Ac 9:43, 10:6, 17, 32).

SIN "Missing the mark." Theologians define it as "any want of conformity unto, or transgression of the law of God." In the genesis of the moral history of the race the rights and liberties of our first parents were defined by a divine law, the violation of which would be sin upon which would fall the judgment of God (Ge 2:16–17). Sin is transgression of the divine law; where no law is, there is no transgression (Ro 4:15). There are two forms of sin—a sin of commission, the doing of anything forbidden by the law, and a sin of omission, not doing what the law requires. The effect of Adam's sin upon the moral life of the Adamic race is what is meant by original sin, the consequences of that sin being universal (Ro 5:12). There is great controversy as to the result of this sin on the human race. Calvinism contends that since Adam was the head of the race, his sin is imputed to every member of the race causing everyone to be guilty (1 Co 15:22). The Arminian view rejects the doctrine that such guilt is imputed and holds that the effect of Adam's sin is that of an inherited proneness to sin, but that guilt is imputed only when sin is actually committed (Eze 18:20; Ro 14:12). The Pelagian doctrine claims that there is no connection between the sin of Adam and the moral character of his race. It says that everyone is pure until he acts sinfully. By never acting sinfully one would be in no need of redemption. This concept is rejected by all evangelical Christians because the Bible clearly states that

197

all have sinned (Ro 3:9–10, 23, 5:12; Ga 3:22; 1 Jo 1:8). The wages of sin is death (Ge 2:15–17; Eze 18:20; Ro 6:23, 8:2; Jam 1:13–15) unless man accepts the atonement provided by God through his Son, Jesus Christ (Is 53:5; Jo 3:14–18; Ro 3:25; 1 Jo 1:5–2:2). See SALVATION. Jesus said that sin originates in the heart (Ma 15:11; Mk 7:15) and warned against sin against the Holy Ghost (Ma 12:30–32; Lu 12:8–10; Jo 16:7–11). This sin is unpardonable, not because God cannot or will not forgive it, but because the sinner refuses to be led by the Spirit to accept the terms of forgiveness (Is 59:1–3; Ep 4:30; 1 Th 5:19; He 3:7–19, 10:26–27; 1 Pe 2). The man of sin is mentioned in 2 Th 2:3–12.

SISERA **1.** Commander of a Canaanite army. He fled after his defeat by Deborah and Barak. He hid in the home of Heber, the Kenite, whose wife, Jael, killed him as he slept (Ju 4:2–22, 5:20–30; 1 Sa 12:9; Ps 83:9). **2.** Ancestor of Nethinim (Ez 2:53; Ne 7:55).

SLAVE Slavery is an ancient institution. A slave might be purchased (Ge 37:28, 36; Eze 27:13), or one might become a slave because of inability to pay a debt. To enslave a debtor or his children was against the Mosaic law (Ex 22:3; 2 Ki 4:1; Am 2:6). Some were taken captive in war (Nu 31:9; 2 Ki 5:2). One might sell himself or a child (Ex 21:2, 7; Le 25:39, 47). The brothers of Joseph sold him for twenty pieces of silver (Ge 37:28). The Jewish laws protected the treatment of Hebrew slaves, and after six years of service he could have his freedom. In the year of Jubilee all Hebrew slaves were liberated (Le 25:40). Foreign slaves had the rights of the people in regard to the Sabbath, religious festivals and sacrifices (Ex 12:44; De 12:12, 18, 16:11, 14). Under Christian conditions obedience was enjoined (Ep 6:5–8; Col 3:22–25). The master was also required to recognize the rights of the slave (Ep 6:9; Col 4:1).

SODOM One of the five cities of the plain of the Jordan (Ge 13:10). It was famous for its wickedness (Ge 13:13, 18:20; Is 3:9; La 4:6). It was the home of Lot and his family. However, before the Lord destroyed the city because of its evilness, Lot was allowed to escape with all of his family except his wife who turned to salt as she gazed back at the city (Ge 19:1-26).

SOLOMON The son of David and Bathsheba; born in Jerusalem. He was king of united Israel (973?-933? B.C.). As king he strengthened the fortifications of Jerusalem, and embellished it with royal buldings and the famous Temple (1 Ki 9:15, 24, 11:27). He had a large army with many chariots and horsemen (1 Ki 4:26, 10:26) and he also controlled a navy and a lucrative sea trade. His reign was one of luxury and extravagance. According to the Scriptures he had 700 wives and 300 concubines (1 Ki 11:3). His lavishness caused much popular discontent and laid the groundwork for the later disruption of the kingdom. He began his career as a king renowned for his wisdom (1 Ki 3:3-14). He was author of 3000 proverbs and 1005 songs (1 Ki 4:32). However, later he lapsed into idolatry, an occurrence attributed to the influence of his wives (1 Ki 11:4). He died after a forty-year rule and was succeeded by his son, Rehoboam (1 Ki 11:42, 43).

SON A term denoting a male child (Ge 17:16, 19; Ma 1:21, 23), but also a grandson (Ge 29:5) or a more distant descendant (Ez 8:15; Ma 1:1). It is also used to denote a foster son (Ex 2:10; He 11:24) and a subject or disciple (1 Ki 20:35; 2 Ki 16:7). It also indicates a member of a tribe, for example, the Israelites were called the sons of Jacob (Lu 1:16). Believers in the Lord Jesus are called sons of God (Jo 1:12-13; Ro 8:14-17; Ga 3:26; 1 Jo 3:1-2).

SON OF GOD The sonship of Christ. In the N.T. it occurs nearly fifty times and is expressive of the relation that exists between the Father and the eternal Son (Ma 16:16, 27:43; Mk 1:1; Jo 3:18). He has all the perfections of God and is equal with God (Jo 1:1-14, 5:17-25; Ph 2:6). In receiving the commission of the Father, in his mode of operation he is subordinate, but not inferior (Jo 3:1, 17, 8:42; Ga 4:4; He 1:2). It was because he claimed he was the Son of God that he was charged with blasphemy by the Sanhedrin (Ma 26:63-66; Mk 14:61). At his baptism and transfiguration he was divinely acknowledged as the Son of God (Ma 3:16-17, 17:5).

SON OF MAN Daniel saw "one like the son of man" in a vision (Da 7:13). This title was applied by Christ to himself. His use of it does not denote that he was merely human, for he frequently declared that he was divine. He identified himself with man in his human nature and in his sufferings for mankind (Ma 20:28; Jo 1:14).

SONS OF GOD A designation for certain godlike beings or angels (Ge 6:2-4; Job 1:6, 2:1).

SOUL An incorporeal being which may or may not be embodied. God is Spirit. Dichtomists believe that man has two parts—body and soul. Trichotomists believe he consists of three parts—body, soul and spirit. The scriptures speak usually of man as body and soul, or body and spirit. The animal is sentient and has, like man, a soul. It is the principle of life but perishes with the body. In man the soul is the principle of the rational and immortal life comprising reason and the moral and religious natures. In addition to the soul-powers of the brute, the human soul has higher powers, intellectual, moral and religious, and will have an immortal existence (Ma 10:28; Re 16:3, 20:4). Trichotomists appeal to 1 Th 5:23 and He 4:12 for support though dichotomists do not feel that these are adequate proof.

SOWER One who scatters seeds. While sowing the sower walked down a furrow distributing the seed with his hand. Jesus referred to a sower in one of his parables (Ma 13:4). The seed was supposed to be ceremonially clean and mixed seed was not to be sown in the same field (Le 11:37–38, 19:19; De 22:9).

SPIRIT See SOUL, HOLY SPIRIT.

STAR It is not strange that the stars, on account of their number and constellations, should have attracted the attention of the ancients (Ge 22:17; Is 13:10). In Job there is reference to Orion, Pleiades, the Bear, Mazzaroth—the Zodiac (Job 9:9, 38:31–32). With the exception of the sun and moon, all heavenly bodies were designated stars by the Hebrews. They recognized the stars as the handiwork of God (Ps 8:3) and under his power (Is 13:10; Je 31:35). But apart from the ordinary observations of the heavens there is nothing in the Scriptures to show that the ancient Hebrews had any real knowledge of astronomy. Following the heathen nations, Israelites who left the pure worship of Jehovah made the stars objects of worship (De 4:19; 2 Ki 17:16, 23:5). It was believed that the stars directly influenced human affairs, and it may be that Deborah in her song had something of this in mind when she spoke of the stars fighting against Sisera (Ju 5:20). The star in the East, of the wise men, the star of Bethlehem, guided the Magi to the Christ child (Ma 2:1–12). Jesus is spoken of as the "the bright and morning star" (Re 22:16).

STEPHEN (a crown) His Greek name would indicate that he was a Hellenist but his birthplace is unknown. He is first mentioned in connection with his appointment as one of seven deacons of the church of Jerusalem (Ac 6:5). He was a man of great faith (Ac 6:8). The activities of Stephen aroused the opposition of foreign Jews who had synagogues in Jerusalem, beginning with the synagogue of the Libertines (freed men), the Cyrenians and Alexandrians. They charged Stephen with blasphemy. They claimed to have heard him say that Jesus would set aside the Mosaic institutions (Ac 6:11–14). Those who testified against him were false witnesses (Ac 6:13). In his defense (Ac 7:2–60), he set forth God's selection of Israel for divine ends but he pointed out that the Israelites were often in opposition to God and his purpose. When he said that he saw Christ, they rushed upon him to put him to death. With Saul of Tarsus holding the clothes of the mob, they stoned him to death. Stephen was the first Christian martyr.

STONING This was the usual mode of inflicting capital punishment provided by the Mosaic law. See PUNISHMENT. The witnesses placed their hands on the head of the criminal to indicate he was the bearer of his guilt (Le 24:14) and the first stones were hurled by the witnesses (De 13:9; Jo 8:7). The law required death by stoning for eighteen different crimes including idolatry, wizardry, blasphemy, and Sabbath breaking (Le 20:27, 24:16; Nu 15:32–36; De 17:2–5).

STRANGER As specified by the Mosaic law, one living among the Hebrew people but not of that nationality. He might also be a visitor in the land (Le 16:29, 17:8; 2 Sa 1:13). While in the land he had claims upon the kind treatment of the Hebrews (De 10:18–19) and his rights were safeguarded (Ex 22:21, 23:9). He was required to refrain from the things prohibited to the Israelites (Le 17:10, 20:2, 24:16). While he must observe the laws regarding the sanctity of the Sabbath, he was not required to perform religious duties peculiar to the Hebrews (Ex 12:43–46).

STRONG DRINK When about to engage in their sacred duties the priests were not allowed to use strong drink (Le 10:9). The same was true of the Nazarite during the period of his vow. He not only should not partake of the fruit of the vine in the way of wine, but was forbidden to eat the grapes (Nu 6:3; Ju 13:4; Lu 1:15).

SUN A radiant heavenly body around which the earth and other planets revolve. In the account of its creation it is described as "the greater light to rule the day" (Ge 1:16). It was referred to as the vital power bringing forth vegetation (De 33:14; 2 Sa 23:4) and was represented as rising and setting and as moving (2 Ki 20:11; Ps 19:4–6; Hab 3:11). Joshua's request that the sun stay up until the Israelites defeated the Amorites was granted (Jos 10:12–13). Many of the peoples with whom the Israelites came in contact worshipped the sun. The Egyptian sun god was called Ra; the Phoenician, Baal; and the Assyrian, Shamash. In the time of the divided kingdom some of the Israelites built altars and burned incense to the sun (2 Ki 23:5). They also dedicated horses to it (2 Ki 23:11). In Mal 4:2 the promised Messiah was called the "Sun of righteousness".

SWINE A word used collectively, usually in regard to domestic hogs. It was ceremonially unclean (Le 11:7; De 14:8). Using its flesh for food in hot countries is believed to be conducive to sickness. Phoenicians, Ethiopians, and Egyptians considered it unclean, but it was eaten by the latter at the time of their festival of the moon god. A swineherd was debarred from a temple, and his wife had to be from a family of swineherds. The Jew regarded a pig as the symbol of filth (Ma 7:6; 2 Pe 2:22). Christ's picture of the prodigal implied that the lowest state to which a Jew could be reduced was that of attending swine (Lu 15:15). Jesus allowed a legion of demons to go into a herd of swine when he cast them out of a man (Mk 5:12–13).

SWORD A weapon with an iron or bronze blade, which was sometimes two-edged. It was worn in a scabbard on the left side (2 Sa 20:8; Eze 32:27). It was the symbol of war (Is 2:4).

SYNAGOGUE (assembly) A local assembly of Jews organized chiefly for worship; also its building or place of meeting. Quite strangely the word appears but once in Old Testament (Ps 74:8) but repeatedly in the New Testament. With the destruction of the Temple by Nebuchadnezzar (586 B.C.) came the necessity for a religious institution which would supplant the one destroyed. The synagogue was accordingly instituted during or soon after the Exile. In its services the emphasis shifted from sacrifice to teaching the law and the prophets. Its ultimate origin is veiled in obscurity. Some trace it to the house meetings or gatherings of elders at the home of Ezekiel in Babylonia (Eze 8:1, 20:1, 3). Great impetus was given to its development by the religious reforms of Ezra and Nehemiah (about 444 B.C.) which, among other things, provided for a systematic reading of the law (Ne 8:1–8). Synagogue buildings were usually rectangular with entrances preferably facing Jerusalem. Galilaean synagogues would thus face the south. The furniture consisted chiefly of a chest (ark) in which were kept the sacred rolls of the law and the prophets. In front of the chest a lamp burned continually. There was usually a raised platform on which stood the reader's desk. There were benches for the worshippers. A few of these, placed in front of the platform and facing the audience, were the "chief seats" in which the Pharisees coveted the honor to sit (Ma 23:6). The service was in four parts as follows: (*a*) recitation of three brief passages of the law including De 6:4–9; (*b*) prayer; (*c*) reading from the law and the prophets; and (*d*) pronouncement of the priestly benediction (Nu 6:24–26). The reading in Hebrew was accompanied by an interpretation into Aramaic. Eventually a sermon was included in the service. Visitors, as Paul, were sometimes asked to address the synagogue (Ac 13:14–16).

T

TABERNACLE a portable sanctuary carried by the Israelites throughout their wilderness wanderings. The Pentateuch describes it as a large tent thirty cubits long, ten cubits broad, with sides ten cubits high. It was the visible symbol of God's presence. When Moses entered this Tabernacle, the cloudy pillar would descend to the doorway and the Lord would talk with Moses face to face (Ex 33:7–11). Elaborate directions for its construction (together with that of its furniture) were divinely given to Moses at Sinai (Ex 25–27, 30–31, 35–40). The structure was built according to pattern (Ex 25:9, 40) and was variously designated as the Tabernacle, tent of the congregation, or tent of meeting (Ex 26:1, 36:18–19, 40:26, 34–35). Forming the outside portion of the square Israelitish camp were the tents of the twelve tribes. Inside this square were stationed the priests and Levites. The center was the court of the Tabernacle (Ex 27:9). Within the court, just halfway between the entrance and the Tabernacle, stood the brazen altar or altar of burnt-offering (Ex 27:1–8). Halfway between it and the Tabernacle was the brazen laver (Ex 30:17–21). Behind the laver was the Tabernacle, a curtain-covered structure 15x45 feet in area, with the entrance at the exact center of the court. Its wooden framework of acacia boards fifteen feet in height, set in silver sockets, and the many curtains supported by the frame are elaborately described (Ex 26). The front or east compartment (15x30 feet) was the holy place.

TABERNACLES, FEAST OF One of the three great annual festivals at which the men of Israel were required to appear (De 16:16; 2 Ch 8:12–13; Ze 14:16). During this time the celebrants lived in tents (tabernacles) in commemoration of the period of wandering in the wilderness (Le 23:40–42).

TABITHA See DORCAS.

TAMAR (a palm tree) **1.** The wife of Er son of Judah. After the death of Er she became the mother of Pharez and Zarah by Judah (Ge 38:6–30). From them several tribal families sprang (Nu 26:20–21). She is an ancestress of Jesus (Ma 1:3). **2.** Absalom's sister, who was violated by their half-brother Amnon (2 Sa 13). **3.** A daughter of Absalom, probably named after Absalom's sister (2 Sa 14:27). **4.** A place on the southern border of the land promised to Ezekiel by the Lord (Eze 47:19).

TAMARISK TREE A small tree, having small leaves which it sheds at maturity. There are several species in Palestine, the largest of which attains a height of from twenty to thirty feet. One was planted by Abraham in Beersheba (Ge 21:33). Beneath another Saul lived (1 Sa 22:6).

TARES A weed, or bearded darnel, that in the blade state could not be distinguished from wheat but in the ear state was quite dissimilar and could then be easily separated (Ma 13:25–30).

TARSHISH **1.** A prince of Persia in the time of Xerxes I (Ex 1:14). **2.** Son of Bilhan of Benjamin (1 Ch 7:10). **3.** Son of Javan, grandson of Japheth, and great-grandson of Noah (Ge 10:4; 1 Ch 1:7). **4.** The city of Tarshish, often mentioned in the Old Testament. It was on the Mediterranean, and a considerable distance from Palestine (Is 66:19; Jon 1:3). From this city the Phoenicians imported silver, iron, tin, and lead (Eze 27:12).

TARSUS The capital of Cilicia, on the river Cydnus in Asia Minor (Ac 9:30, 11:25, 21:39, 22:3).

TATNAI A Persian governor who opposed the plan of Zerubbabel and others to build the second Temple (Ez 5:3, 6, 6:6, 13).

TAXES When the Israelites became settled in Palestine, taxation took on an organized form. In the time of the judges the Jews were obliged to pay tithes and the redemption money of the firstborn. The tabernacle, priesthood and Levites were thus provided for. Under the monarchy, to meet the greater expenditure, heavier taxes were imposed by Solomon on livestock and products of the field (1 Ki 4:7–28), and those peoples under the domination of the king paid tribute (Sa 8:6, 14; 1 Ki 10:15; 2 Ki 3:4). These measures became oppressive and contributed largely to the division of the kingdom under Rehoboam (1 Ki 12:4). Under the Persians the Jews were heavily taxed in addition to taxes levied for their own national interests (Ne 5:4, 9:37). The same was true under the Egyptian and Syrian kings. At this time and during the Roman period taxes were collected by a member of a company which purchased the right from the government to collect taxes in a certain region. Called publicans in the Roman period, these men were hated by the people because of their harsh methods. During the reign of Julius Caesar (about 45 B.C.) the right of these men to operate in Judea was abolished. See PUBLICAN.

TAXING Two instances are given of tax registrations, or enrollments, one object of which was doubtless to determine the levying of taxes. The first was under Augustus when Mary and Joseph went to Bethlehem. This led to the fulfilment of Micah's prophecy relative to Jesus (Mi 5:2; Ma 2:5–6; Lu 2:1–20).

TEMPLE 1. *Solomonic Temple* The permanent house of the Lord in Jerusalem proposed by David, who purchased the site (2 Sa 7; 1 Ki 5:3–5, 8:17; 1 Ch 22, 28:11–29:9). He collected immense quantities of gold and silver for it, including 3,000 talents of gold and 7,000 talents of silver from his own coffers (1 Ch 22:14, 29:4, 7). The temple was built by Solomon on a Jerusalem hilltop, west of Kidron and north of the ancient city of David. Zerubbabel and Herod later reconstructed temples there. It was a small oblong building about 45 feet high with inner dimensions of 30x90 feet. An east front porch, fifteen feet wide, extended across the breadth of the building. The Temple building was divided into two chambers by a partition of olive wood. The chamber of the east corresponded to the Holy Place in the tabernacle. The west chamber, called oracle, corresponded to the Holy of Holies (1 Ki 6:2–3, 20, 31). The walls of both chambers were of cedar and the floor was overlaid with gold (1 Ki 6:9, 15–22, 29–35). Within the oracle were two giant cherubim of olive wood overlaid with gold, and about fifteen feet high. Their outstretched wings were spread above the ark (1 Ki 6:20, 22, 8:5–7). This bulding was plundered and destroyed by Nebuchadnezzar in 586 B.C. **2.** Zerubbabel's Temple. The erection of this structure was authorized by Cyrus after Zerubbabel led about 50,000 people back to Jerusalem. It was begun about 520 B.C. (Hag 1:1–4, 8) and was finished about four years later. It differed with its predecessor, Solomon's Temple, chiefly in regard to simplicity. The wooden partition between the holy place and the Holy of Holies was replaced by a veil. One golden candlestick instead of ten stood in the holy place. The ark, which had been destroyed, was not replaced. **3.** *Herodian Temple.* To secure the favor of the Jews, Herod the Great promised them a new temple. Before the second Temple was taken down, the materials for the new temple were gathered. Work on this temple began in 19 B.C. After eighteeen months the main building was constructed but the entire work including buildings and courts was not completed until about A.D. 64 or six years before it was destroyed. It was the costliest, the greatest, and most magnificent of the three temples. It was the Temple of New Testament times and to it Jesus was brought when he was an infant (Lu 2:22–34). Later he taught in it (Mk 14:49). This temple was the scene of the driving out of the money-changers by Jesus (Ma 21:12–14; Mk 11:15–17; Lu 19:45–47; Jo 2:13–16). This Temple was destroyed in A.D. 70.

TEN COMMANDMENTS Called by the Hebrews the Ten Words (Decalogue). Divinely inscribed on two tablets of stone on Sinai (Ex 31:18). Basic law of the Hebrew state, first of the Sinaitic institutions to be given, the "Magna Charta" of Israel. See Ex 20 and De 5.

TENT The moveable habitation used by shepherds and soldiers (Ge 25:27; Ju 8:11). Tent material was often made from the coarse, black hair of goats (Son 1:5). The tents were made in various shapes—round and oblong—and they were fastened to the ground by stakes (Ex 35:18; Is 54:2). Tent-making was the vocation of Paul and Aquila, the man with whom he worked at this trade while in Corinth. (Ac 18:3).

TERAH 1. The father of Abraham. During the greater part of his life he lived in Ur of the Chaldees. He was an idolater (Jos 24:2), and like the people among whom he dwelt, he was a worshipper of the moon god. His family migrated to Haran whre he died at the age of 205 (Ge 11:25–32). 2. An encampment of the Israelties (Nu 33:27–28).

TERAPHIM A household image, greatly venerated because it was regarded as a guardian through which came prosperity and comfort. They were of different sizes, some small enough to be carried or concealed easily (Ge 31:19, 30, 34). When Jacob left Padan-aram, his wife, Rachel, stole

Laban's teraphim (Ge 31:19–35). Micah, who lived in Mount Ephraim, set up a sanctuary for himself having ephod and teraphim (Ju 17:5).

TEREBINTH The turpentine tree from which the ancients extracted turpentine and resin. Although not in the Authorized Version, it is used in the Revised Version for teil tree (Is 6:13). It ranges in height from about fifteen feet to forty feet.

TETRARCH Originally the ruler of the fourth part of a country. The term also applied to subordinate princes or petty kings. The title was applied to Herod Antipas, ruler of Galilee and Perea (Ma 14:1; Lu 3:1, 19, 9:7; Ac 13:1).

THADDAEUS See JUDAS.

THEOCRACY (rule of God) A form of government in which God is regarded as the head of the state and the one responsible for the institution of the laws. This was the form of government of the ancient Hebrews. To them God was king and the law was the Ten Commandments, or Decalogue (Ex 20:1–22; De 4:12, 33).

THOMAS (twin) An apostle who was also called Didymus, the Greek form of his name (Ma 10:3). It was he who expressed concern for the safety of Jesus when the latter went to Bethany at the time of the death of Lazarus. Thomas proposed that all the apostles go with Jesus and die with him if necessary (Jo 11:16). Known for his doubting nature, Thomas refused to believe the testimony of the others regarding the resurrection of Jesus. He preferred to trust only his own senses (Jo 20:24–25).

THORNS, THISTLES Prickly plants like the thorn, bramble, thistle, brier, and nettle, flourish in Palestine. To torture and insult Jesus, the Roman soldiers placed a crown of thorns on his head as he was being led to the cross (Ma 27:29). Paul used the expression "thorn in the flesh" to describe his physical infirmity (2 Co 12:7).

THRESHING The process by which the grain is separated from wheat stalks. Among the ancients this was done by pounding it out with a stick or flail (Ju 6:11; Is 28:27). In other cases the unthreshed grain was placed in a circular pathway on the threshing floor and oxen were driven over it to trod out the grain (De 25:4).

THRONE An elevated seat occupied by a person of authority. He might be a king, a governor, a military officer, a high priest, a judge (1 Sa 1:9; 2 Sa 3:10; Ps 122:5; Je 1:15; Ma 19:28). Solomon's throne, overlaid with gold and inlaid with ivory, was six steps from the ground and a stone lion stood at each end of the steps (1 Ki 10:18–20; 2 Ch 9:17–19). When administering justice, issuing royal orders, or granting an audience, the king occupied the throne (1 Ki 2:19, 7:7, 10:18–20, 22:10). The throne of God is in heaven (Ps 11:4, 103:19; Is 66:1; Ma 5:33–35) and he set up the throne of David (2 Sa 3:10) to be established forever (2 Sa 7:13; 1 Ki 2:45; Ps 89:35–37). This prophecy (Is 9:6–7; Je 33:15–17) was fulfilled in Christ (Lu 1:31–33).

THUMMIM See URIM AND THUMMIM.

TIBERIAS A city on the Sea of Galilee, built by Herod Antipas, and named after Tiberius who was then emperor. It was the capital of Galilee until the reign of Herod Agrippa II. The Sea of Galilee is also called the Sea of Tiberias (Jo 6:1, 21:1).

TIBERIUS CAESAR See CAESAR.

TIMOTHY (worshipping God) Paul's companion and assistant. A native of Lystra, Timothy was the child of a mixed marriage. His mother was Jewish, his father was Greek (Ac 16:1). He was given religious instruction at an early age by his mother, Eunice, and his grandmother, Lois (2 Ti 1:5, 3:15). To forestall criticism of Timothy on the part of the Jews, Paul caused him to be circumcised (Ac 16:3).

TITHE A tenth part of one's income. Tithing was practiced by various ancient nations. The Egyptians gave a fifth of their crops to Pharaoh (Ge 47:24). Abraham gave a tenth of the spoils of his victory to Melchizedek, the priest-king of Salem (Ge 14:20). Under the Mosaic law the Jews were required to give a tenth of the products of the soil and of cattle "to the Lord" (Le 27:30, 32). Of the cattle every tenth animal was set apart. The tithe offered as a heave offering was given to the Levites (Nu 18:21, 24) because of their service at the sanctuary and the fact that they did not receive a portion of the land. The tithe was taken to the sanctuary where a portion was eaten by the giver and the Levites in a eucharistic feast and the balance went to the Levites. Every third year the tithe was stored in the town of the givers, and the widow, the stranger, the fatherless, and Levite could partake of it (De 14:28–29).

TITUS A companion and fellow-laborer of Paul. A Christian convert of Greek parentage, he is first mentioned in the Bible when he accompanied Paul to Jerusalem where a church council considered the question of circumcision as it related to Gentile Christians. Titus was not required by the council to be circumcised (Ga 2:1–3). Paul's epistle to him was written to guide his activities in Crete (Tit 1:5–3:11).

TOMB See SEPULCHER.

TONGUE The organ of speech (Job 29:10; Ps 39:3, 71:24; Jam 3:6). It denotes the language or dialect of a people (Es 1:22; Da 1:4; Ac 1:19, 2:4, 8, 11). In the story of the tower of Babel God purposely confuses the language of the people, causing the various peoples of the earth to understand only their own tongue, or language. This story explains the rise of all languages from a single origin (Ge 11:1–9). On the day of Pentecost, when the Holy Spirit descended, tongues of fire appeared and the Apostles began to speak as the Spirit gave them utterance (Ac 2:1–21). The gift of tongues is listed among the other spiritual endowments (1 Co 12:1–13, 28–30, 14:2–33).

TOPAZ A precious stone found mainly in Ethiopia (Job 28:19). It was in the first row of the breastplate of the high priest (Ex 28:17) and in the foundation of the New Jerusalem (Re 21:20).

TRANSFIGURATION A moment in the life of Jesus in which, while on a high mountain with Peter, James, and John, he suddenly was visited by Moses and Elijah who spoke of his coming death (Lu 9:28–31). During this time his face shone brightly and his clothes appeared white as light (Ma 17:2). It was believed that the purpose of this visit was to prepare the disciples for the coming events which were to culminate in the crucifixion. The site of the transfiguration is thought to be Mount Hermon. It occurred at night (Lu 9:32), about six or eight days after Peter's confession to Jesus that he (Jesus) was the Messiah (Ma 16:13–17). After this event Jesus told the disciples to tell no one of the transfiguration until after the "Son of man be risen again from the dead" (Ma 17:9; Mk 9:9).

TRESPASS OFFERING See OFFERINGS.

TRUMPET A musical instrument made of the horn of an animal which could be heard at a great distance (Ex 19:16, 19; 2 Sa 6:15). Militarily it was used in mobilizing an army (Ju 6:34), signaling an attack, and calling off pursuit (2 Sa 2:28). It was used when a king was crowned (1 Ki 1:34; 2 Ki 9:13). By it the year of jubilee was ushered in (Le 25:9). At the resurrection of the dead the trumpet will sound (1 Co 15:52).

TYRE (a rock) A very ancient city of Phoenicia on a strongly protected island about half a mile from the shore. Its importance was frequently referred to by ancient writers (Eze 26:1–27:32). Its rise came after the rise of the city of Sidon (Is 23). In the fifteenth century B.C. it was under the dominion of Egypt, and it was a strong city when the Israelites came into Canaan under Joshua (Jos 19:29). At no time did it come into the hands of the Israelites. In the time of David and Solomon very friendly relations existed. Hiram, king of Tyre, furnished David with materials and craftsmen for his palace (2 Sa 5:11). He also provided materials for Solomon's Temple and other building enterprises (1 Ki 5:1, 9:10–14; 2 Ch 2:3, 11). Sometime after the kingdom was divided in 921 B.C., Ahab, the second king of the fourth dynasty of Israel, married the daughter of Ethbaal, king of the Zidonians (1 Ki 16:31). The Tyrians wre not a warlike people; they were mainly interested in commerce, colonization, manufacture. They traded with the remotest peoples, their productions consisting of glassware, dyes, work in metal. In the ninth century B.C. Carthage was founded by Tyrians and became one of Rome's strongest rivals. Jeremiah and Ezekiel prophesied against Tyre (Je 27:1–11; Eze 26:1–28:19, 29:18–20). Jesus once came to the coasts of Tyre and Sidon (Ma 15:21–31; Mk 7:24–31). A Christian Church was founded at Tyre and here Paul spent some time (Ac 21:3–4).

U

UNCLEAN ANIMALS According to Mosaic law unclean animals—those unfit for food—included: **1.** Those who do not have cloven hooves and do not chew the cud (Le 11:3–8); hence all carnivorous and most other animals except oxen, sheep, goats, and certain deer and gazelles (De 14:4–8). **2.** Carnivorous birds, including the owl, eagle, vulture, kite, swan, pelican, stork, bat, and several others (Le 11:13–19; De 14:12–18). **3.** Water animals which lack either fins or scales, notably eels (Le 11:9–12). **4.** Insects not provided with leaping legs similar to those of a locust (Le 11:20–23). **5.** All creeping things, including certain small quadrupeds (Le 11:29–31, 41–43).

UNCLEANNESS The Mosaic law distinguishes between the ceremonially clean and unclean, as well as between holy and unholy (Le 10:10). Ceremonially unclean persons could become clean through the rites of purification. Mosaic rules pertaining to uncleanness fall roughly into five groups: those having to do with sexual impurity (Le 15:16–18), with blood (Le 15:19–30; 1 Sa 14:33), with food (De 14:7–21), with death (Nu 19:11–22), and with leprosy (Le 13–14).

UR 1. A city of the Chaldees in northern Mesopotamia slightly west of the Euphrates. It was the place in which Abraham lived before moving to Canaan (Ge 11:28, 31, 15:7; Ne 9:7). **2.** The father of Eliphal (1 Ch 11:35).

URIAH (light of Jehovah) **1.** One of David's warriors; a Hittite (2 Sa 23:39; 1 Ch 11:41). He was the husband of Bathsheba, with whom David committed adultery. As a result David had Uriah placed in a dangerous position in the line of battle and Uriah was killed. David then married

215

Bathsheba (2 Sa 11:1–27; Ma 1:6). **2.** A priest who was a witness to a written prophecy of Isaiah concerning Maher-shalal-hashbaz (Is 8:2). He was probably the Urijah who built the altar for Ahaz (2 Ki 16:10–16). **3.** Son of Shemaiah and a prophet of Kirjath-jearim. Jehoiakim sought to kill him for the judgment he predicted would fall upon Judah. He fled to Egypt but was brought back and put to death (Je 26:20–23). He was also called Urijah. **4.** A priest in the time of Ezra and father of Meremoth (Ez 8:33). In Ne 3:4, 21 he is called Urijah. **5.** A priest who assisted Ezra (Ne 8:4).

URIM AND THUMMIM Small sacred objects in the breastplate of the high priest (Ex 28:30; Le 8:8) and which, as a form of divination by lot, were used to ascertain the Lord's will (Nu 27:21; De 33:8; 1 Sa 14:37–42, 28:6). Some regard the Urim and Thummim as two small stones which were cast as lots to determine guilt or innocence.

UZZIAH 1. A Levite of the line of Kohath (1 Ch 6:24) **2.** Father of Jonathan. The son was an overseer of David (1 Ch 27:25). **3.** A man of Judah (Ne 11:4). **4.** Son of Harim, a priest. He renounced his foreign wife (Ez 10:21). **5.** A king of Judah (2 Ki 15:13, 30–34; Ze 14:5; Ma 1:9). In 2 Ki 14:21, 15:1–8, 17–27 he is called Azariah. He was the son of Amaziah whom he succeeded at the age of sixteen (2 Ki 14:21).

V

VASHTI The first queen of Ahasuerus king of Persia (Es 1:9–2:17).

VINE This word usually refers to the grape vine. It was extensively cultivated by the people of the East as an important means of livelihood (Ge 40:9–11; Ps 78:47). Palestine was very favorable to the growth of the vine, especially in the hill country (Nu 13:23; Ju 9:27, 21:20; Je 31:5). The Eshcol grape is particularly noted (Nu 13:23). The vineyard was often on the hillside protected by a stone wall (Nu 22:24; Pr 24:31; Son 2:15; Is 5:1, 5). The vintage was a festive season and was attended with singing and shouting as the grapes were trodden in the press (Is 16:10; Je 25:30, 48:33). Jesus compared himself to the vine and his disciples to the branches (Jo 15:1–8).

VISIONS An order of mental phenomena in which God communicated to the mind in accordance with the mind's constitution. In the case of the prophets these visions were given to men committed to the will and service of God, and were of such a nature as to establish the fact of their divine source (Je 23:16, 21–22, 27). The genuineness of visions containing predictions was established by the fulfillment of the predictions. "They belong to an age of revelation and came to men who in manifold manner proved themselves to be vehicles of revelation." Those who falsely declared they had received visions wre denounced (Je 14:14, 23:16; Eze 13:7). Dreams should be distinguished from visions.

VOW A promise to God to perform some service for him on condition that he in return grant a specific favor, such as a safe journey (Ge 28:20–22), victory (Ju 11:30–31), or offspring (1 Sa 1:11). A more disinterested vow was made by the Nazarite who sought God's good will, in return for which he promised to give up strong drink, cutting his hair, and to dedicate himself wholly to the Lord (Nu 6:1–21).

W

WAGES Payment for labor or service. The Mosaic law required that wages be paid at the end of each day (Le 19:13; De 24:14–15). To withhold what was due a hired man was severely denounced by the prophets (Je 22:13; Mal 3:5). In the time of Jesus the wage for a day's labor was a denarius, or penny, equivalent to about seventeen cents (Ma 20:2).

WAR An armed conflict. Among the early Hebrews war was little more than a skirmish between opposing sides, usually of a few men each. However, from the time of Saul, the menace of the Philistines and other foes necessitated a standing army. War was regarded by the Hebrews as essentially religious. Their God was the God of hosts, their battles were the Lord's battles (1 Sa 18:17, 25:28; Ps 80:7, 19). Before going to war it was customary for primitive nations to use divination to determine favorable conditions and a propitious time. The Hebrews inquired of God (Ju 20:23, 27; 1 Sa 14:37, 23:2). Spies were sent into a county before invading it to ascertain what would be needed in making an attack (Jos 2:1; Ju 7:10; 1 Sa 26:4). The signal for an attack was the blowing of a trumpet (Jos 6:5; Ju 7:20) and the advance was accompanied with shouting (1 Sa 17:52; Am 1:14). When a city was captured, it was common to destroy it and massacre the inhabitants (Jos 8:24–29, 10:22–27; 2 Ki 15:16).

WASHING See BATHING.

WAVE OFFERING A portion of the peace offering dedicated to the priest. See OFFERINGS. During the wave offering the breast of the sacrificed animal was waved to and fro as it was carried toward the altar by the priest. This symbolized its presentation to the Lord and the Lord's return of it to the priests (Ex 29:19–28; Le 7:28–36, 10:12, 15). Waving was a horizontal motion made in line with the altar while the heave offering was up and down. At harvest time a sheaf of firstfruits was waved on the second day of the Passover, thereby dedicating the harvest to the Lord (Le 23:10–11).

WEEK A period of seven days. From the earliest institution of the Sabbath after the creation of the world, the Bible refers to seven-day periods (Ge 2:1–3). Although the word *week* is not used, the implication is the same. The term is implied at the time of the flood (Ge 7:4, 10, 8:10, 12) and the use of the seven-day division of time is also used in Babylonian accounts of this event. The only day of the seven named by the Hebrews was the Sabbath. They numbered the days of the week (Ma 28:1; Ac 20:7).

WEEKS, FEAST OF One of the three annual feasts during which all the men of Israel were required to present themselves at the sanctuary (Ex 34:22–23). It fell seven weeks after the waving of the sheaf and is also called Pentecost (Ac 2:1) or the feast of harvest because the first fruits of the wheat harvest were presented (Ex 23:16, 34:22; Nu 28:26). All labor was avoided and the day was observed as a Sabbath (Le 23:21). Sacrifices attended the offering of the loaves (Le 23:17–19).

WIDOW Because of the helpless position of widows, the Mosaic law required that they be treated kindly. Those who disregarded this law were to be punished (De 10:18, 24:17, 19, 27:19; Ze 7:10–12; Mal 3:5; Mk 12:40). Some Hebrew widows were cared for by their children or their relatives (Ge 38:11) or had the means to support themselves (Ju 17:1–6). In addition, a brother-in-law or close relative could be required to marry a young and childless widow (De 25:5–10; Ru 4:1–13). However, those widows who had no family, or whose relatives were poor, were in a very difficult position. Ruth, for example, gleaned the field after the reapers to support herself and Naomi (Ru 2:2, 17–18). In the early church, care for the widows was a duty of the congregation, and provisions were made to cover their needs (Ac 6:1; 1 Ti 5:3–16; Jam 1:27).

WIFE See MARRIAGE.

WILDERNESS OF THE WANDERING The land in which the Israelites wandered for forty years before entering Canaan. It was in the peninsula of Sinai formed by the Gulf of Suez and the Gulf of Akabah, the two branches of the Red Sea. About Mount Sinai was the granite region, while along the shore of the Mediterranean was the sandy region. The northern and central districts consisted of limestone (Ex 16:1–35; Nu 14:25, 33–45, 20:2–13).

WINE The Hebrew word *Yayim* is used to denote wine or fermented grape juice and its intoxicating character is obvious from the Scriptural use of the word. Palestine was a wine-producing country, and wine was commonly used. Lot drank wine and became intoxicated (Ge 19:32). It was used as a drink-offering in connection with the daily sacrifice (Ex 29:40) and other offerings (Le 23:13; Nu 15:5). The priests were forbidden to use wine during their sacred ministrations (Le 10:9) and the Nazarite, during the period of his vow, had to abstain from wine as well as from eating grapes (Nu 6:3–4). Mixed wine was wine mixed with water (Is 1:22) or with spices and strong drink (Ps 75:8; Is 5:22). The Scriptures set forth in striking forms the effects of the intemperate use of wine. Some of these effects are the enslavement of the drinker to wine (Ho 4:11), the redness of the eye (Ge 49:12), improper speech (Pr 20:1, 23:29–32; Is 28:7), distorted judgment (Pr 31:5). What was used by

Jesus in the institution of the Lord's Supper is called the "fruit of the vine" (Ma 26:29).

WISDOM The ability to judge fairly and to understand and make wise use of facts. The Hebrew conception was that wisdom is an attribute of God (Job 28; Is 40:12–14; Ro 11:33–35) and that he shared it with certain men (Pr 2:1–22; Ec 2:26; 1 Co 2:4–12, 12:7–8; Ep 1:17; Col 1:9). Wisdom is personified in Pr. 8. The portion of the Bible known as wisdom literature consists of Job, Proverbs, Ecclesiastes, and Song of Solomon. Paul condemned worldy wisdom (1 Co 1:19–31; Col 2:8; 1 Ti 6:20).

WITNESS 1. A memorial to an event. One such witness was the heap of stones set up by Jacob and Laban in witness of their covenant (Ge 31:46–52). Joshua set up a stone in witness of his covenant with the people of Israel (Jos 24:27). **2.** A person who gave testimony, especially in legal matters. Witnesses were needed to attest to a property transaction or a betrothal (Ru 4:9; Je 32:10). Under Mosaic law, in criminal cases, it was necessary to have two witnesses (De 17:6; Ma 18:16). If it were discovered that a witness had given false testimony, then he was punished with the same penalty the accused would have drawn (De 19:16–19). In carrying out a death sentence the witnesses were the first to cast the stones (De 17:6–7; 1 Ki 21:10). **3.** One who testifies to his faith in Christ (Lu 24:48; He 12:1). The Greek word for witness is martyr, a word that came to denote one who had suffered death rather than abandon his faith (Ac 22:20; Re 2:13). **4.** Witness of God for Christ (Ma 3:16–17; Lu 9:28–35; 1 Jo 5:7–12). **5.** Witness of the Spirit in man (Ro 8:14–16).

WOMAN In her creation she was the helpmeet and equal of man (Ge 2:21–24). See EVE. For the principle of monogamy see MARRIAGE. In early times women labored in the fields and took care of sheep (Ge 29:6; Ex 2:16; Ru 2:3, 8) but their main duties were of a household nature such as grinding grain (Ma 24:41), caring for the physical needs of the family (1 Sa 2:19; 2 Sa 13:8; Pr 31:13, 19; Ac 9:36–39), supervising the home (1 Ti 5:14), and instructing the children (Pr 1:8, 31:1; 2 Ti 3:15). Unde the Mosaic law the wife and mother was respected and honored (Ex 20:12; Pr 1:8, 18:22; Ec 9:9). In the New Testament she was further ennobled by Jesus through his teachings on adultery, marriage, and divorce (Ma 5:27–32) and through his attitude toward his mother, the sisters at Bethany, and the woman at the well (Lu 10:38–42; Jo 4:7–30, 19:25–27).

WORSHIP Religious reverence and homage, especially the act of paying divine honors to God (Ex 34:14; Ma 4:10). In the Bible four stages of public worship are discernible. In the patriarchal age and the time of the judges it was meagerly described and scarcely distinguishable from private worship (Jos 24:14–31). Temple worship, besides featuring sacrifice, was highly ritualistic as evidenced by its use of the Psalms. Synagogue worship after the Exile and through New Testament times made of prime importance the reading of the law and the prophets (Lu 4:14–21). Early Christian worship included preaching, prayer, reading of Scripture, singing, administration of the Lord's Supper, and the giving of alms (Ac 12:5, 20:7; 1 Co 11:18–29, 16:1–2; Col 3:16; 1 Th 5:27). See CHURCH.

X

XERXES King of Persia from 484–464 B.C. Six years after Xerxes was assassinated in the palace, Ezra conducted the second expedition to Jerusalem.